COLLECTION EDITOR: **JENNIFER GRÜNWALD**
ASSISTANT EDITOR: **SARAH BRUNSTAD**
ASSOCIATE MANAGING EDITOR: **ALEX STARBUCK**
EDITOR, SPECIAL PROJECTS: **MARK D. BEAZLEY**
SENIOR EDITOR, SPECIAL PROJECTS: **JEFF YOUNGQUIST**
SVP PRINT, SALES & MARKETING: **DAVID GABRIEL**

EDITOR IN CHIEF: **AXEL ALONSO**
CHIEF CREATIVE OFFICER: **JOE QUESADA**
PUBLISHER: **DAN BUCKLEY**
EXECUTIVE PRODUCER: **ALAN FINE**

AVENGERS VOL. 6: INFINITE AVENGERS. Contains material originally published in magazine form as AVENGERS #29-34. First printing 2015. ISBN# 978-0-7851-8922-0. Published by MARVEL WORLDWIDE, INC., a subsidiary of MARVEL ENTERTAINMENT, LLC. OFFICE OF PUBLICATION: 135 West 50th Street, New York, NY 10020. Copyright © 2015 MARVEL No similarity between any of the names, characters, persons, and/or institutions in this magazine with those of any living or dead person or institution is intended, and any such similarity which may exist is purely coincidental. **Printed in the U.S.A.** ALAN FINE, President, Marvel Entertainment; DAN BUCKLEY, President, TV, Publishing and Brand Management; JOE QUESADA, Chief Creative Officer; TOM BREVOORT, SVP of Publishing; DAVID BOGART, SVP of Operations & Procurement, Publishing; C.B. CEBULSKI, VP of International Development & Brand Management; DAVID GABRIEL, SVP Print, Sales & Marketing; JIM O'KEEFE, VP of Operations & Logistics; DAN CARR, Executive Director of Publishing Technology; SUSAN CRESPI, Editorial Operations Manager; ALEX MORALES, Publishing Operations Manager; STAN LEE, Chairman Emeritus. For information regarding advertising in Marvel Comics or on Marvel.com, please contact Jonathan Rheingold, VP of Custom Solutions & Ad Sales, at jrheingold@marvel.com. For Marvel subscription inquiries, please call 800-217-9158. **Manufactured between 5/8/2015 and 6/15/2015 by R.R. DONNELLEY INC., SALEM, VA, USA.**

10 9 8 7 6 5 4 3 2 1

AVENGERS

WRITER: **JONATHAN HICKMAN**

PENCILER: **LEINIL FRANCIS YU**

INKER: **GERRY ALANGUILAN**

COLORISTS: **SUNNY GHO** WITH **MATT MILLA** [ISSUE 34]

LETTERERS: **VC'S CORY PETIT** [ISSUES 29-31, 33-34] AND
CLAYTON COWLES [ISSUE 32]

COVER ART: **FRANK CHO & JASON KEITH** [ISSUE 29] AND
LEINIL FRANCIS YU & SUNNY GHO [ISSUES 30-34]

ASSISTANT EDITOR: **JAKE THOMAS**

EDITORS: **TOM BREVOORT** WITH **WIL MOSS**

AVENGERS CREATED BY STAN LEE & JACK KIRBY

PREVIOUSLY IN AVENGERS

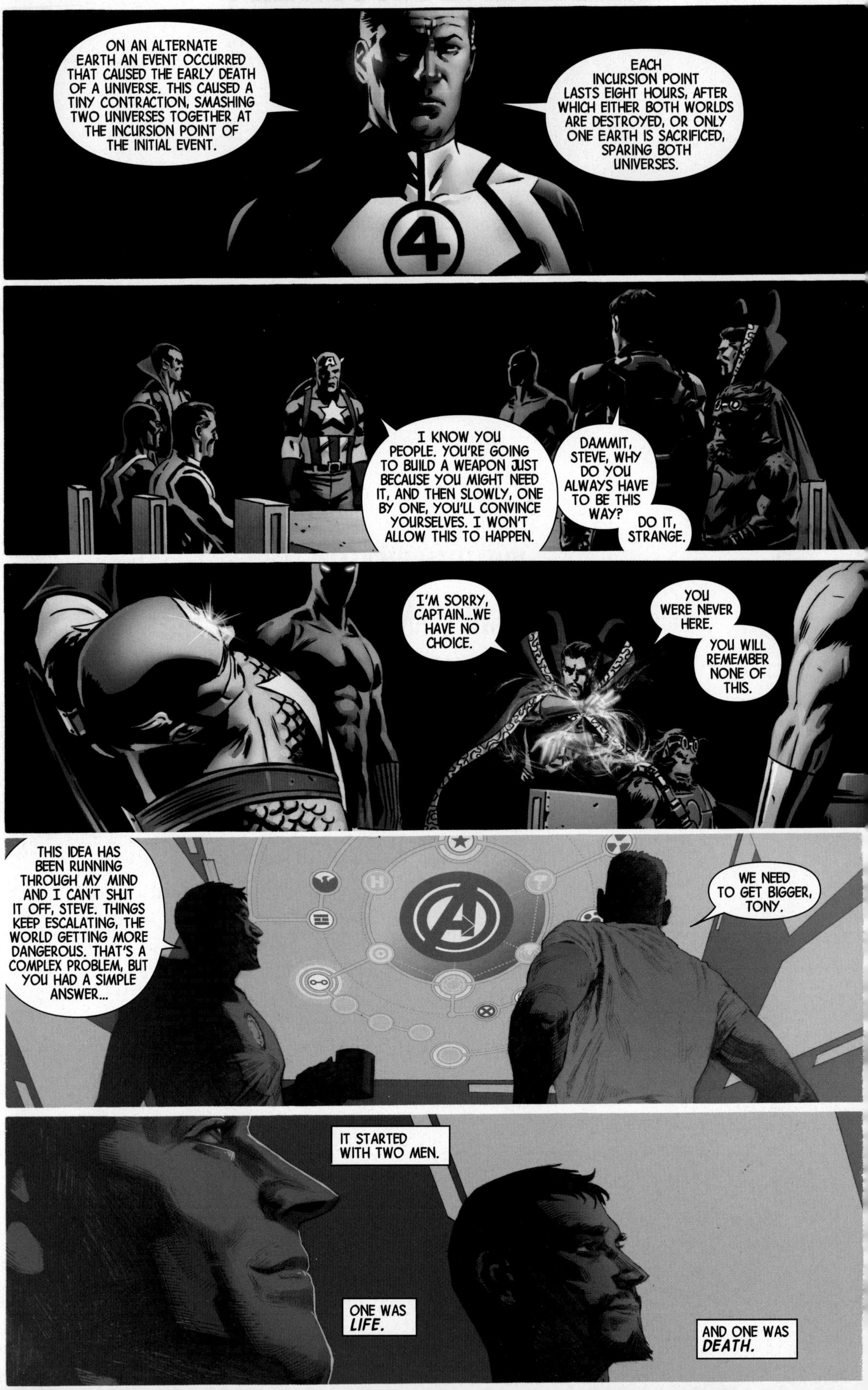
ON AN ALTERNATE EARTH AN EVENT OCCURRED THAT CAUSED THE EARLY DEATH OF A UNIVERSE. THIS CAUSED A TINY CONTRACTION, SMASHING TWO UNIVERSES TOGETHER AT THE INCURSION POINT OF THE INITIAL EVENT.
EACH INCURSION POINT LASTS EIGHT HOURS, AFTER WHICH EITHER BOTH WORLDS ARE DESTROYED, OR ONLY ONE EARTH IS SACRIFICED, SPARING BOTH UNIVERSES.
I KNOW YOU PEOPLE. YOU'RE GOING TO BUILD A WEAPON JUST BECAUSE YOU MIGHT NEED IT, AND THEN SLOWLY, ONE BY ONE, YOU'LL CONVINCE YOURSELVES. I WON'T ALLOW THIS TO HAPPEN.
DAMMIT, STEVE, WHY DO YOU ALWAYS HAVE TO BE THIS WAY?
DO IT, STRANGE.
I'M SORRY, CAPTAIN...WE HAVE NO CHOICE.
YOU WERE NEVER HERE.
YOU WILL REMEMBER NONE OF THIS.
THIS IDEA HAS BEEN RUNNING THROUGH MY MIND AND I CAN'T SHUT IT OFF, STEVE. THINGS KEEP ESCALATING, THE WORLD GETTING MORE DANGEROUS. THAT'S A COMPLEX PROBLEM, BUT YOU HAD A SIMPLE ANSWER...
WE NEED TO GET BIGGER, TONY.
IT STARTED WITH TWO MEN.
ONE WAS *LIFE.*
AND ONE WAS *DEATH.*

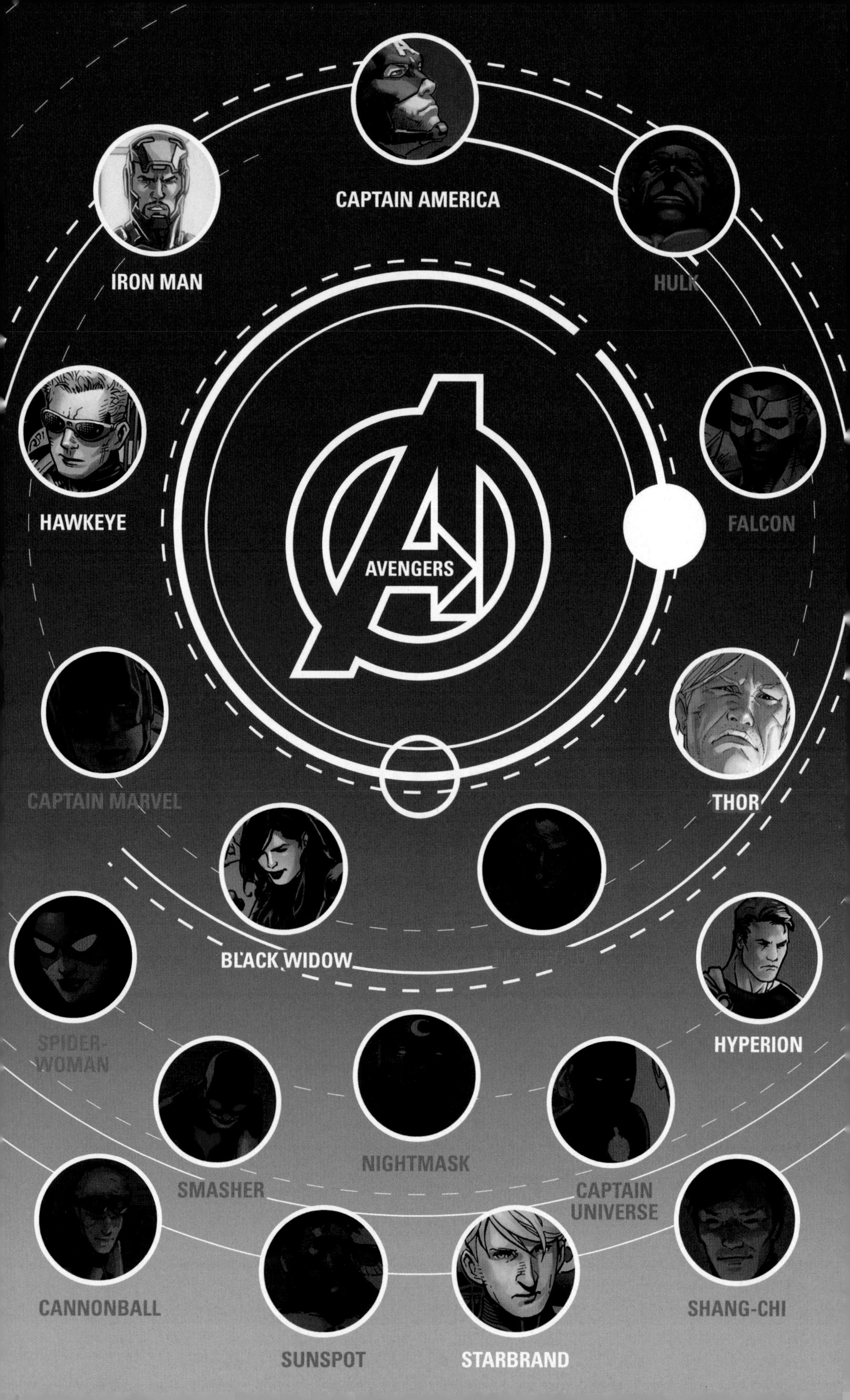

CAPTAIN AMERICA
IRON MAN
HULK
HAWKEYE
AVENGERS
FALCON
CAPTAIN MARVEL
THOR
BLACK WIDOW
SPIDER-WOMAN
HYPERION
NIGHTMASK
SMASHER
CAPTAIN UNIVERSE
CANNONBALL
SHANG-CHI
SUNSPOT
STARBRAND

"INFINITE AVENGERS"

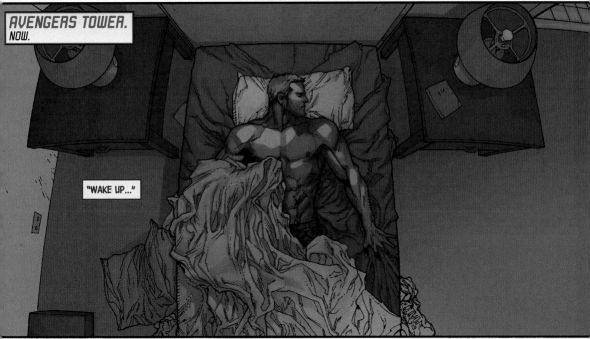

"WAKE UP..."

THEN.

NHHMMM?

WAKE UP, OLD MAN.

I HAVEN'T BEEN ABLE TO SLEEP.

I COULDN'T STOP THINKING ABOUT SOMETHING YOU SAID, AND, WELL...*I'VE BEEN BUSY.*

I'M SORRY. I KNOW IT'S LATE.

IT'S FINE, TONY.

I'M GRATEFUL.

BAD DREAMS?

"SOMETHING LIKE THAT."

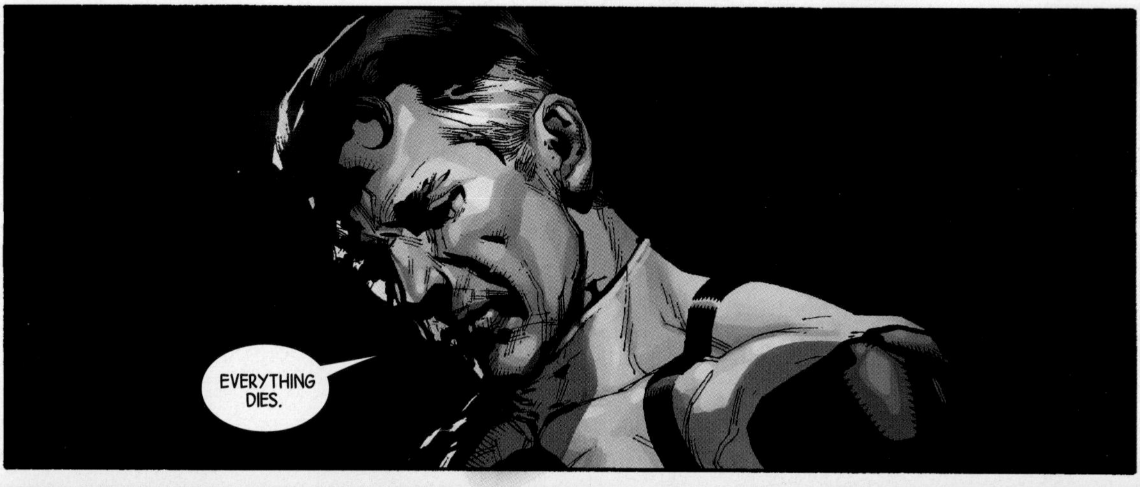
EVERYTHING DIES.

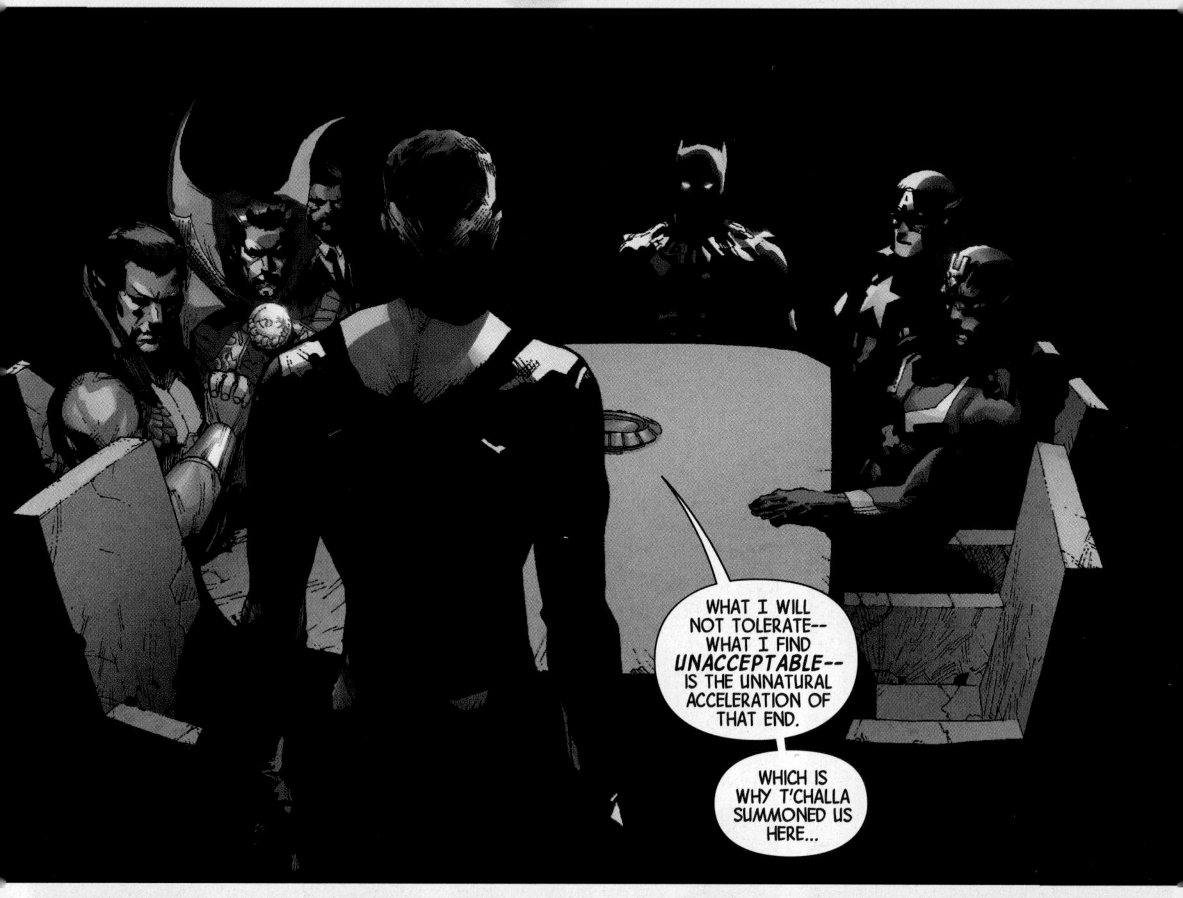
WHAT I WILL NOT TOLERATE-- WHAT I FIND *UNACCEPTABLE--* IS THE UNNATURAL ACCELERATION OF THAT END.
WHICH IS WHY T'CHALLA SUMMONED US HERE...

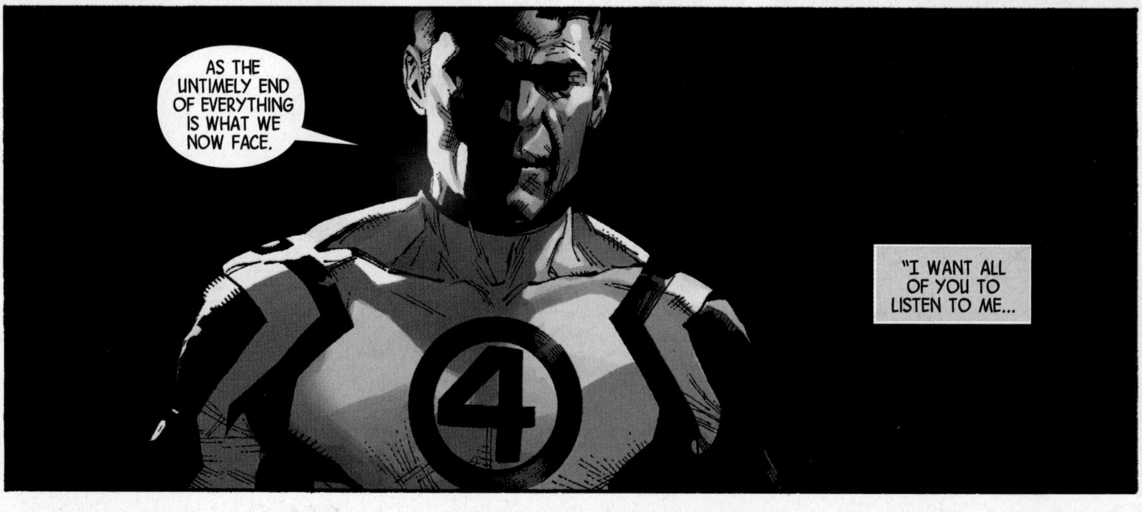
AS THE UNTIMELY END OF EVERYTHING IS WHAT WE NOW FACE.
"I WANT ALL OF YOU TO LISTEN TO ME...

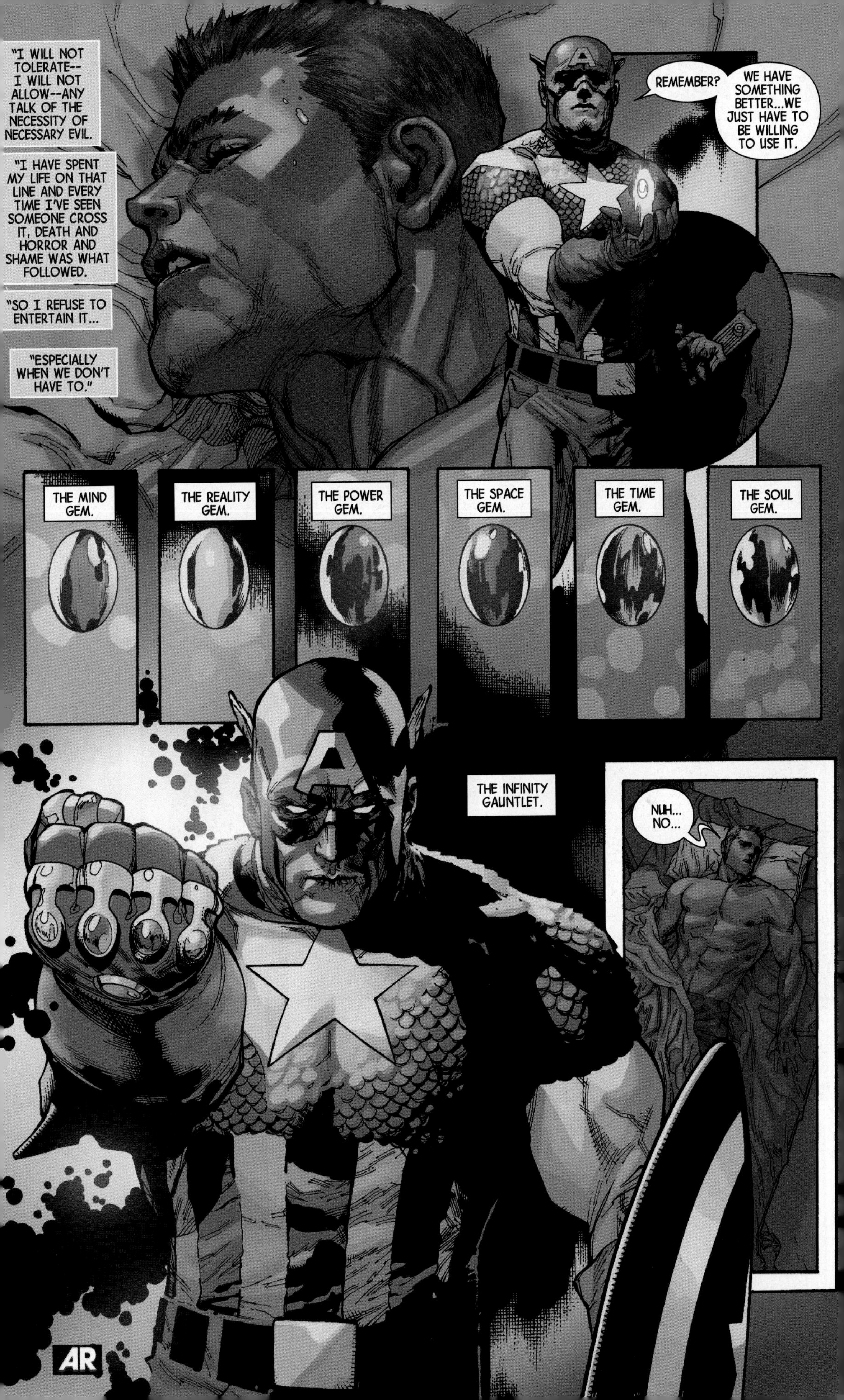
"I WILL NOT TOLERATE--I WILL NOT ALLOW--ANY TALK OF THE NECESSITY OF NECESSARY EVIL.
"I HAVE SPENT MY LIFE ON THAT LINE AND EVERY TIME I'VE SEEN SOMEONE CROSS IT, DEATH AND HORROR AND SHAME WAS WHAT FOLLOWED.
"SO I REFUSE TO ENTERTAIN IT...
"ESPECIALLY WHEN WE DON'T HAVE TO."
REMEMBER?
WE HAVE SOMETHING BETTER...WE JUST HAVE TO BE WILLING TO USE IT.
THE MIND GEM.
THE REALITY GEM.
THE POWER GEM.
THE SPACE GEM.
THE TIME GEM.
THE SOUL GEM.
THE INFINITY GAUNTLET.
NUH... NO...
AR

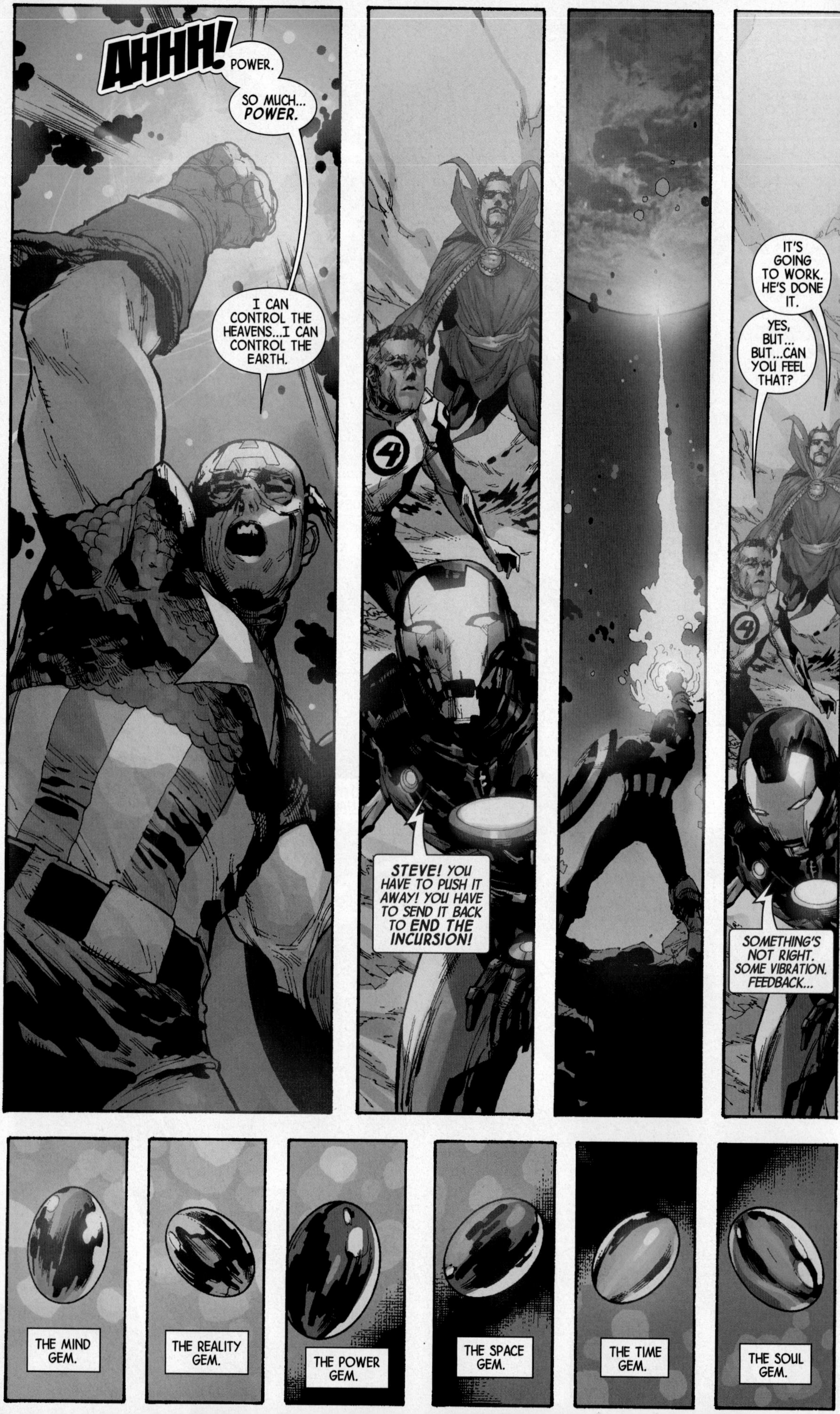
AHHH!
POWER.
SO MUCH... POWER.
I CAN CONTROL THE HEAVENS...I CAN CONTROL THE EARTH.
STEVE! YOU HAVE TO PUSH IT AWAY! YOU HAVE TO SEND IT BACK TO END THE INCURSION!
IT'S GOING TO WORK. HE'S DONE IT.
YES, BUT... BUT...CAN YOU FEEL THAT?
SOMETHING'S NOT RIGHT. SOME VIBRATION. FEEDBACK...
THE MIND GEM.
THE REALITY GEM.
THE POWER GEM.
THE SPACE GEM.
THE TIME GEM.
THE SOUL GEM.

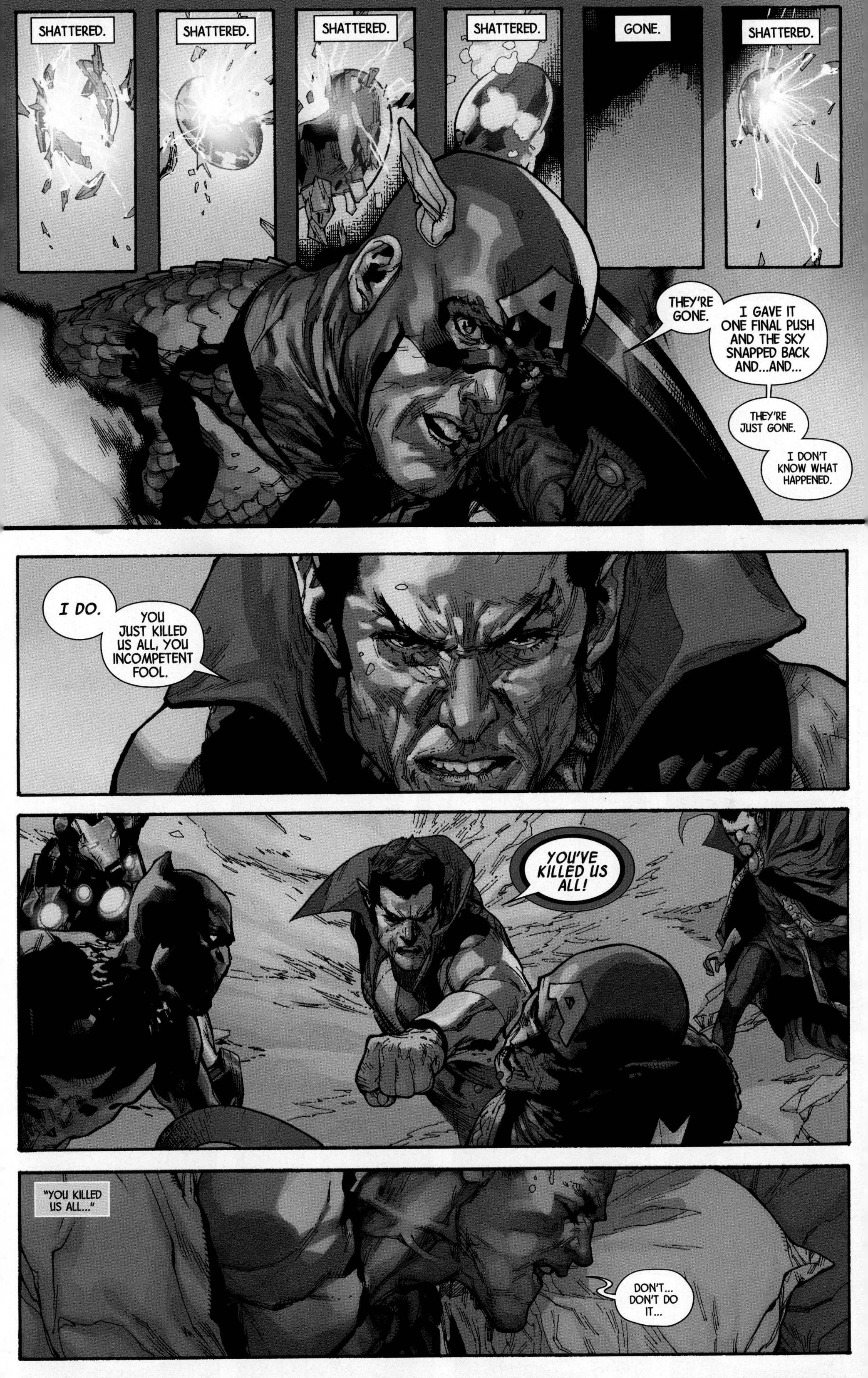

SHATTERED.
SHATTERED.
SHATTERED.
SHATTERED.
GONE.
SHATTERED.
THEY'RE GONE.
I GAVE IT ONE FINAL PUSH AND THE SKY SNAPPED BACK AND...AND...
THEY'RE JUST GONE.
I DON'T KNOW WHAT HAPPENED.
I DO.
YOU JUST KILLED US ALL, YOU INCOMPETENT FOOL.
YOU'VE KILLED US ALL!
"YOU KILLED US ALL..."
DON'T... DON'T DO IT...

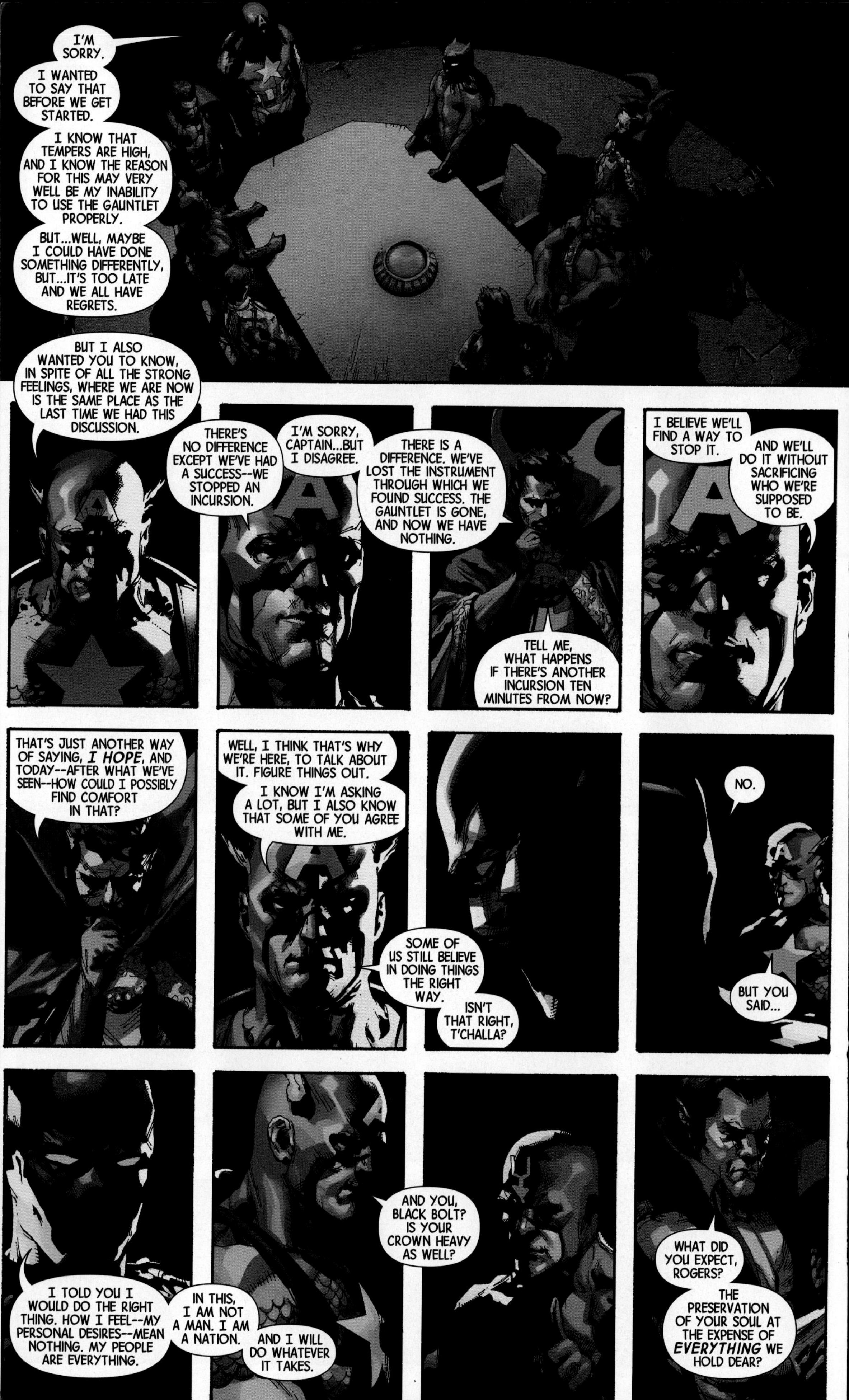
I'M SORRY.
I WANTED TO SAY THAT BEFORE WE GET STARTED.
I KNOW THAT TEMPERS ARE HIGH, AND I KNOW THE REASON FOR THIS MAY VERY WELL BE MY INABILITY TO USE THE GAUNTLET PROPERLY.
BUT...WELL, MAYBE I COULD HAVE DONE SOMETHING DIFFERENTLY, BUT...IT'S TOO LATE AND WE ALL HAVE REGRETS.
BUT I ALSO WANTED YOU TO KNOW, IN SPITE OF ALL THE STRONG FEELINGS, WHERE WE ARE NOW IS THE SAME PLACE AS THE LAST TIME WE HAD THIS DISCUSSION.
THERE'S NO DIFFERENCE EXCEPT WE'VE HAD A SUCCESS--WE STOPPED AN INCURSION.
I'M SORRY, CAPTAIN...BUT I DISAGREE.
THERE IS A DIFFERENCE. WE'VE LOST THE INSTRUMENT THROUGH WHICH WE FOUND SUCCESS. THE GAUNTLET IS GONE, AND NOW WE HAVE NOTHING.
TELL ME, WHAT HAPPENS IF THERE'S ANOTHER INCURSION TEN MINUTES FROM NOW?
I BELIEVE WE'LL FIND A WAY TO STOP IT.
AND WE'LL DO IT WITHOUT SACRIFICING WHO WE'RE SUPPOSED TO BE.
THAT'S JUST ANOTHER WAY OF SAYING, *I HOPE*, AND TODAY--AFTER WHAT WE'VE SEEN--HOW COULD I POSSIBLY FIND COMFORT IN THAT?
WELL, I THINK THAT'S WHY WE'RE HERE, TO TALK ABOUT IT. FIGURE THINGS OUT.
I KNOW I'M ASKING A LOT, BUT I ALSO KNOW THAT SOME OF YOU AGREE WITH ME.
SOME OF US STILL BELIEVE IN DOING THINGS THE RIGHT WAY.
ISN'T THAT RIGHT, T'CHALLA?
NO.
BUT YOU SAID...
I TOLD YOU I WOULD DO THE RIGHT THING. HOW I FEEL--MY PERSONAL DESIRES--MEAN NOTHING. MY PEOPLE ARE EVERYTHING.
IN THIS, I AM NOT A MAN. I AM A NATION.
AND I WILL DO WHATEVER IT TAKES.
AND YOU, BLACK BOLT? IS YOUR CROWN HEAVY AS WELL?
WHAT DID YOU EXPECT, ROGERS?
THE PRESERVATION OF YOUR SOUL AT THE EXPENSE OF *EVERYTHING* WE HOLD DEAR?

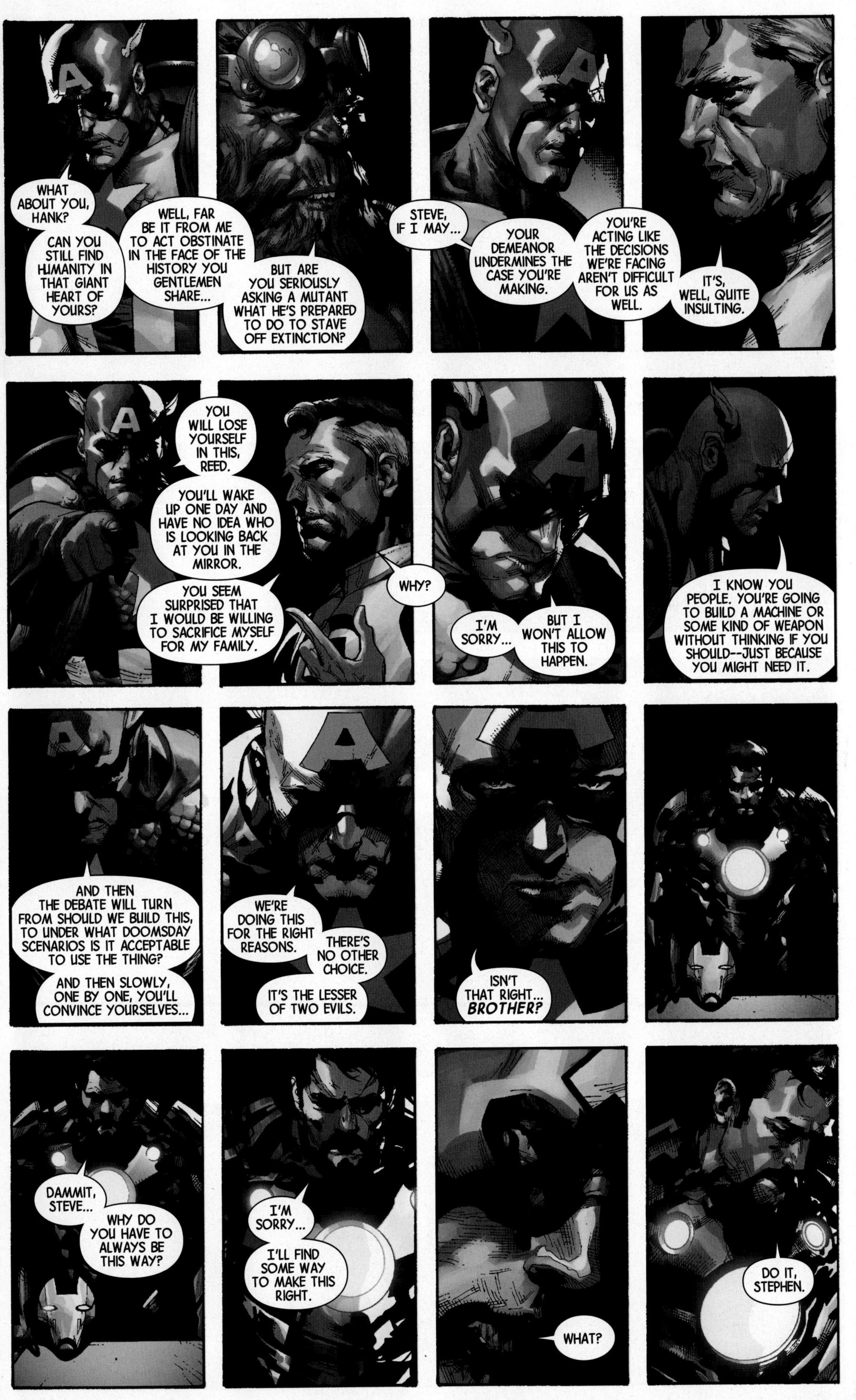
WHAT ABOUT YOU, HANK?
CAN YOU STILL FIND HUMANITY IN THAT GIANT HEART OF YOURS?
WELL, FAR BE IT FROM ME TO ACT OBSTINATE IN THE FACE OF THE HISTORY YOU GENTLEMEN SHARE...
BUT ARE YOU SERIOUSLY ASKING A MUTANT WHAT HE'S PREPARED TO DO TO STAVE OFF EXTINCTION?
STEVE, IF I MAY...
YOUR DEMEANOR UNDERMINES THE CASE YOU'RE MAKING.
YOU'RE ACTING LIKE THE DECISIONS WE'RE FACING AREN'T DIFFICULT FOR US AS WELL.
IT'S, WELL, QUITE INSULTING.
YOU WILL LOSE YOURSELF IN THIS, REED.
YOU'LL WAKE UP ONE DAY AND HAVE NO IDEA WHO IS LOOKING BACK AT YOU IN THE MIRROR.
YOU SEEM SURPRISED THAT I WOULD BE WILLING TO SACRIFICE MYSELF FOR MY FAMILY.
WHY?
I'M SORRY...
BUT I WON'T ALLOW THIS TO HAPPEN.
I KNOW YOU PEOPLE. YOU'RE GOING TO BUILD A MACHINE OR SOME KIND OF WEAPON WITHOUT THINKING IF YOU SHOULD--JUST BECAUSE YOU MIGHT NEED IT.
AND THEN THE DEBATE WILL TURN FROM SHOULD WE BUILD THIS, TO UNDER WHAT DOOMSDAY SCENARIOS IS IT ACCEPTABLE TO USE THE THING?
AND THEN SLOWLY, ONE BY ONE, YOU'LL CONVINCE YOURSELVES...
WE'RE DOING THIS FOR THE RIGHT REASONS.
THERE'S NO OTHER CHOICE.
IT'S THE LESSER OF TWO EVILS.
ISN'T THAT RIGHT... BROTHER?
DAMMIT, STEVE...
WHY DO YOU HAVE TO ALWAYS BE THIS WAY?
I'M SORRY...
I'LL FIND SOME WAY TO MAKE THIS RIGHT.
WHAT?
DO IT, STEPHEN.

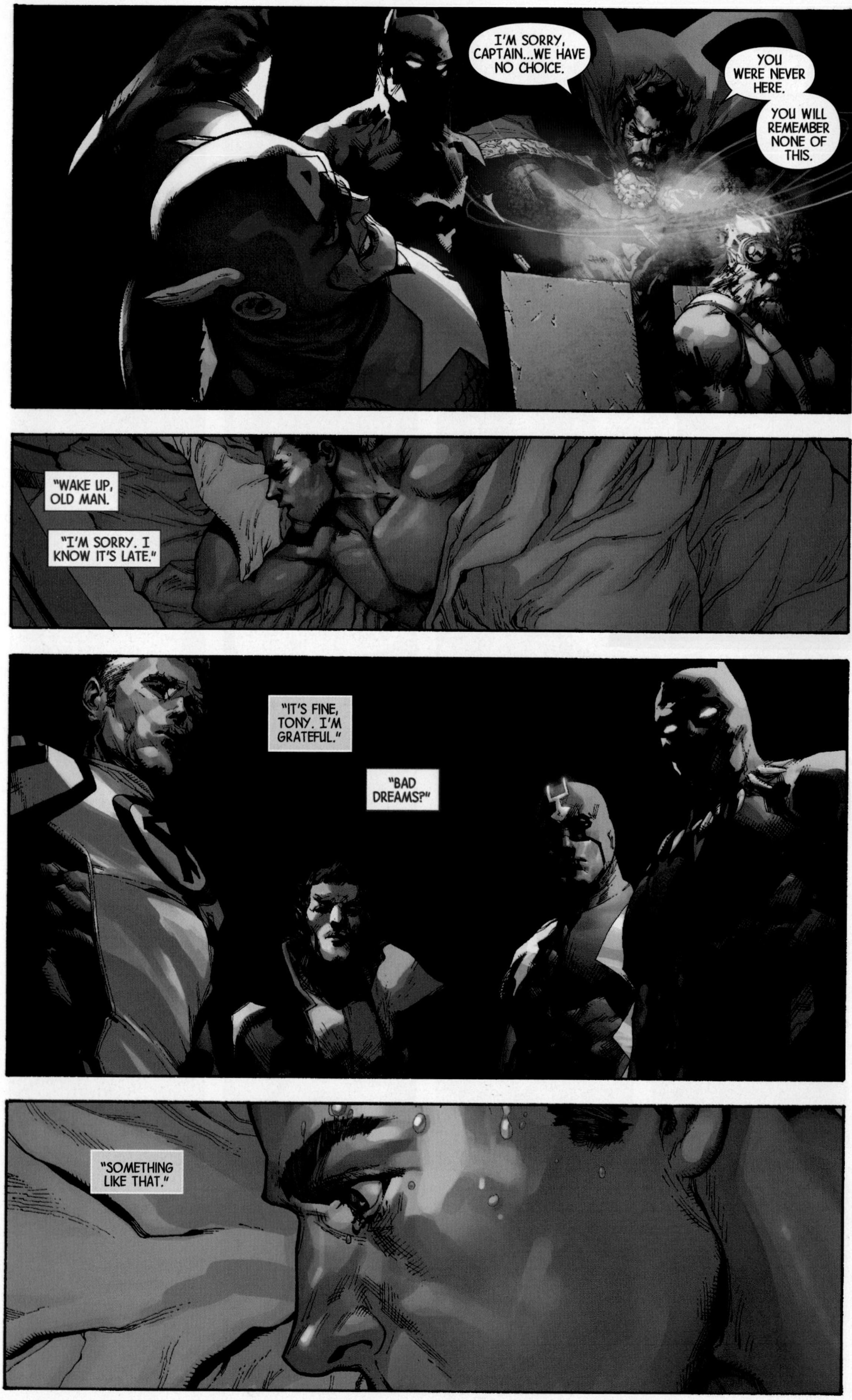
I'M SORRY, CAPTAIN...WE HAVE NO CHOICE.
YOU WERE NEVER HERE.
YOU WILL REMEMBER NONE OF THIS.
"WAKE UP, OLD MAN.
"I'M SORRY. I KNOW IT'S LATE."
"IT'S FINE, TONY. I'M GRATEFUL."
"BAD DREAMS?"
"SOMETHING LIKE THAT."

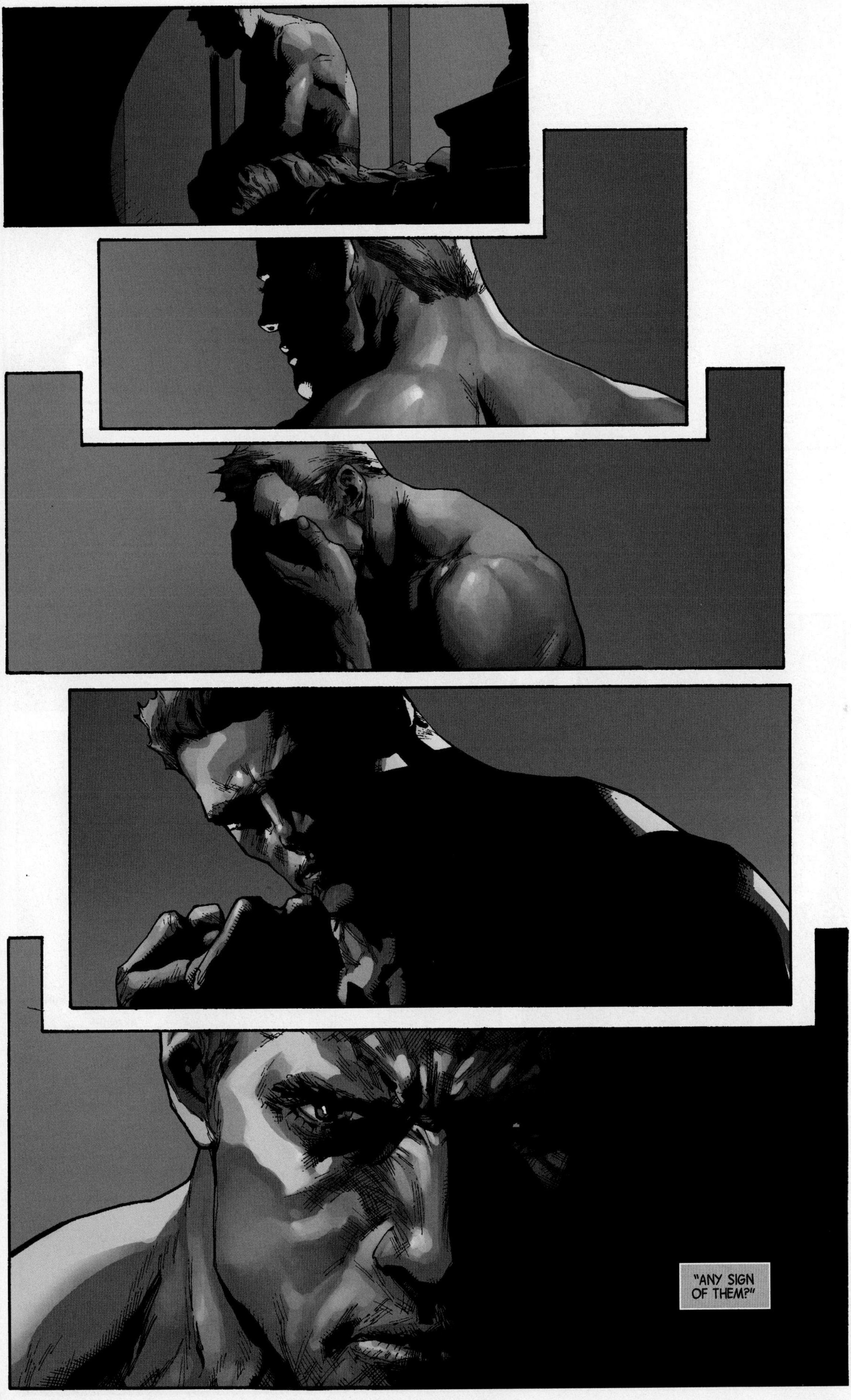
"ANY SIGN
OF THEM?"

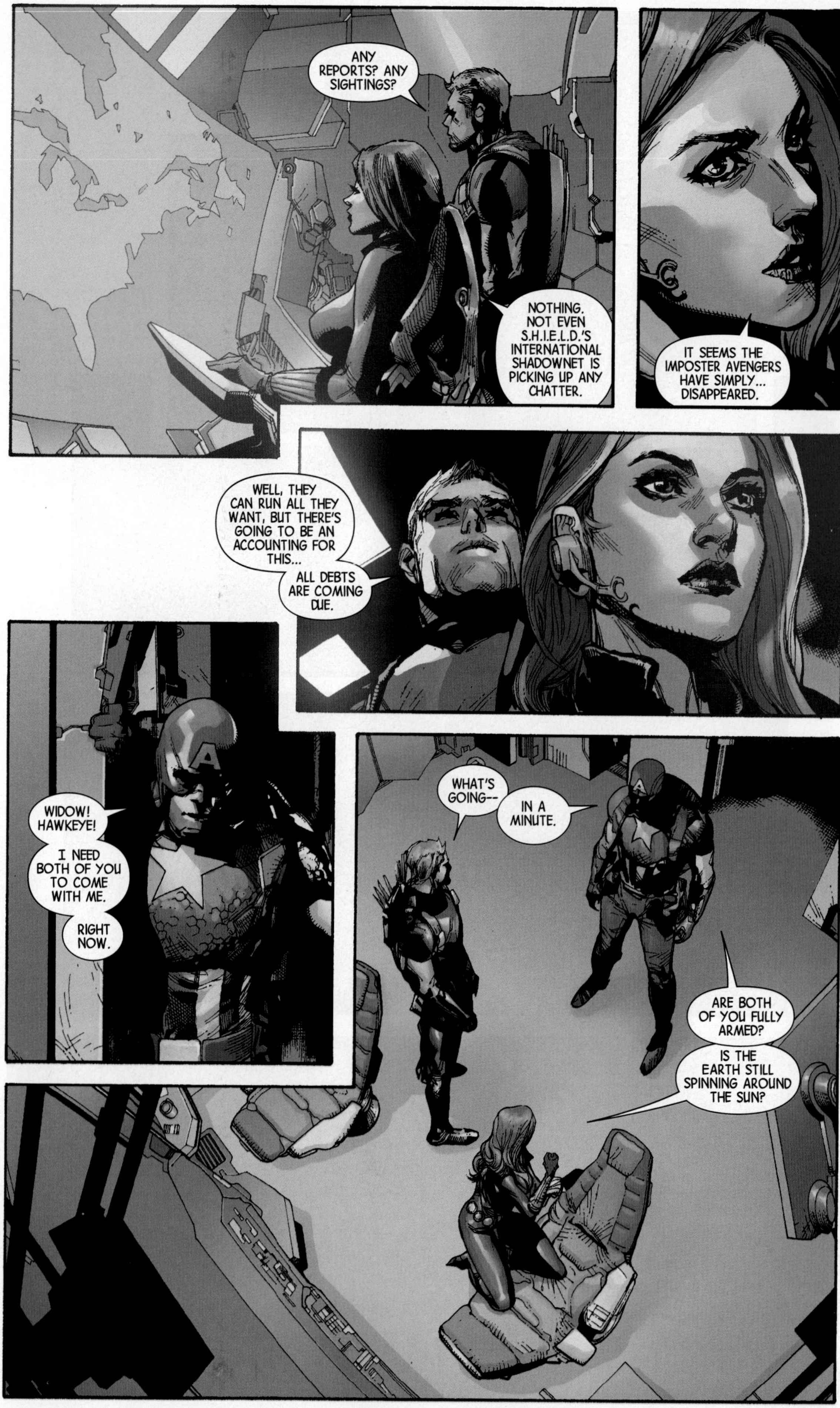
ANY REPORTS? ANY SIGHTINGS?
NOTHING. NOT EVEN S.H.I.E.L.D.'S INTERNATIONAL SHADOWNET IS PICKING UP ANY CHATTER.
IT SEEMS THE IMPOSTER AVENGERS HAVE SIMPLY... DISAPPEARED.
WELL, THEY CAN RUN ALL THEY WANT, BUT THERE'S GOING TO BE AN ACCOUNTING FOR THIS...
ALL DEBTS ARE COMING DUE.
WIDOW! HAWKEYE!
I NEED BOTH OF YOU TO COME WITH ME.
RIGHT NOW.
WHAT'S GOING--
IN A MINUTE.
ARE BOTH OF YOU FULLY ARMED?
IS THE EARTH STILL SPINNING AROUND THE SUN?

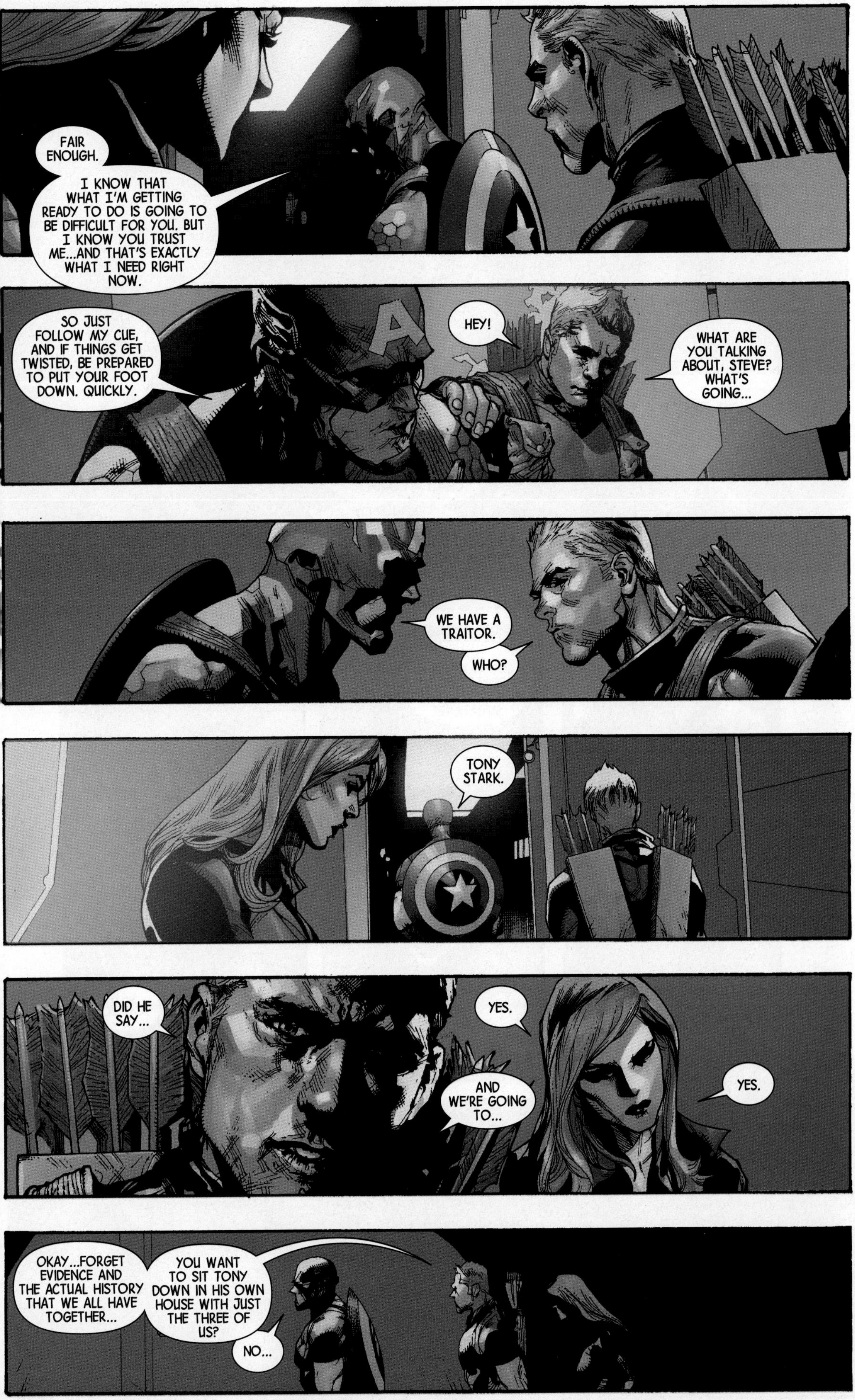
FAIR ENOUGH.
I KNOW THAT WHAT I'M GETTING READY TO DO IS GOING TO BE DIFFICULT FOR YOU. BUT I KNOW YOU TRUST ME...AND THAT'S EXACTLY WHAT I NEED RIGHT NOW.
SO JUST FOLLOW MY CUE, AND IF THINGS GET TWISTED, BE PREPARED TO PUT YOUR FOOT DOWN. QUICKLY.
HEY!
WHAT ARE YOU TALKING ABOUT, STEVE? WHAT'S GOING...
WE HAVE A TRAITOR.
WHO?
TONY STARK.
DID HE SAY...
YES.
AND WE'RE GOING TO...
YES.
OKAY...FORGET EVIDENCE AND THE ACTUAL HISTORY THAT WE ALL HAVE TOGETHER...
YOU WANT TO SIT TONY DOWN IN HIS OWN HOUSE WITH JUST THE THREE OF US?
NO...

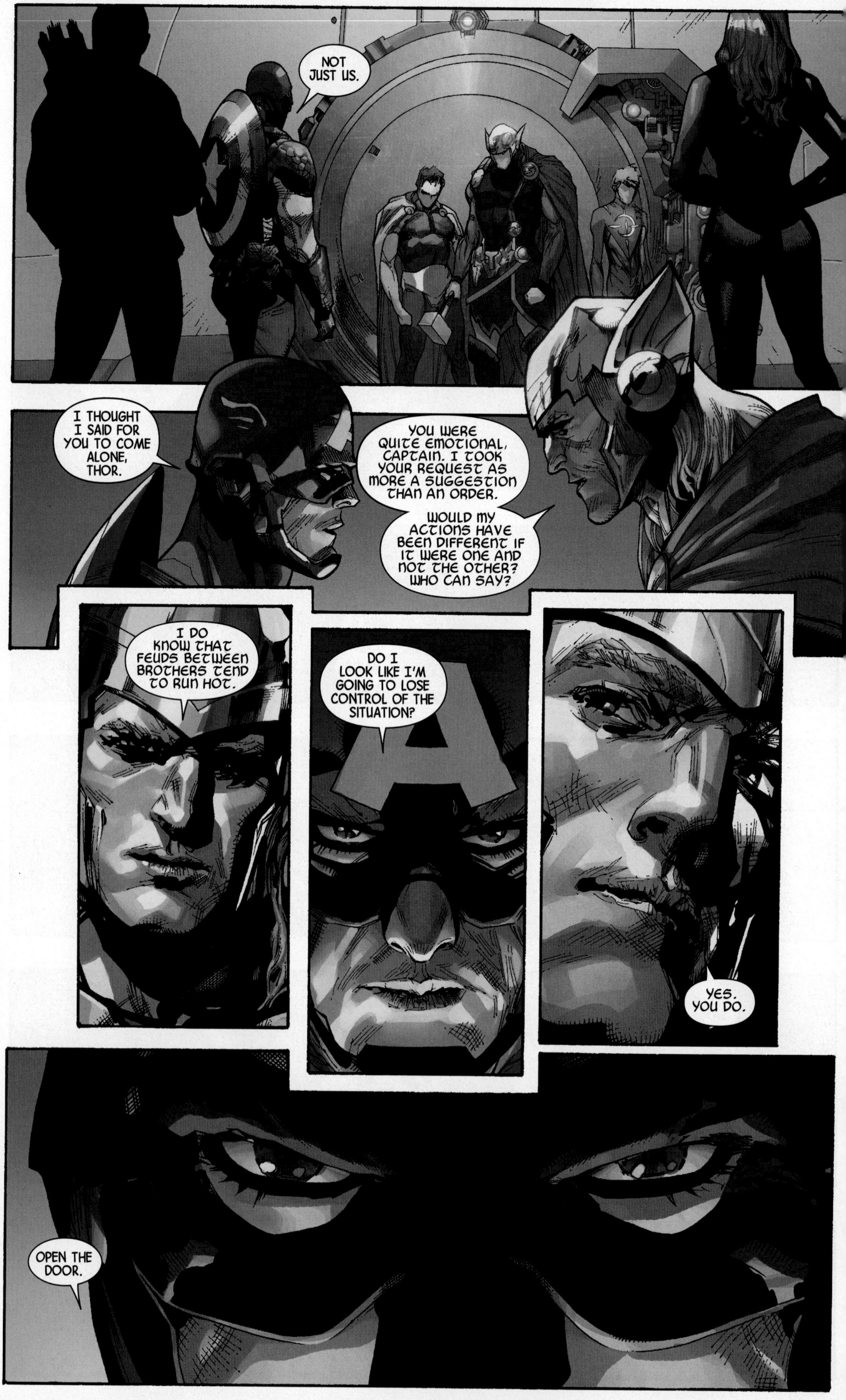
NOT JUST US.
I THOUGHT I SAID FOR YOU TO COME ALONE, THOR.
YOU WERE QUITE EMOTIONAL, CAPTAIN. I TOOK YOUR REQUEST AS MORE A SUGGESTION THAN AN ORDER.
WOULD MY ACTIONS HAVE BEEN DIFFERENT IF IT WERE ONE AND NOT THE OTHER? WHO CAN SAY?
I DO KNOW THAT FEUDS BETWEEN BROTHERS TEND TO RUN HOT.
DO I LOOK LIKE I'M GOING TO LOSE CONTROL OF THE SITUATION?
YES. YOU DO.
OPEN THE DOOR.

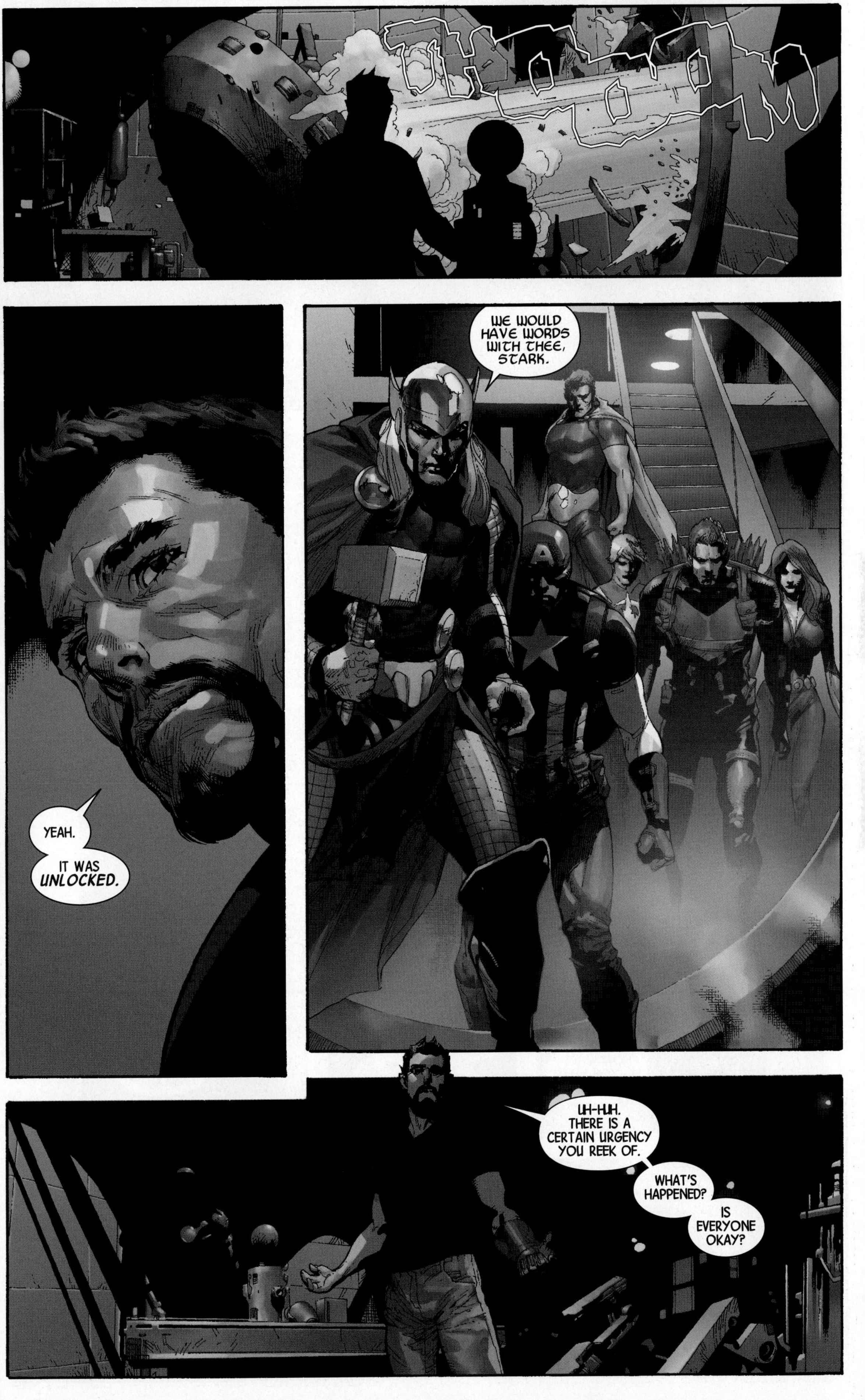
THOOOOOM
WE WOULD HAVE WORDS WITH THEE, STARK.
YEAH.
IT WAS UNLOCKED.
UH-HUH. THERE IS A CERTAIN URGENCY YOU REEK OF.
WHAT'S HAPPENED?
IS EVERYONE OKAY?

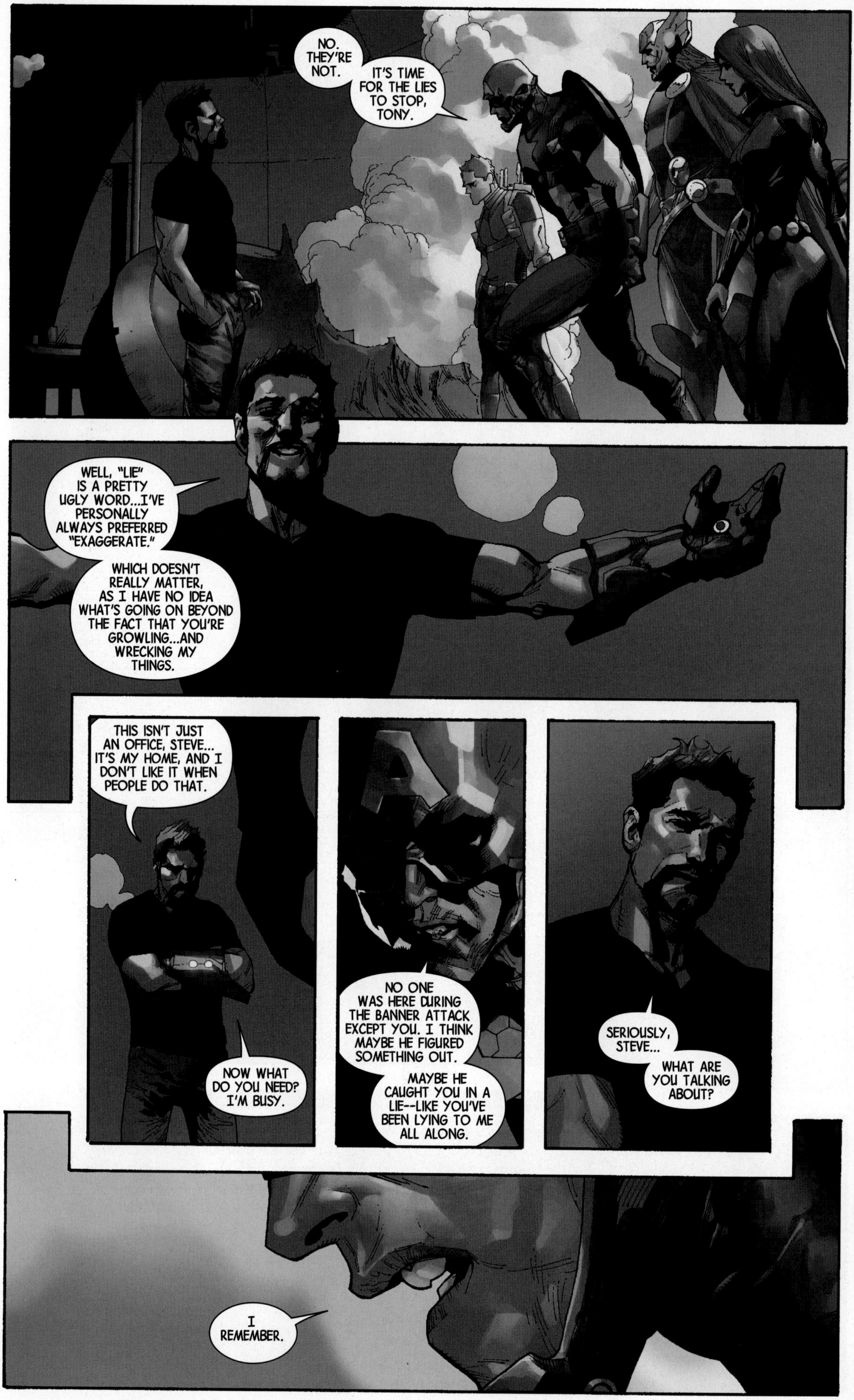
NO. THEY'RE NOT.
IT'S TIME FOR THE LIES TO STOP, TONY.
WELL, "LIE" IS A PRETTY UGLY WORD...I'VE PERSONALLY ALWAYS PREFERRED "EXAGGERATE."
WHICH DOESN'T REALLY MATTER, AS I HAVE NO IDEA WHAT'S GOING ON BEYOND THE FACT THAT YOU'RE GROWLING...AND WRECKING MY THINGS.
THIS ISN'T JUST AN OFFICE, STEVE... IT'S MY HOME, AND I DON'T LIKE IT WHEN PEOPLE DO THAT.
NOW WHAT DO YOU NEED? I'M BUSY.
NO ONE WAS HERE DURING THE BANNER ATTACK EXCEPT YOU. I THINK MAYBE HE FIGURED SOMETHING OUT.
MAYBE HE CAUGHT YOU IN A LIE--LIKE YOU'VE BEEN LYING TO ME ALL ALONG.
SERIOUSLY, STEVE...
WHAT ARE YOU TALKING ABOUT?
I REMEMBER.

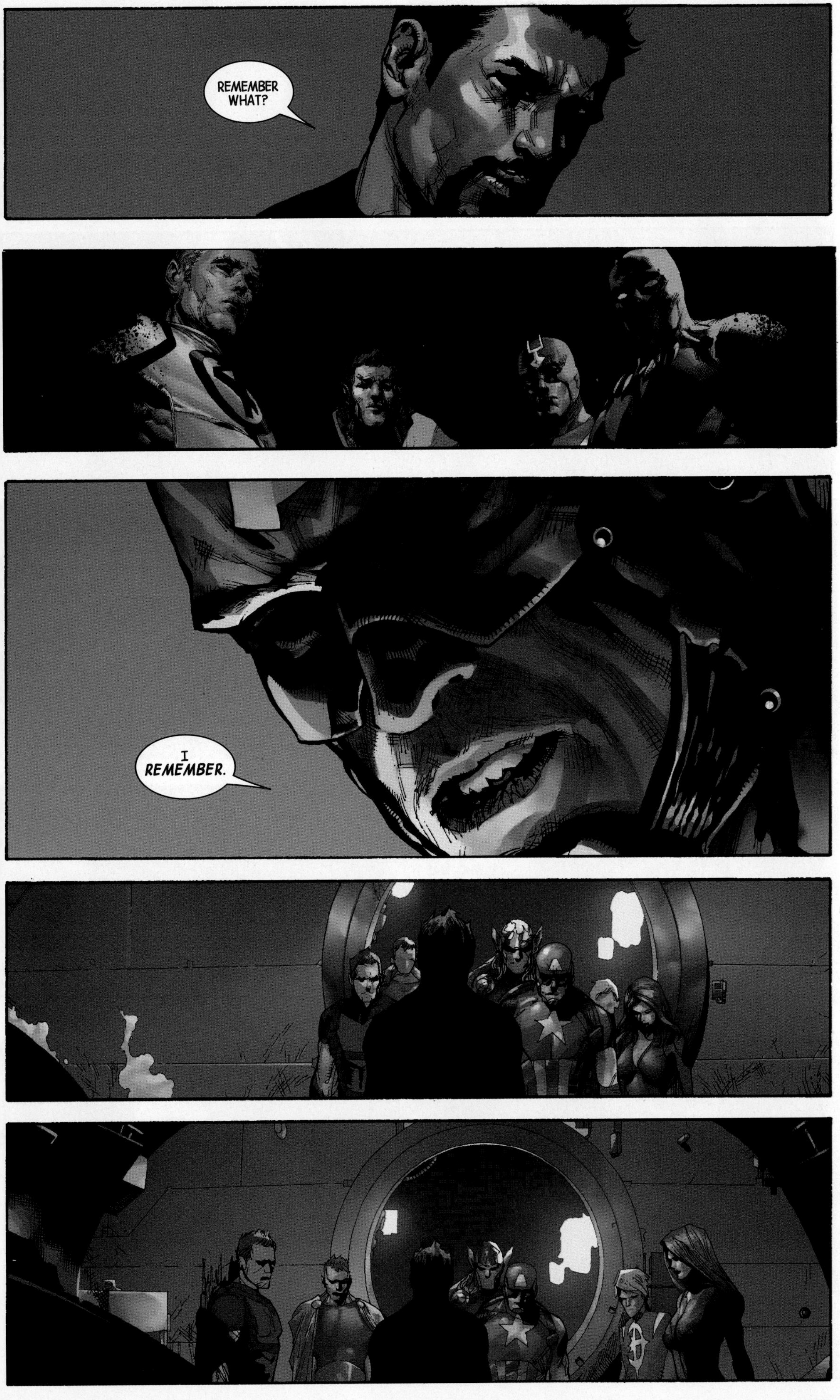
REMEMBER WHAT?
I REMEMBER.

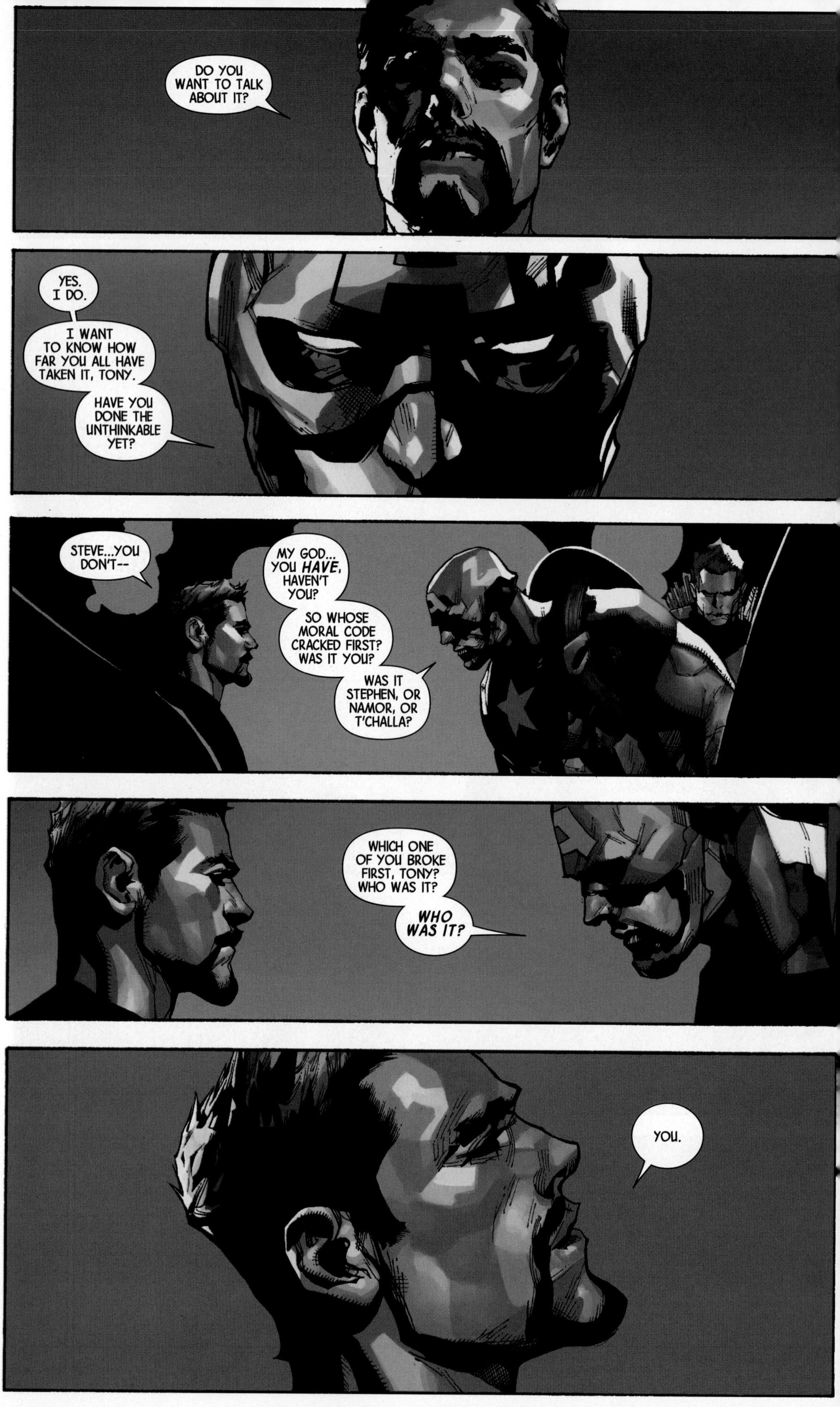
DO YOU WANT TO TALK ABOUT IT?
YES. I DO.
I WANT TO KNOW HOW FAR YOU ALL HAVE TAKEN IT, TONY.
HAVE YOU DONE THE UNTHINKABLE YET?
STEVE...YOU DON'T--
MY GOD... YOU *HAVE*, HAVEN'T YOU?
SO WHOSE MORAL CODE CRACKED FIRST? WAS IT YOU?
WAS IT STEPHEN, OR NAMOR, OR T'CHALLA?
WHICH ONE OF YOU BROKE FIRST, TONY? WHO WAS IT?
WHO WAS IT?
YOU.

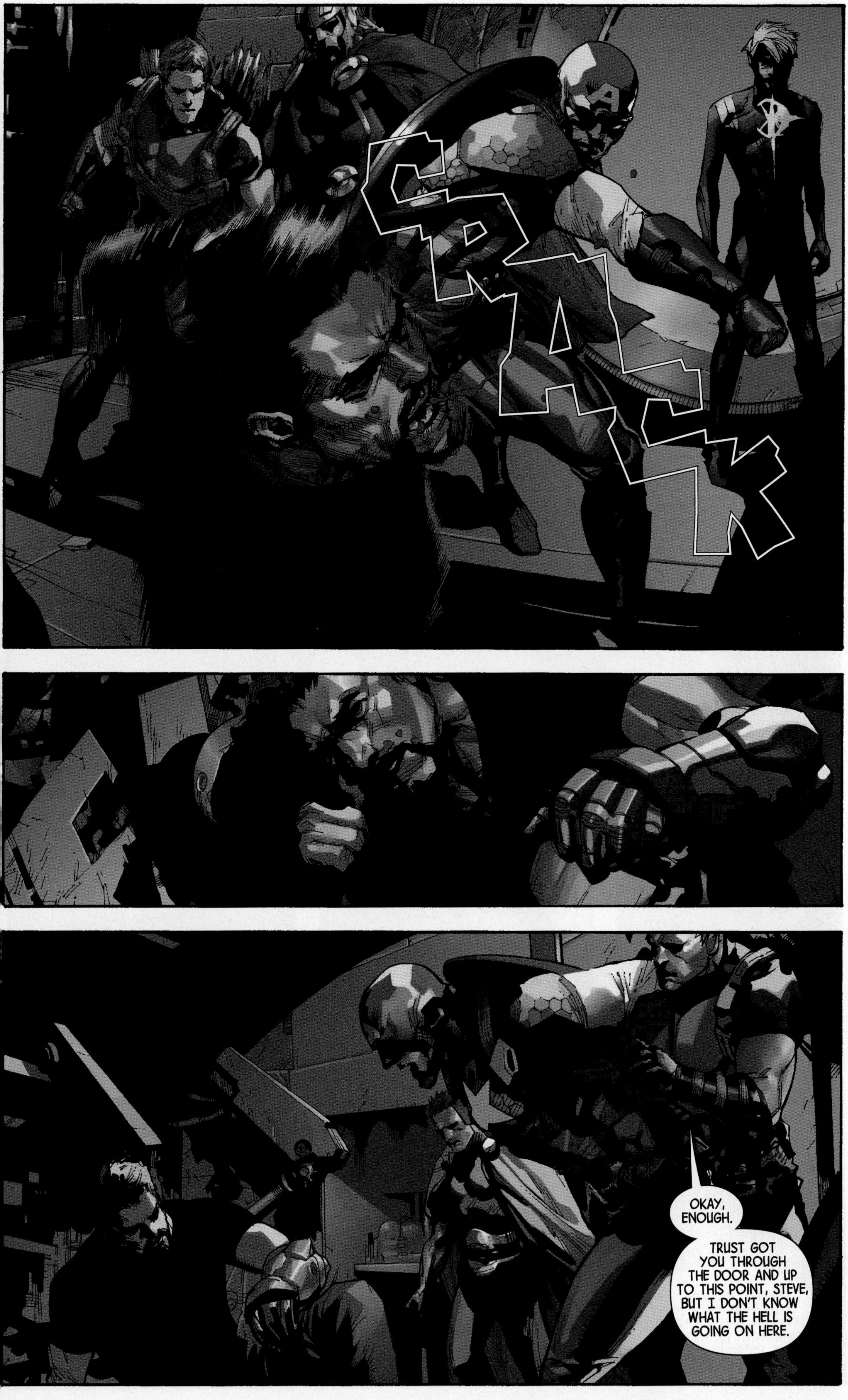
CRACK
OKAY, ENOUGH.
TRUST GOT YOU THROUGH THE DOOR AND UP TO THIS POINT, STEVE, BUT I DON'T KNOW WHAT THE HELL IS GOING ON HERE.

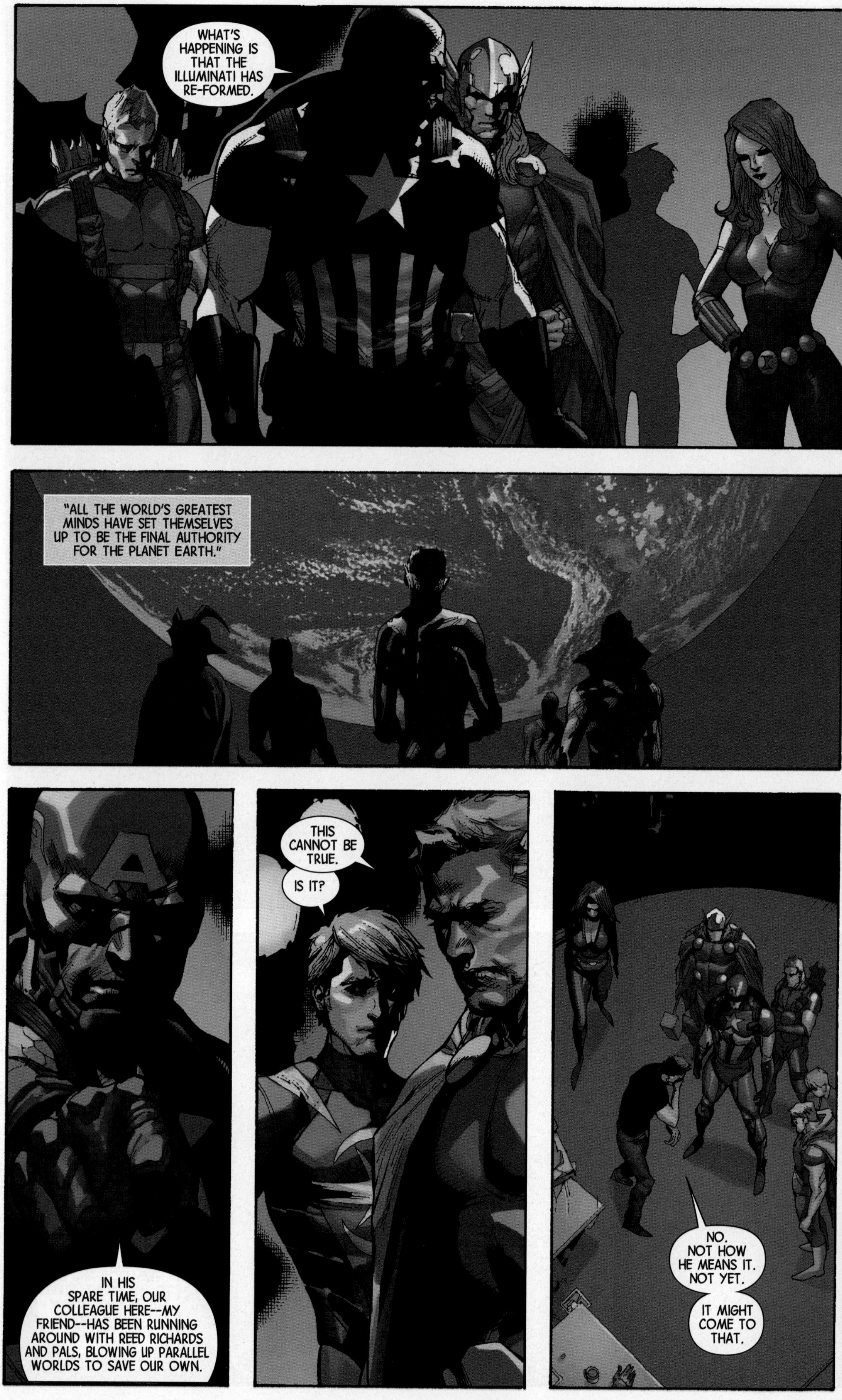
WHAT'S HAPPENING IS THAT THE ILLUMINATI HAS RE-FORMED.
"ALL THE WORLD'S GREATEST MINDS HAVE SET THEMSELVES UP TO BE THE FINAL AUTHORITY FOR THE PLANET EARTH."
IN HIS SPARE TIME, OUR COLLEAGUE HERE--MY FRIEND--HAS BEEN RUNNING AROUND WITH REED RICHARDS AND PALS, BLOWING UP PARALLEL WORLDS TO SAVE OUR OWN.
THIS CANNOT BE TRUE.
IS IT?
NO. NOT HOW HE MEANS IT. NOT YET.
IT MIGHT COME TO THAT.

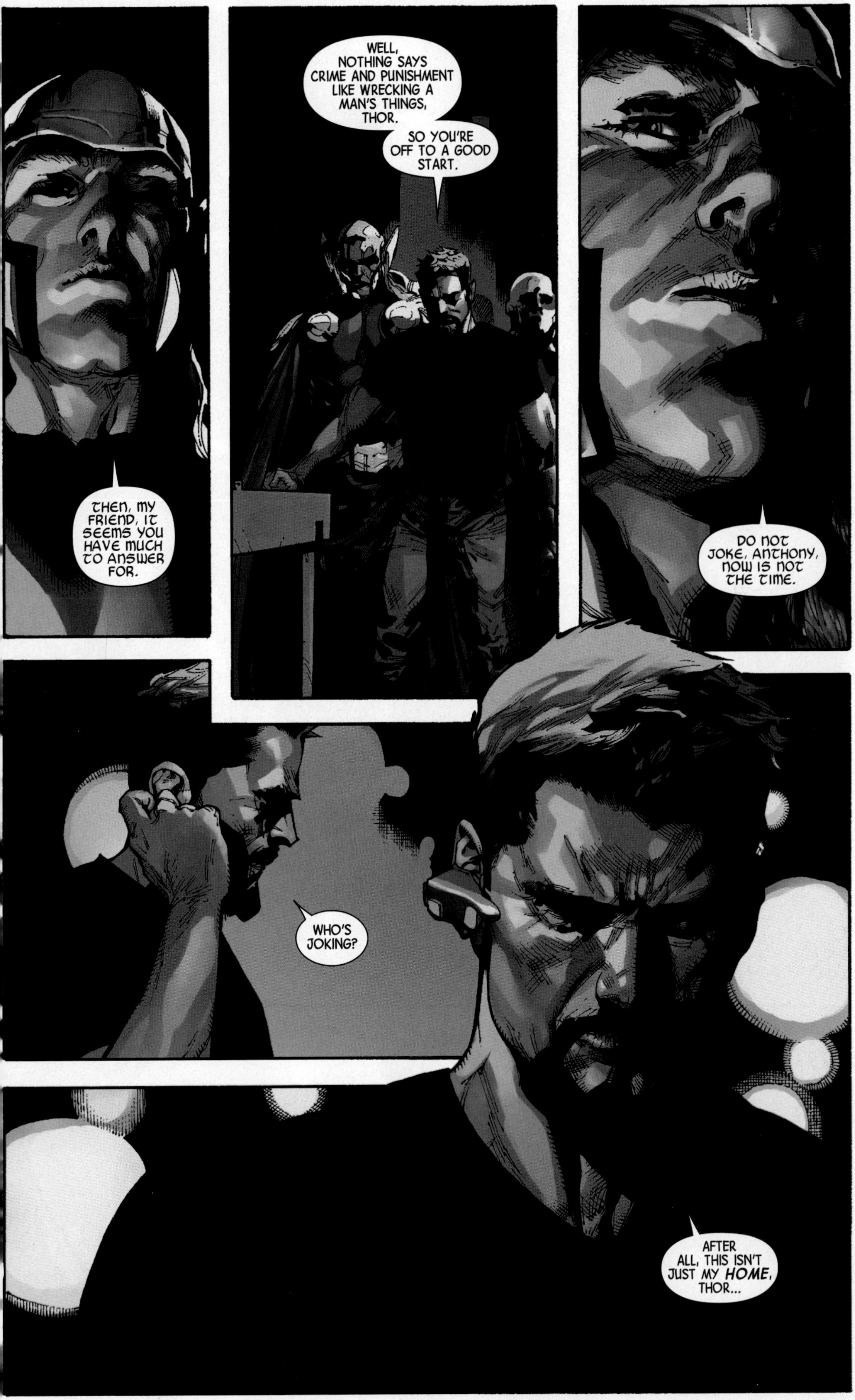
THEN, MY FRIEND, IT SEEMS YOU HAVE MUCH TO ANSWER FOR.
WELL, NOTHING SAYS CRIME AND PUNISHMENT LIKE WRECKING A MAN'S THINGS, THOR.
SO YOU'RE OFF TO A GOOD START.
DO NOT JOKE, ANTHONY, NOW IS NOT THE TIME.
WHO'S JOKING?
AFTER ALL, THIS ISN'T JUST MY HOME, THOR...

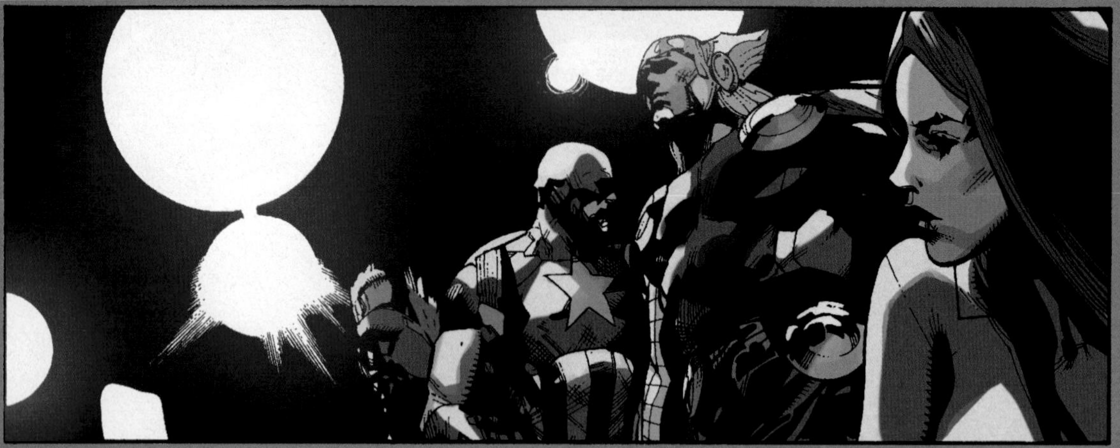
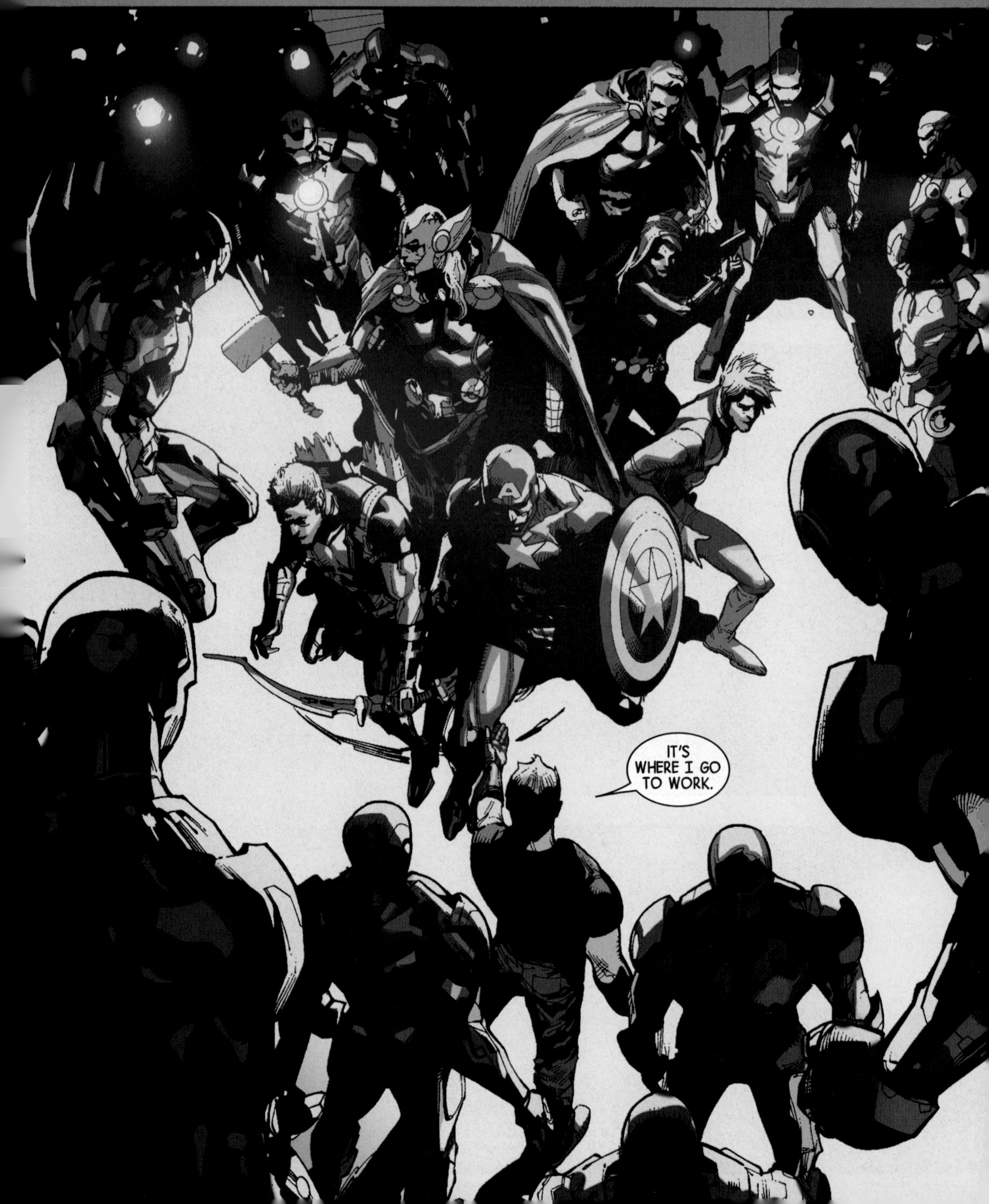
IT'S WHERE I GO TO WORK.

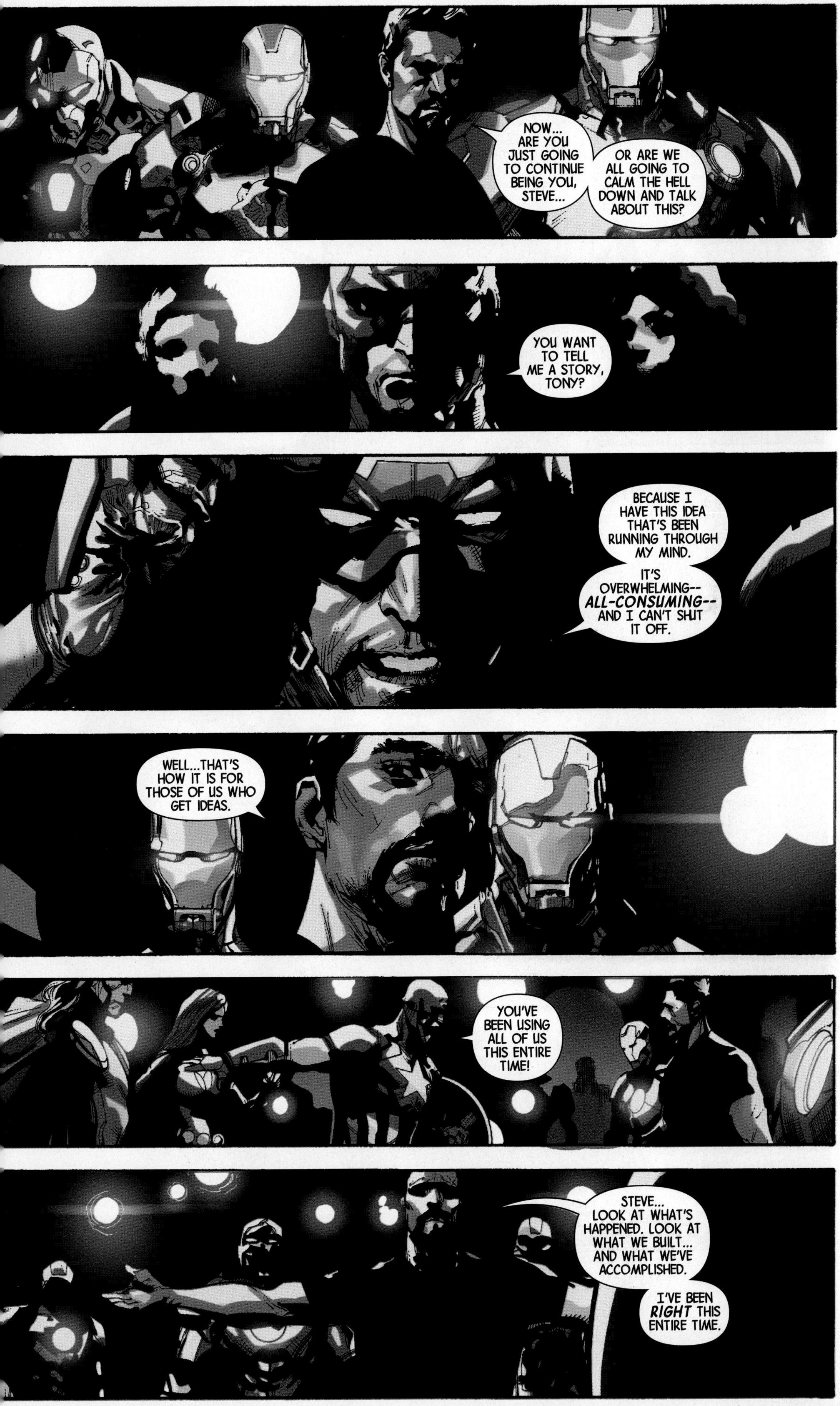
NOW... ARE YOU JUST GOING TO CONTINUE BEING YOU, STEVE...
OR ARE WE ALL GOING TO CALM THE HELL DOWN AND TALK ABOUT THIS?
YOU WANT TO TELL ME A STORY, TONY?
BECAUSE I HAVE THIS IDEA THAT'S BEEN RUNNING THROUGH MY MIND.
IT'S OVERWHELMING-- ALL-CONSUMING-- AND I CAN'T SHUT IT OFF.
WELL...THAT'S HOW IT IS FOR THOSE OF US WHO GET IDEAS.
YOU'VE BEEN USING ALL OF US THIS ENTIRE TIME!
STEVE... LOOK AT WHAT'S HAPPENED. LOOK AT WHAT WE BUILT... AND WHAT WE'VE ACCOMPLISHED.
I'VE BEEN RIGHT THIS ENTIRE TIME.

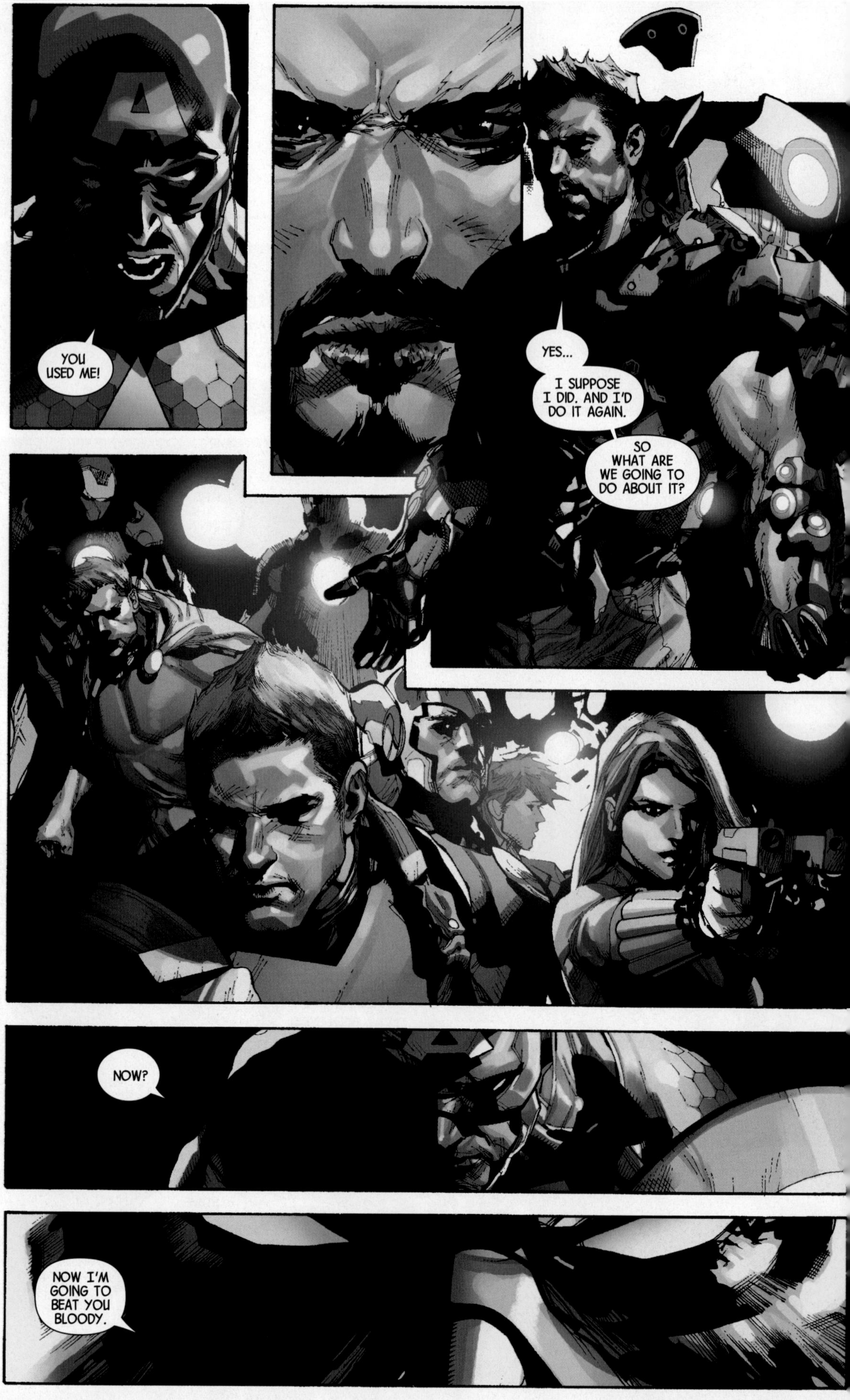
YOU USED ME!
YES...
I SUPPOSE I DID. AND I'D DO IT AGAIN.
SO WHAT ARE WE GOING TO DO ABOUT IT?
NOW?
NOW I'M GOING TO BEAT YOU BLOODY.

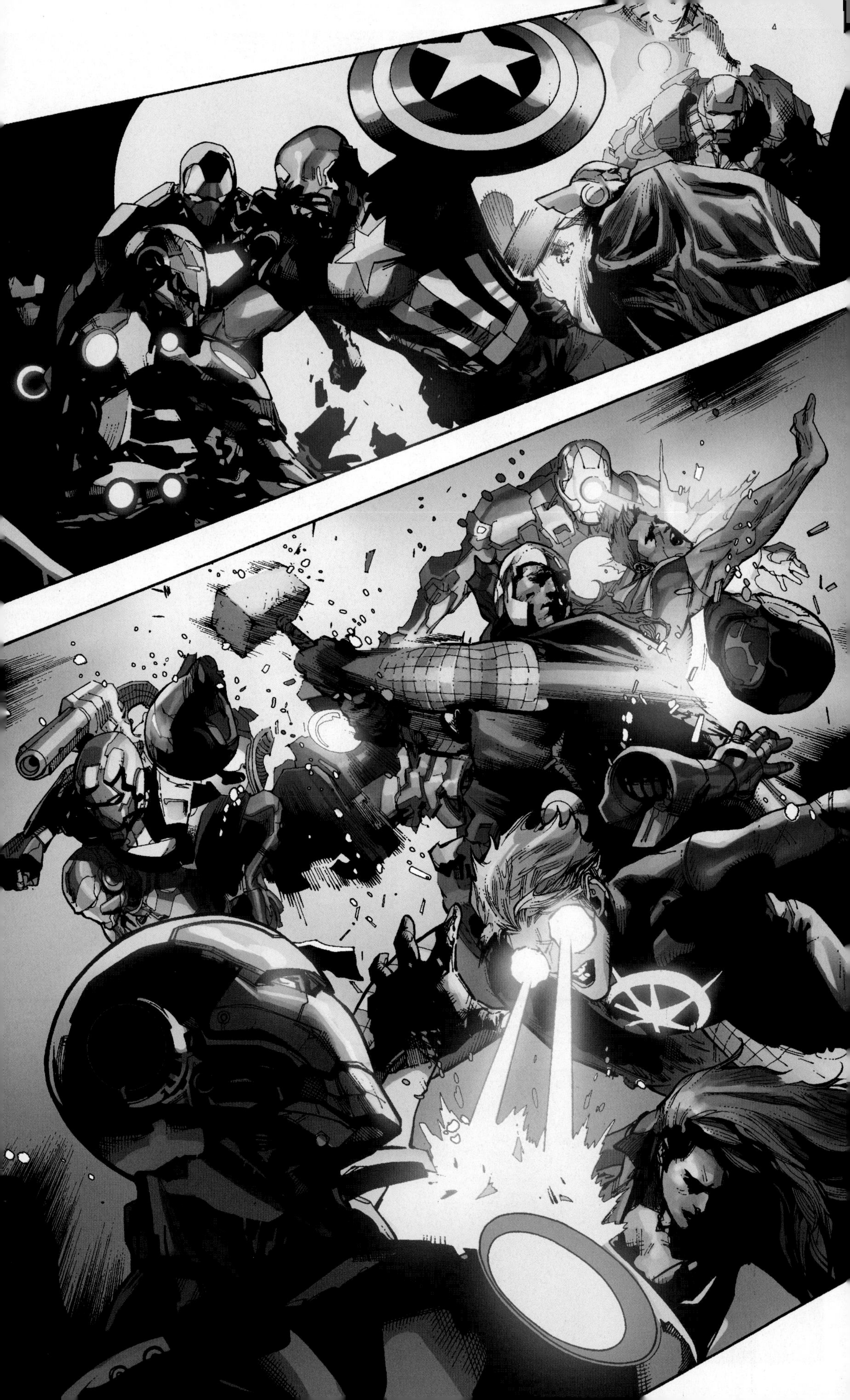

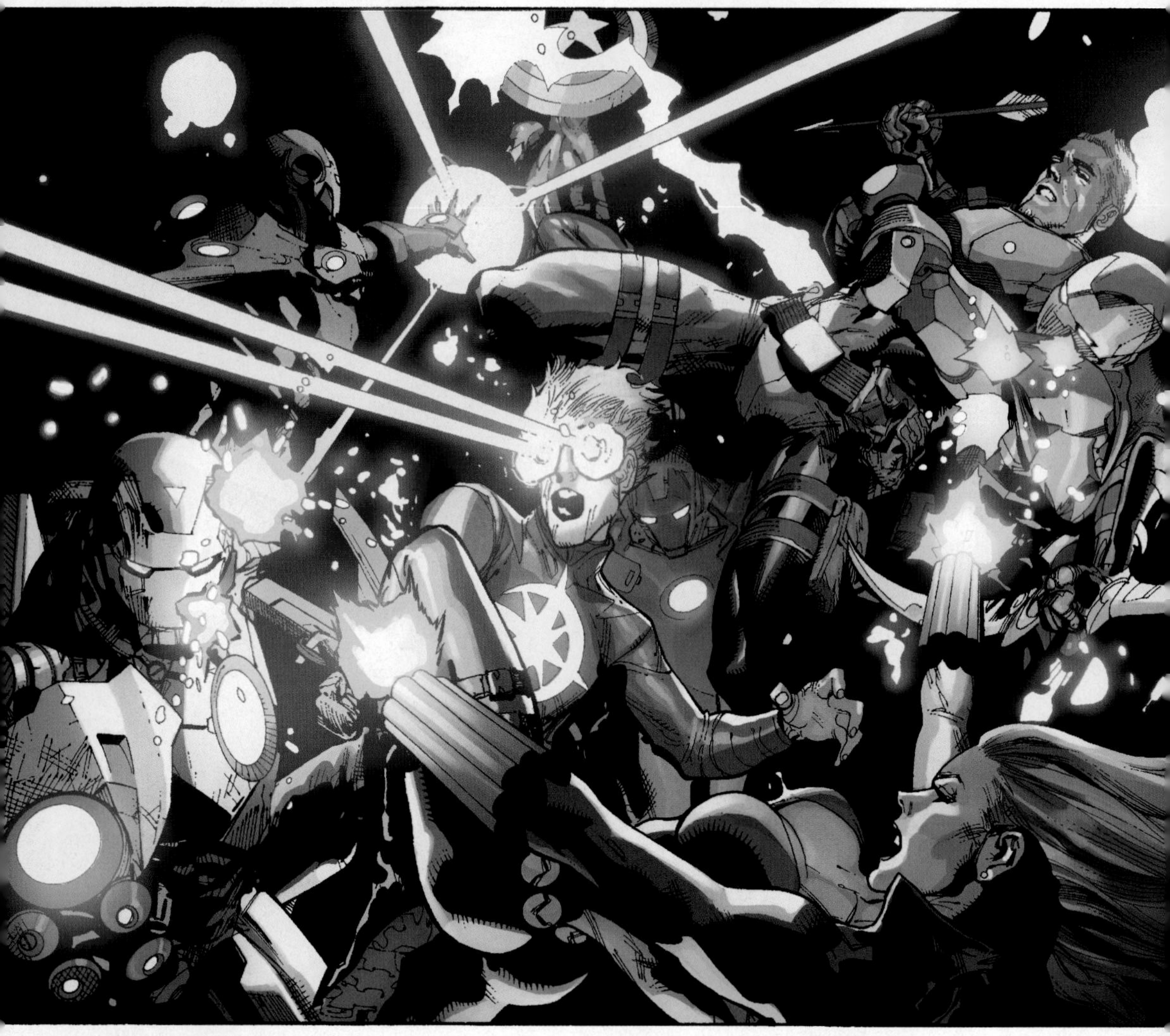

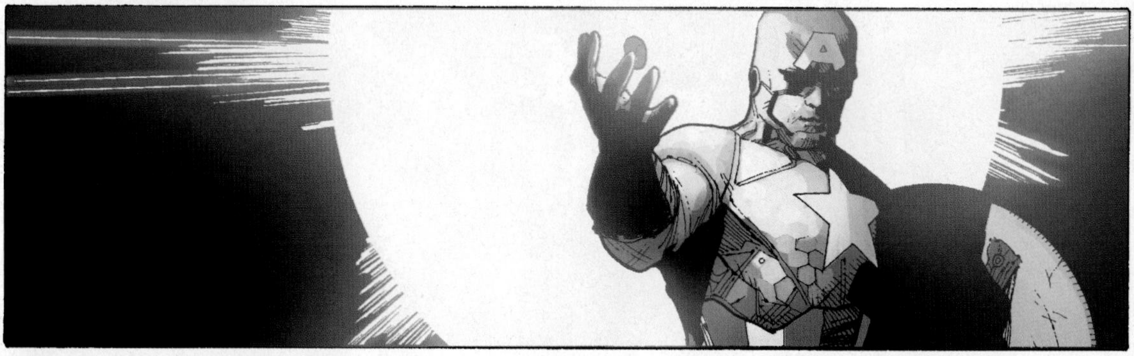

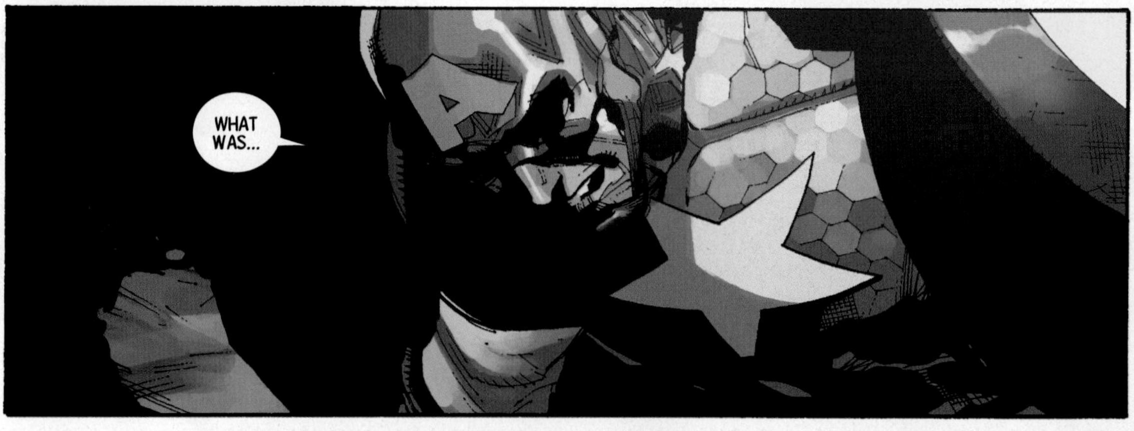
WHAT WAS...

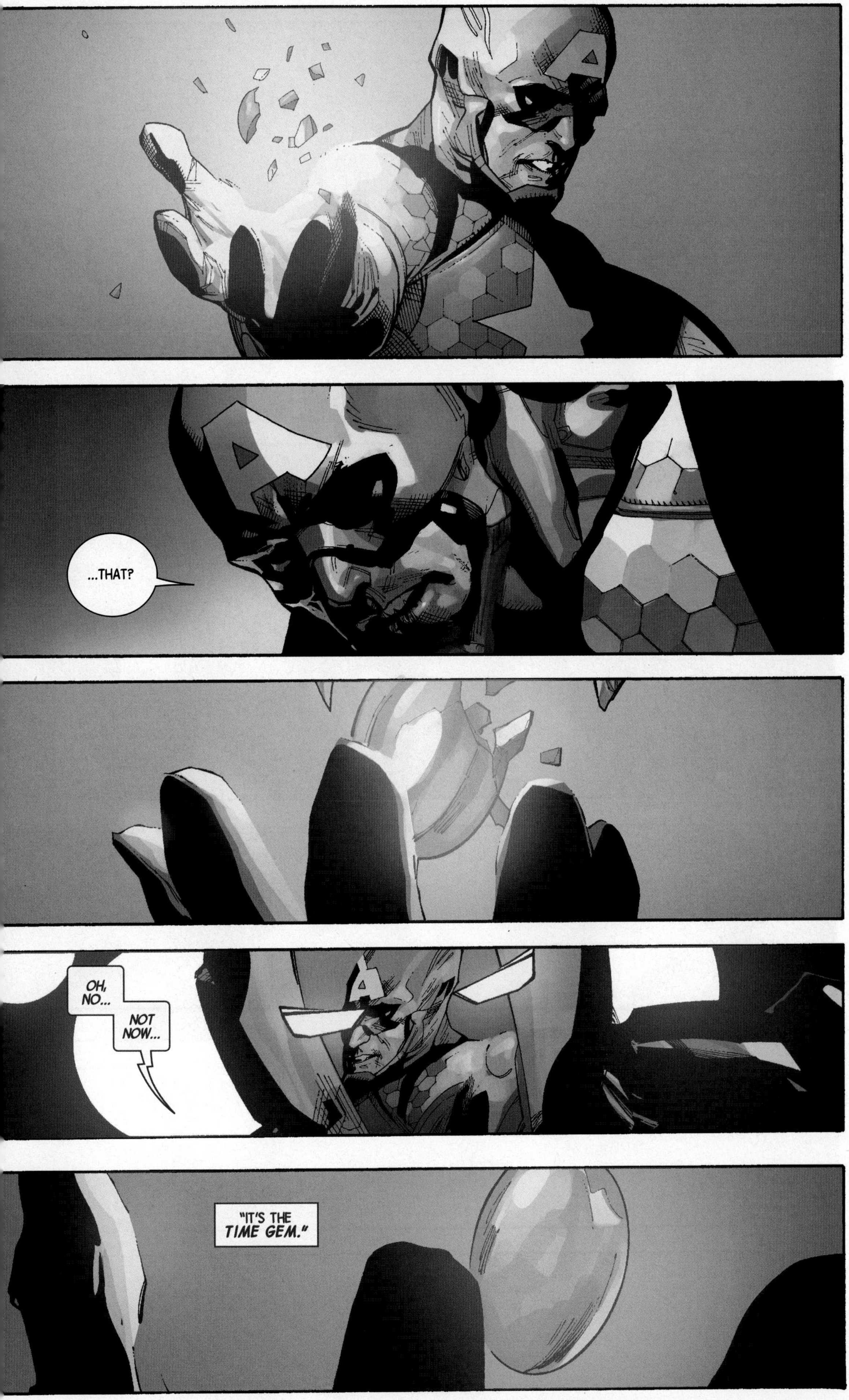
...THAT?
OH, NO...
NOT NOW...
"IT'S THE TIME GEM."

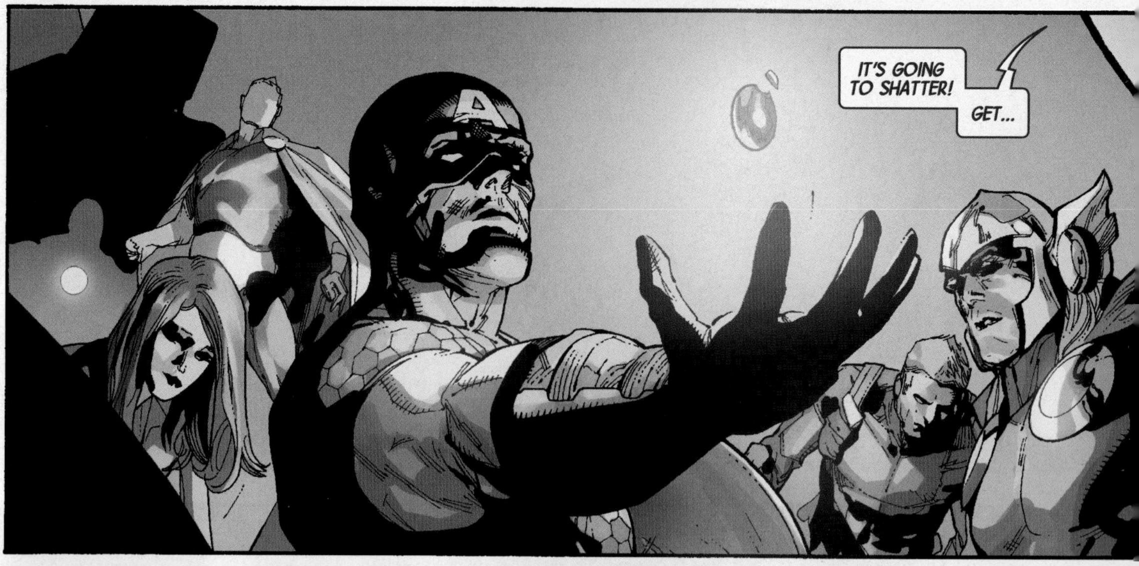
IT'S GOING TO SHATTER!
GET...
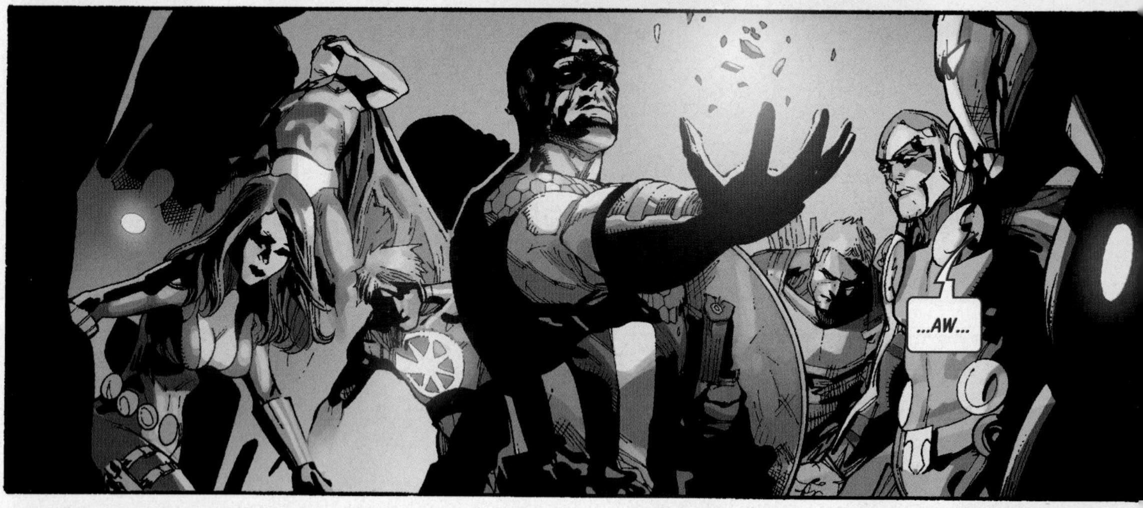
...AW...
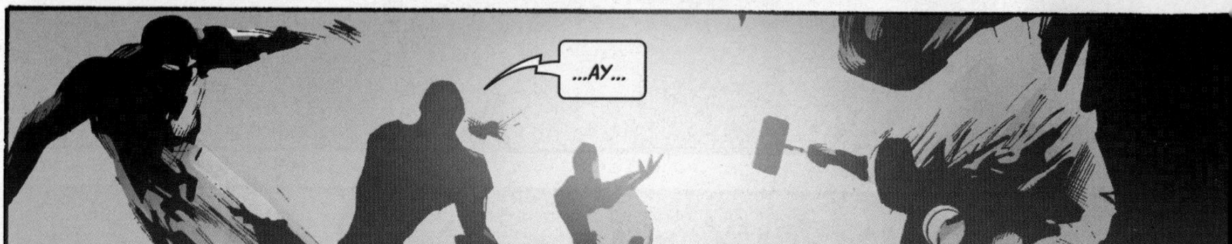
...AY...
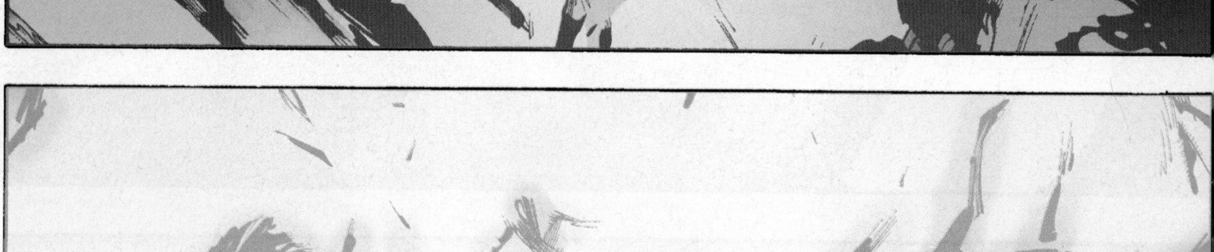
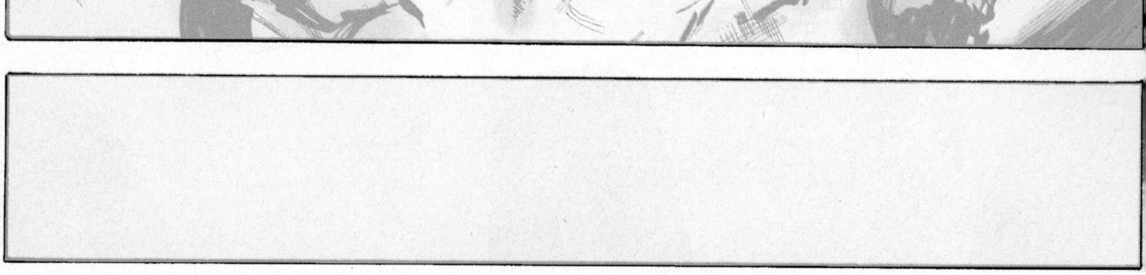

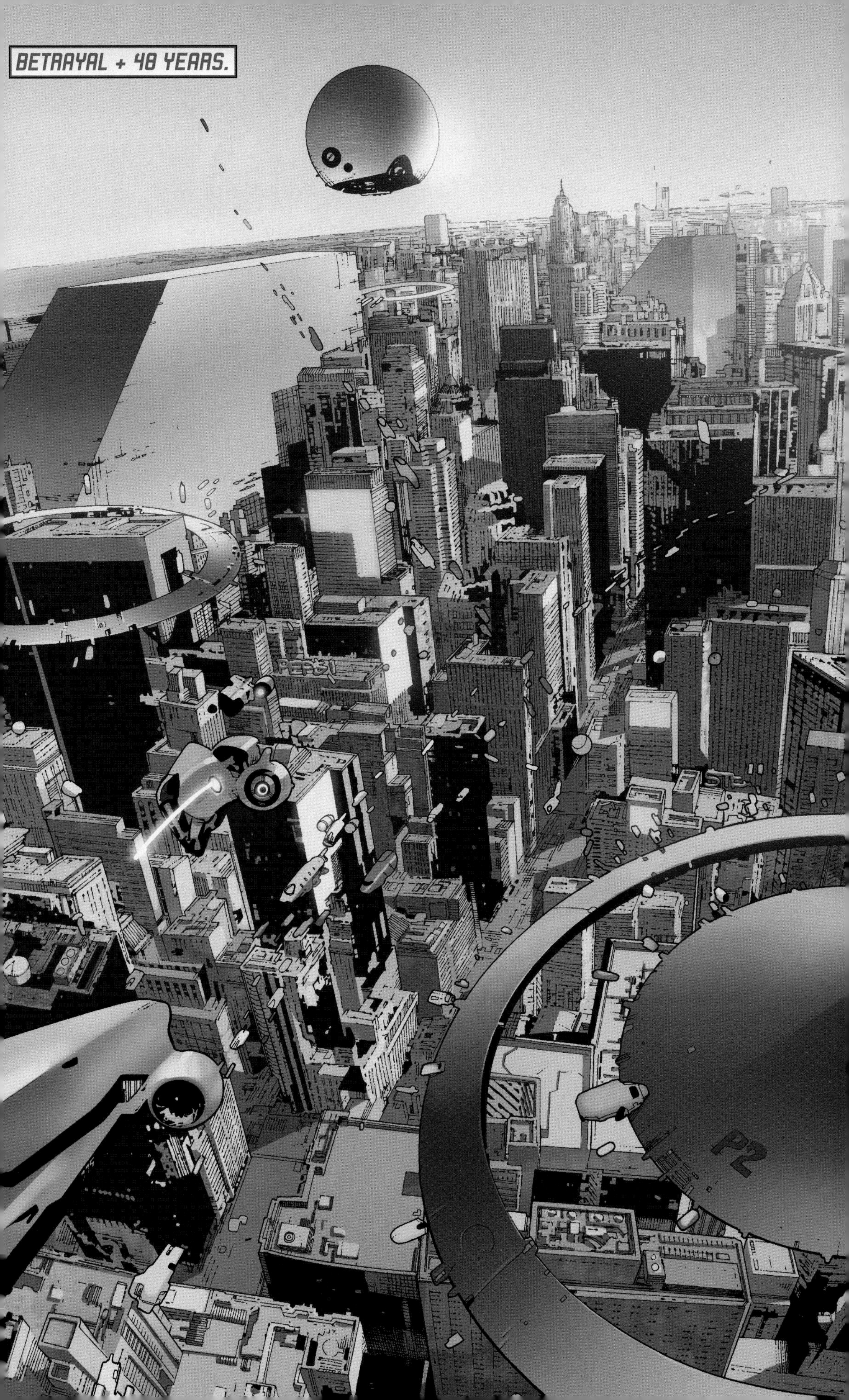
BETRAYAL + 48 YEARS.
P2

"FIFTY INTO THE FUTURE"

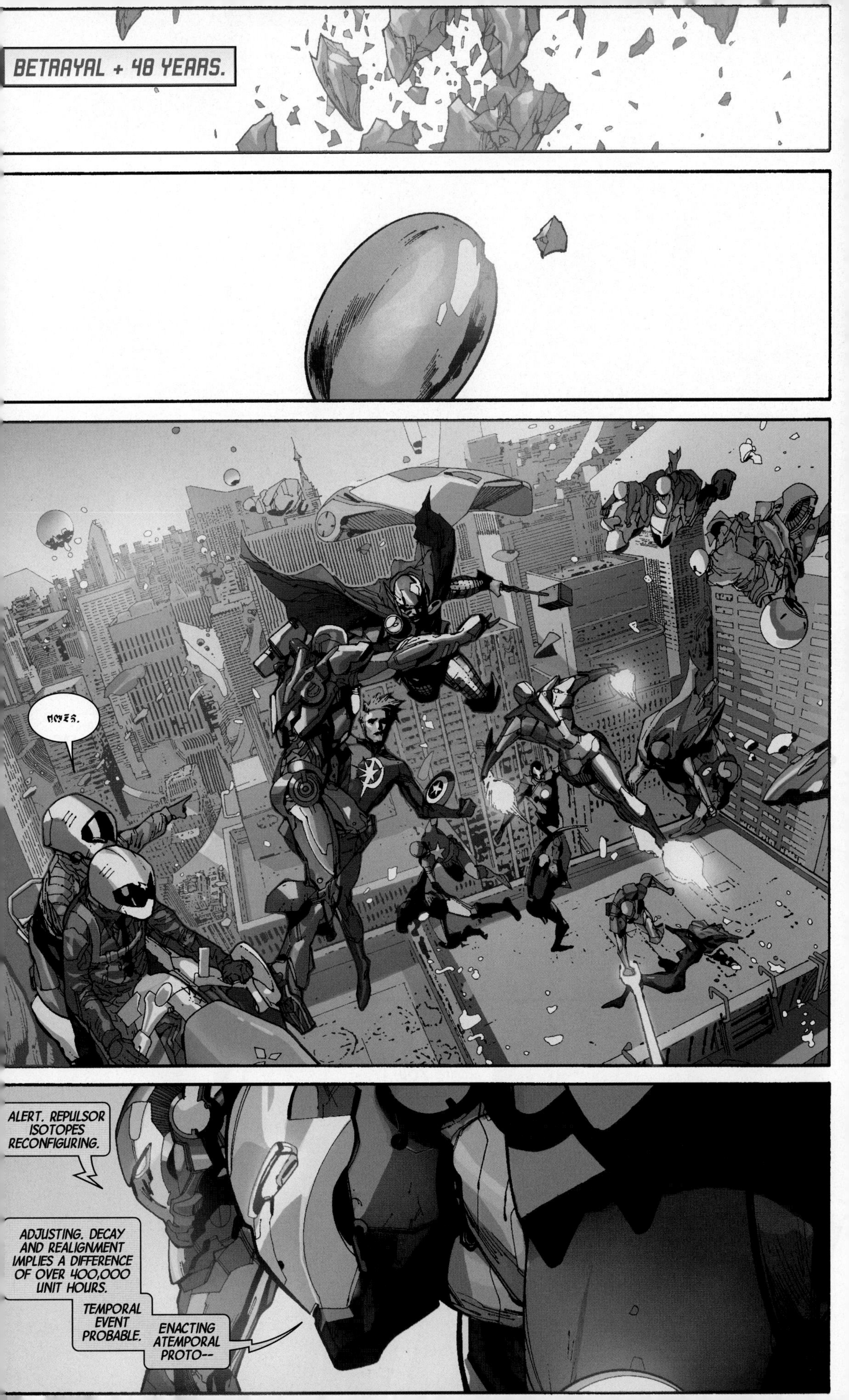
BETRAYAL + 48 YEARS.
ALERT. REPULSOR ISOTOPES RECONFIGURING.
ADJUSTING. DECAY AND REALIGNMENT IMPLIES A DIFFERENCE OF OVER 400,000 UNIT HOURS.
TEMPORAL EVENT PROBABLE.
ENACTING ATEMPORAL PROTO--

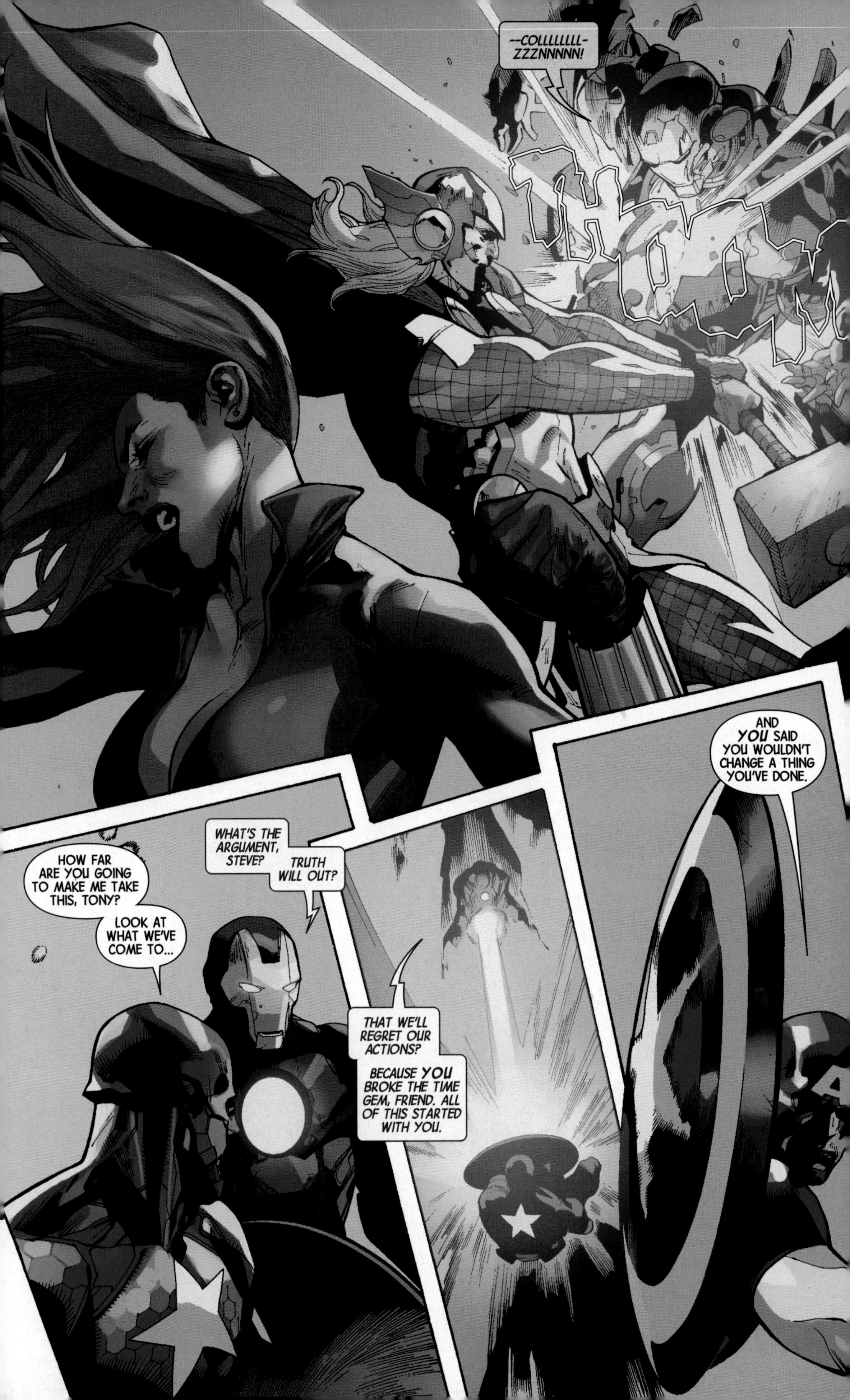
--COLLLLLLLL-ZZZNNNNN!
HOW FAR ARE YOU GOING TO MAKE ME TAKE THIS, TONY?
LOOK AT WHAT WE'VE COME TO...
WHAT'S THE ARGUMENT, STEVE?
TRUTH WILL OUT?
THAT WE'LL REGRET OUR ACTIONS?
BECAUSE YOU BROKE THE TIME GEM, FRIEND. ALL OF THIS STARTED WITH YOU.
AND YOU SAID YOU WOULDN'T CHANGE A THING YOU'VE DONE.

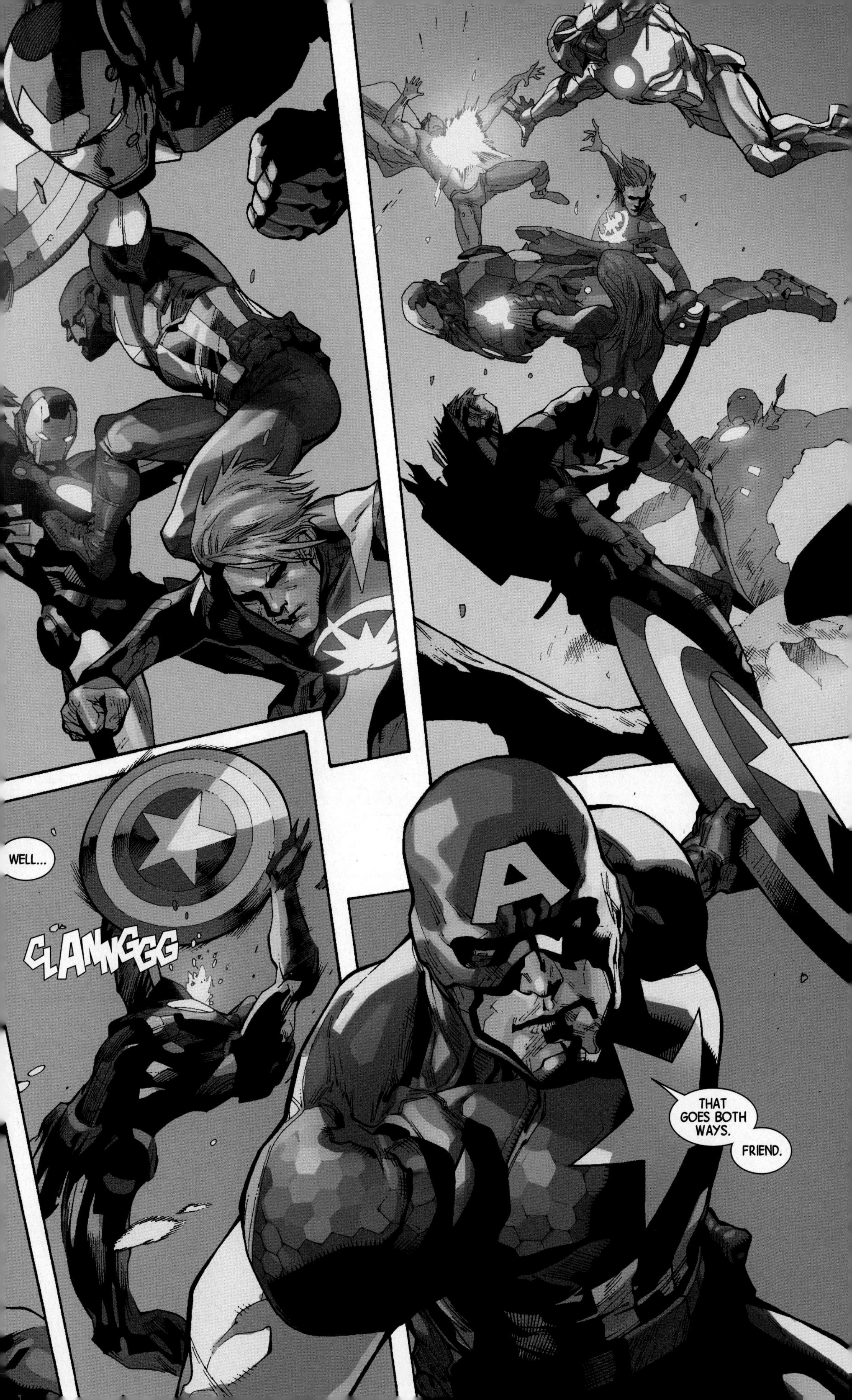
WELL...
CLANNGGG
THAT GOES BOTH WAYS.
FRIEND.

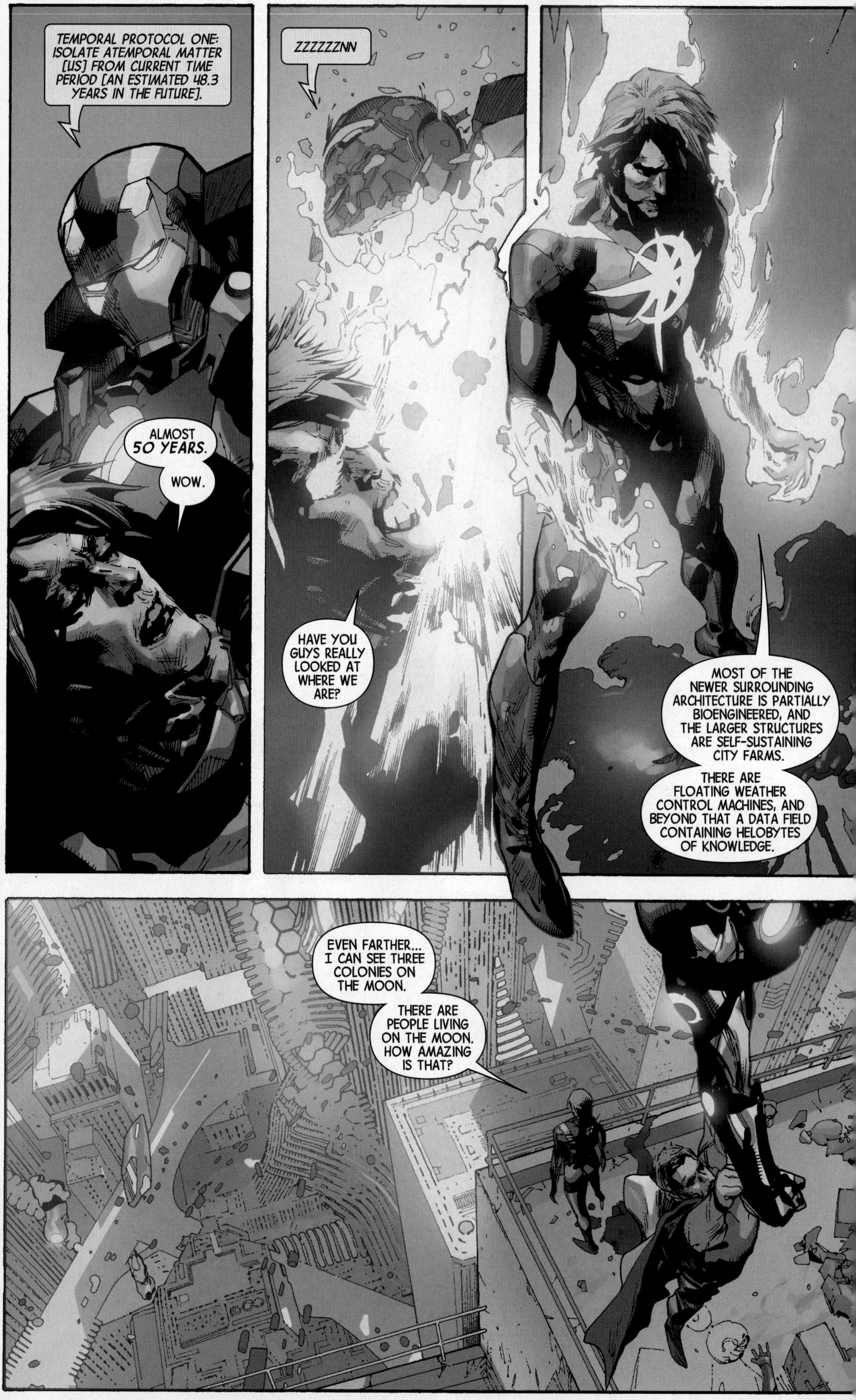
TEMPORAL PROTOCOL ONE: ISOLATE ATEMPORAL MATTER [US] FROM CURRENT TIME PERIOD [AN ESTIMATED 48.3 YEARS IN THE FUTURE].
ALMOST 50 YEARS.
WOW.
ZZZZZZNN
HAVE YOU GUYS REALLY LOOKED AT WHERE WE ARE?
MOST OF THE NEWER SURROUNDING ARCHITECTURE IS PARTIALLY BIOENGINEERED, AND THE LARGER STRUCTURES ARE SELF-SUSTAINING CITY FARMS.
THERE ARE FLOATING WEATHER CONTROL MACHINES, AND BEYOND THAT A DATA FIELD CONTAINING HELOBYTES OF KNOWLEDGE.
EVEN FARTHER... I CAN SEE THREE COLONIES ON THE MOON.
THERE ARE PEOPLE LIVING ON THE MOON. HOW AMAZING IS THAT?

TRULY REMARKABLE.

SHHRRIPPP

WE SHOULD MARVEL AT *OUR* ACHIEVEMENTS, STARBRAND... BUT ALL PROGRESS IS THE RESULT OF A WELL-ORDERED MIND.

SO FIRST THINGS FIRST, YOUNG MAN.

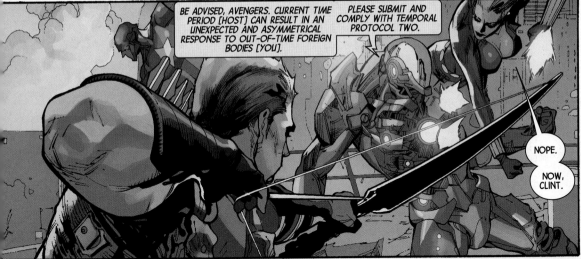

BE ADVISED, AVENGERS. CURRENT TIME PERIOD [HOST] CAN RESULT IN AN UNEXPECTED AND ASYMMETRICAL RESPONSE TO OUT-OF-TIME FOREIGN BODIES [YOU].

PLEASE SUBMIT AND COMPLY WITH TEMPORAL PROTOCOL TWO.

NOPE.

NOW, CLINT.

GOT IT.

BOOM

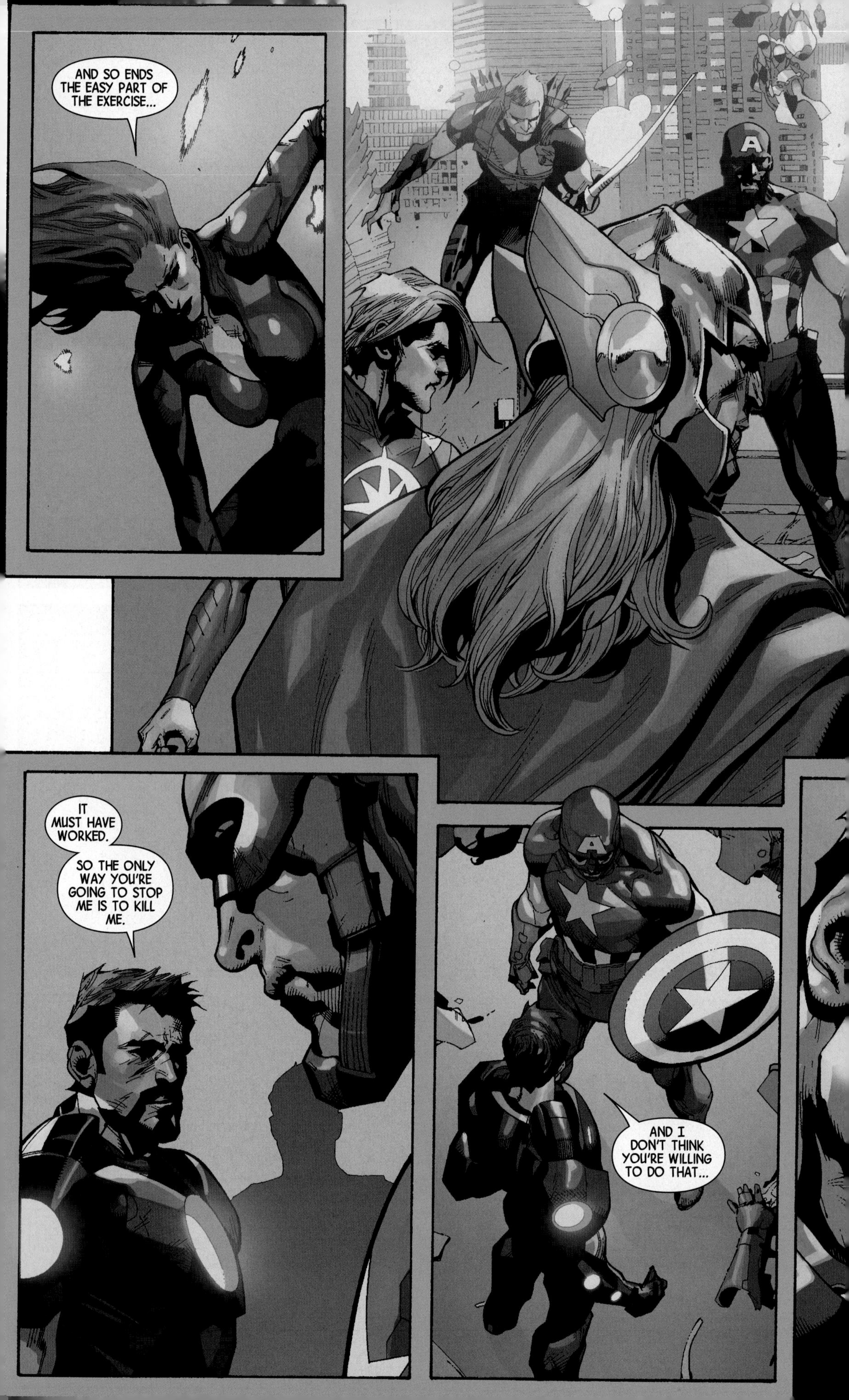
AND SO ENDS THE EASY PART OF THE EXERCISE...
IT MUST HAVE WORKED.
SO THE ONLY WAY YOU'RE GOING TO STOP ME IS TO KILL ME.
AND I DON'T THINK YOU'RE WILLING TO DO THAT...

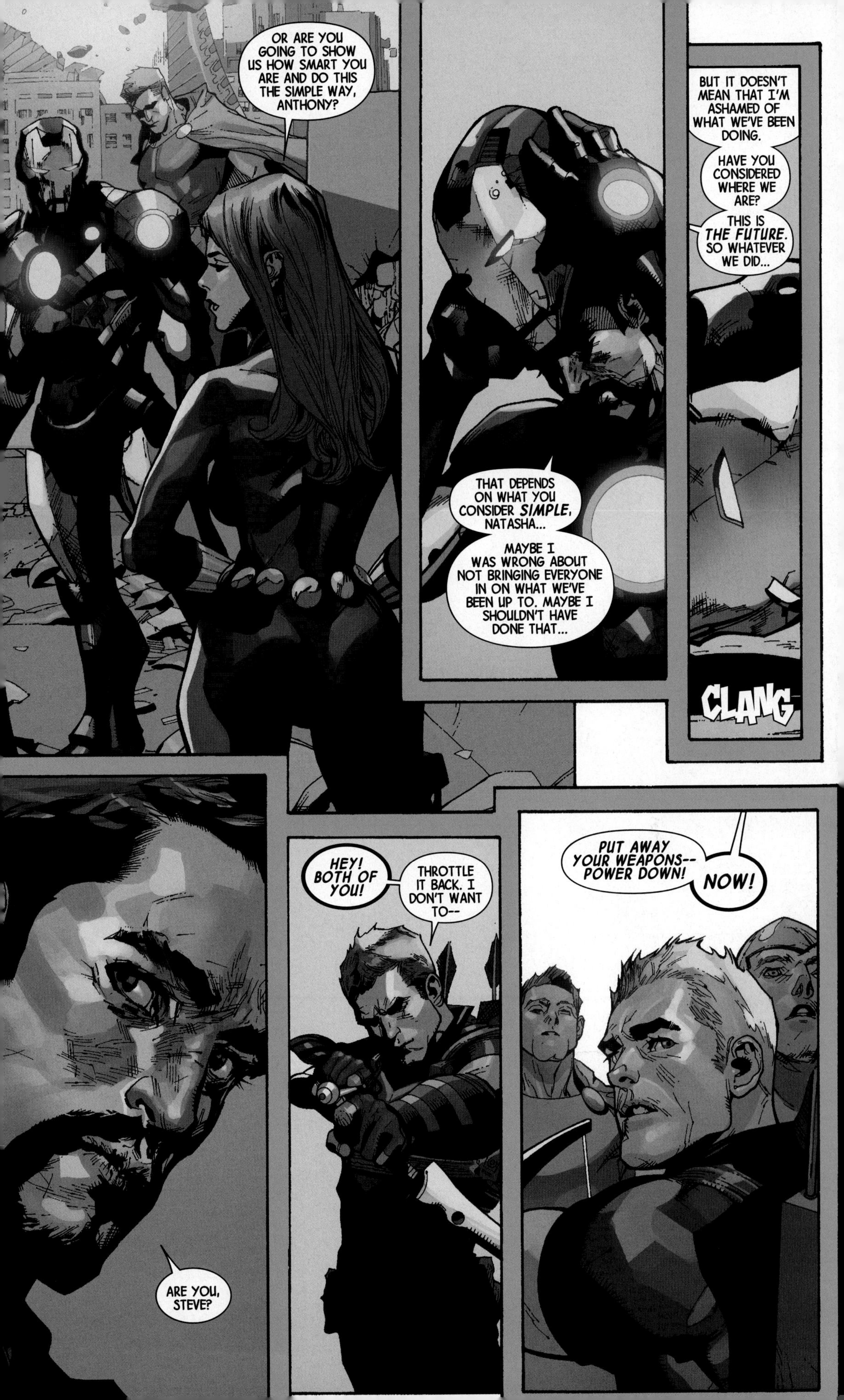
OR ARE YOU GOING TO SHOW US HOW SMART YOU ARE AND DO THIS THE SIMPLE WAY, ANTHONY?
THAT DEPENDS ON WHAT YOU CONSIDER *SIMPLE*, NATASHA...
MAYBE I WAS WRONG ABOUT NOT BRINGING EVERYONE IN ON WHAT WE'VE BEEN UP TO. MAYBE I SHOULDN'T HAVE DONE THAT...
BUT IT DOESN'T MEAN THAT I'M ASHAMED OF WHAT WE'VE BEEN DOING.
HAVE YOU CONSIDERED WHERE WE ARE?
THIS IS *THE FUTURE*. SO WHATEVER WE DID...
CLANG
ARE YOU, STEVE?
HEY! BOTH OF YOU!
THROTTLE IT BACK. I DON'T WANT TO--
PUT AWAY YOUR WEAPONS-- POWER DOWN!
NOW!

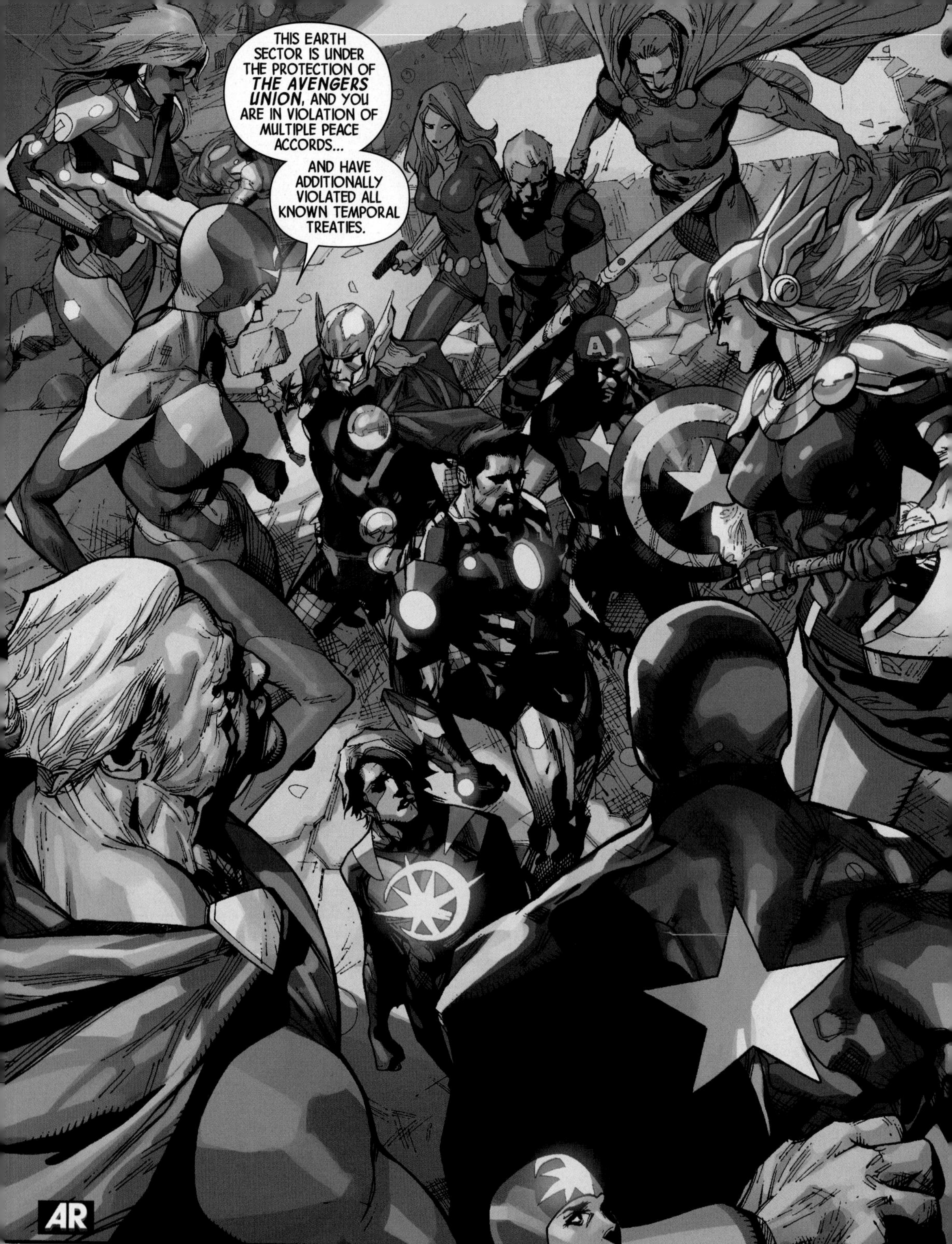
THIS EARTH SECTOR IS UNDER THE PROTECTION OF ***THE AVENGERS UNION***, AND YOU ARE IN VIOLATION OF MULTIPLE PEACE ACCORDS...
AND HAVE ADDITIONALLY VIOLATED ALL KNOWN TEMPORAL TREATIES.
AR

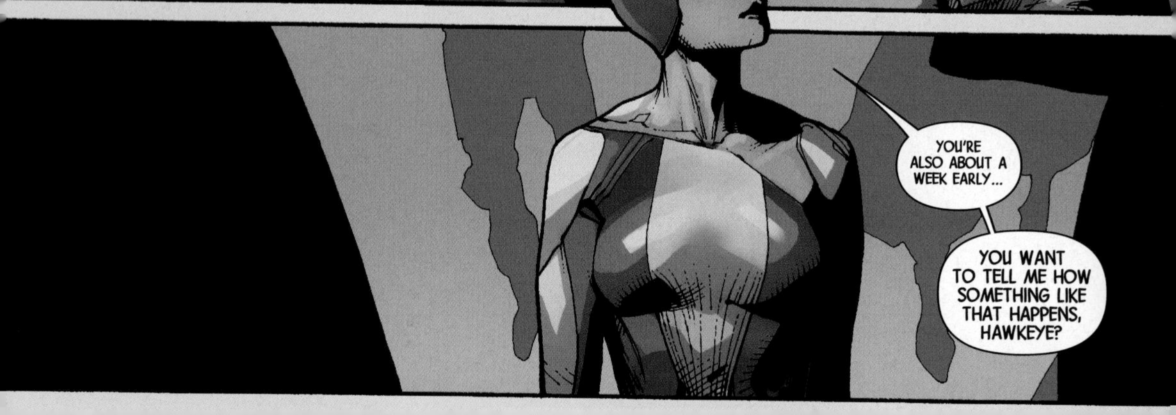
YOU'RE ALSO ABOUT A WEEK EARLY...
YOU WANT TO TELL ME HOW SOMETHING LIKE THAT HAPPENS, HAWKEYE?

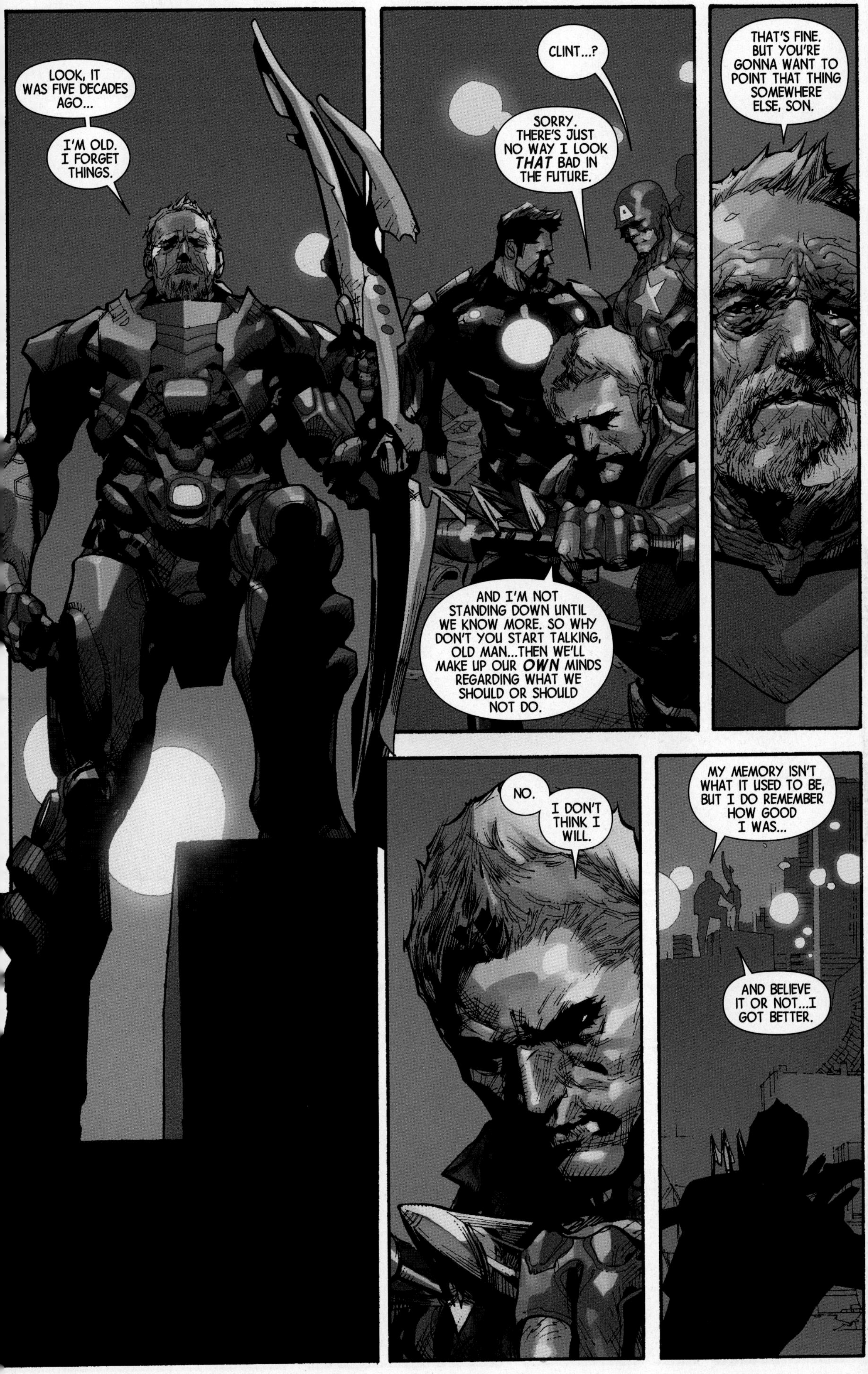
LOOK, IT WAS FIVE DECADES AGO...
I'M OLD. I FORGET THINGS.
CLINT...?
SORRY. THERE'S JUST NO WAY I LOOK THAT BAD IN THE FUTURE.
AND I'M NOT STANDING DOWN UNTIL WE KNOW MORE. SO WHY DON'T YOU START TALKING, OLD MAN...THEN WE'LL MAKE UP OUR OWN MINDS REGARDING WHAT WE SHOULD OR SHOULD NOT DO.
THAT'S FINE. BUT YOU'RE GONNA WANT TO POINT THAT THING SOMEWHERE ELSE, SON.
NO.
I DON'T THINK I WILL.
MY MEMORY ISN'T WHAT IT USED TO BE, BUT I DO REMEMBER HOW GOOD I WAS...
AND BELIEVE IT OR NOT...I GOT BETTER.

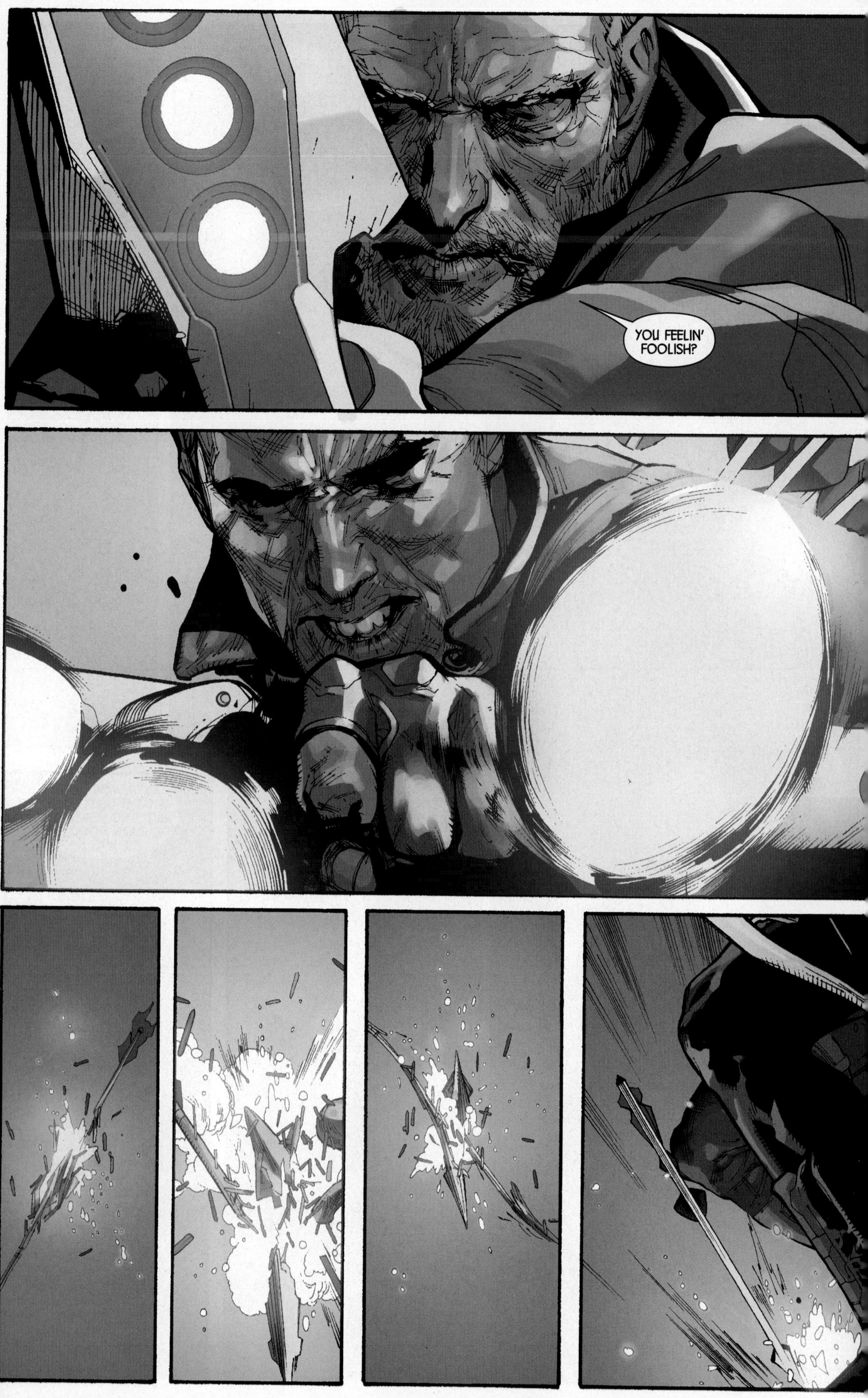
YOU FEELIN' FOOLISH?

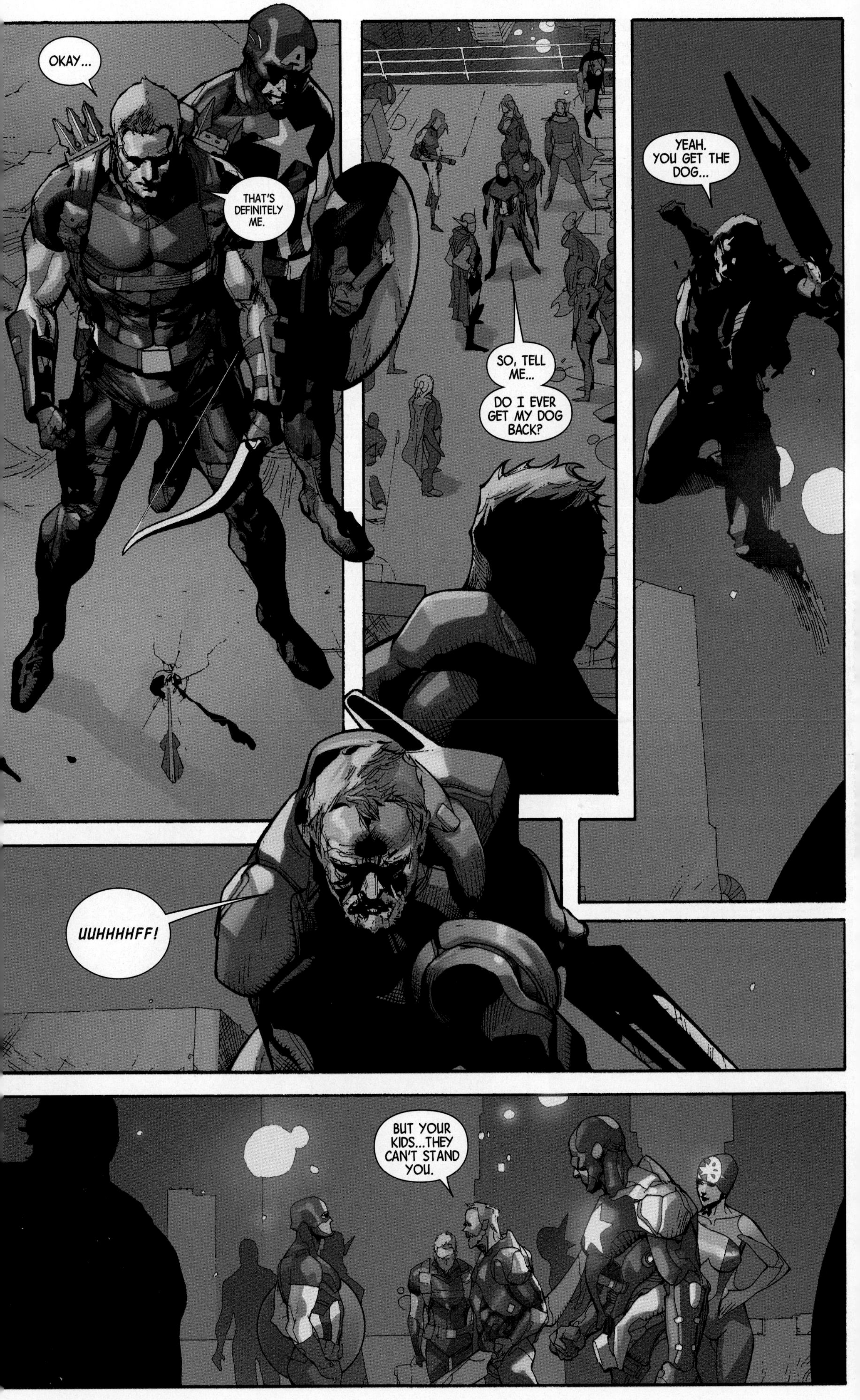
OKAY...
THAT'S DEFINITELY ME.
SO, TELL ME...
DO I EVER GET MY DOG BACK?
YEAH. YOU GET THE DOG...
UUHHHHFF!
BUT YOUR KIDS...THEY CAN'T STAND YOU.

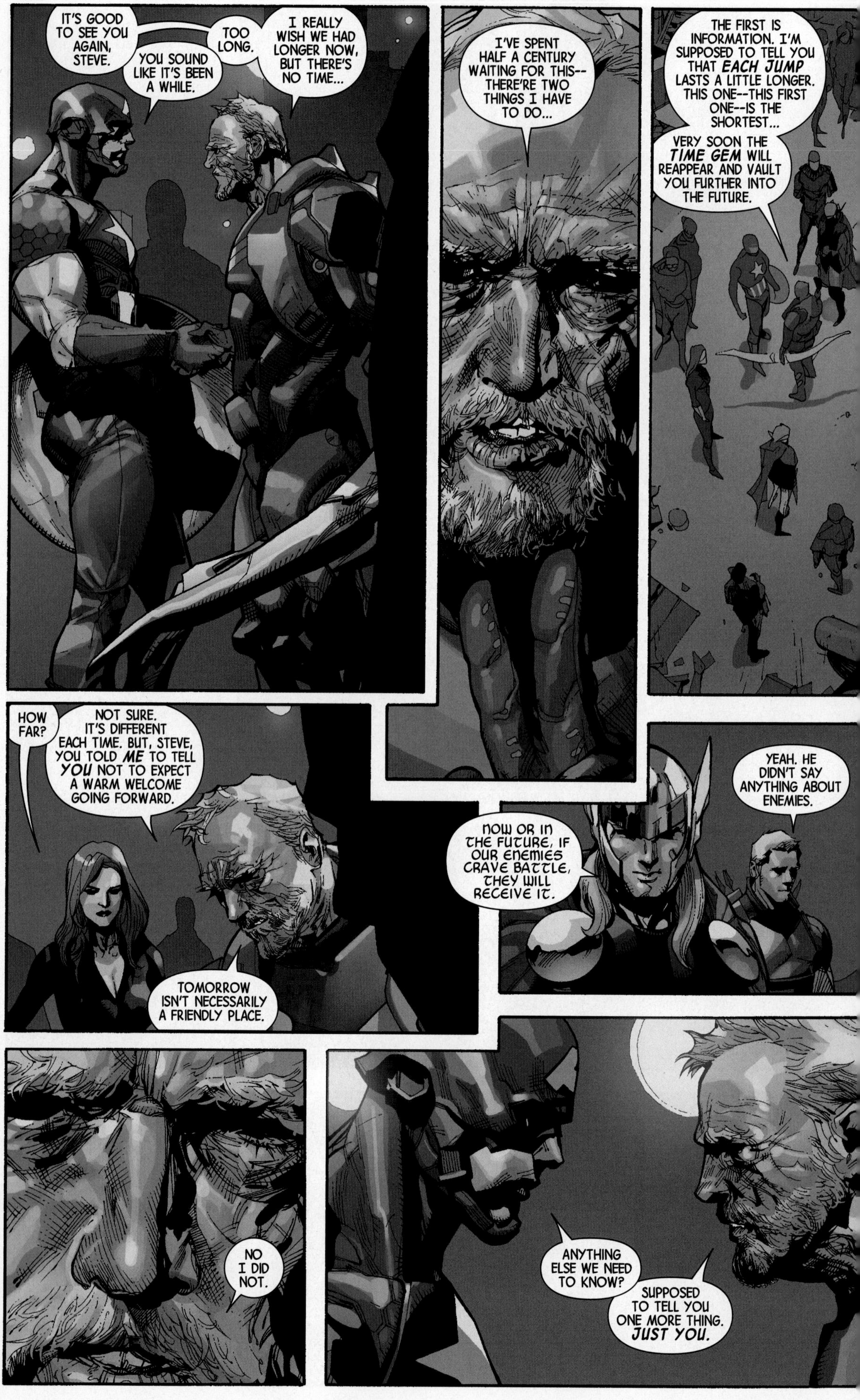
IT'S GOOD TO SEE YOU AGAIN, STEVE.
TOO LONG.
YOU SOUND LIKE IT'S BEEN A WHILE.
I REALLY WISH WE HAD LONGER NOW, BUT THERE'S NO TIME...
I'VE SPENT HALF A CENTURY WAITING FOR THIS-- THERE'RE TWO THINGS I HAVE TO DO...
THE FIRST IS INFORMATION. I'M SUPPOSED TO TELL YOU THAT EACH JUMP LASTS A LITTLE LONGER. THIS ONE--THIS FIRST ONE--IS THE SHORTEST...
VERY SOON THE TIME GEM WILL REAPPEAR AND VAULT YOU FURTHER INTO THE FUTURE.
HOW FAR?
NOT SURE. IT'S DIFFERENT EACH TIME. BUT, STEVE, YOU TOLD ME TO TELL YOU NOT TO EXPECT A WARM WELCOME GOING FORWARD.
TOMORROW ISN'T NECESSARILY A FRIENDLY PLACE.
NOW OR IN THE FUTURE, IF OUR ENEMIES CRAVE BATTLE, THEY WILL RECEIVE IT.
YEAH. HE DIDN'T SAY ANYTHING ABOUT ENEMIES.
NO I DID NOT.
ANYTHING ELSE WE NEED TO KNOW?
SUPPOSED TO TELL YOU ONE MORE THING. JUST YOU.

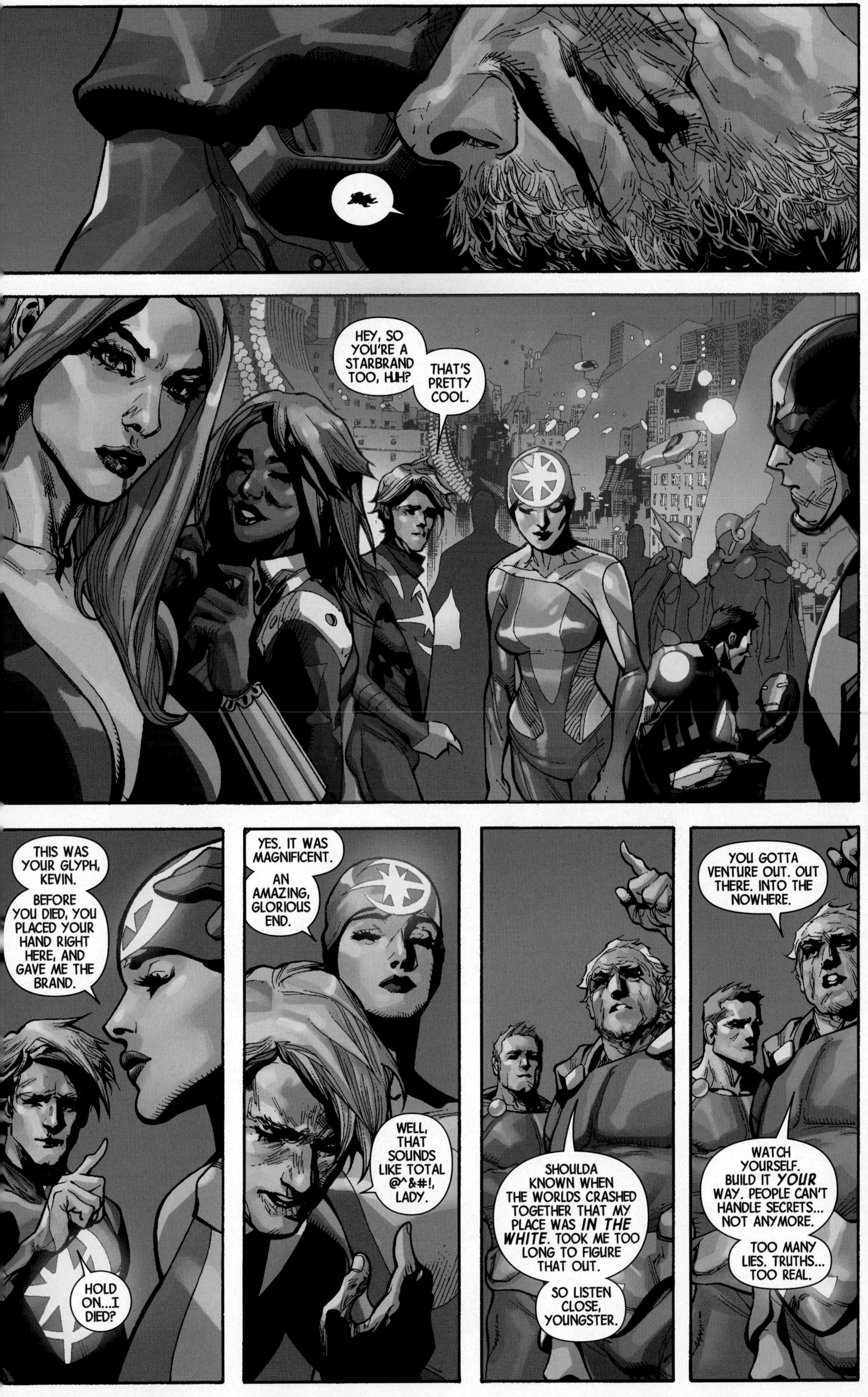

HEY, SO YOU'RE A STARBRAND TOO, HUH?
THAT'S PRETTY COOL.
THIS WAS YOUR GLYPH, KEVIN.
BEFORE YOU DIED, YOU PLACED YOUR HAND RIGHT HERE, AND GAVE ME THE BRAND.
HOLD ON...I DIED?
YES. IT WAS MAGNIFICENT.
AN AMAZING, GLORIOUS END.
WELL, THAT SOUNDS LIKE TOTAL @^&#!, LADY.
SHOULDA KNOWN WHEN THE WORLDS CRASHED TOGETHER THAT MY PLACE WAS IN THE WHITE. TOOK ME TOO LONG TO FIGURE THAT OUT.
SO LISTEN CLOSE, YOUNGSTER.
YOU GOTTA VENTURE OUT. OUT THERE. INTO THE NOWHERE.
WATCH YOURSELF. BUILD IT YOUR WAY. PEOPLE CAN'T HANDLE SECRETS... NOT ANYMORE.
TOO MANY LIES. TRUTHS... TOO REAL.

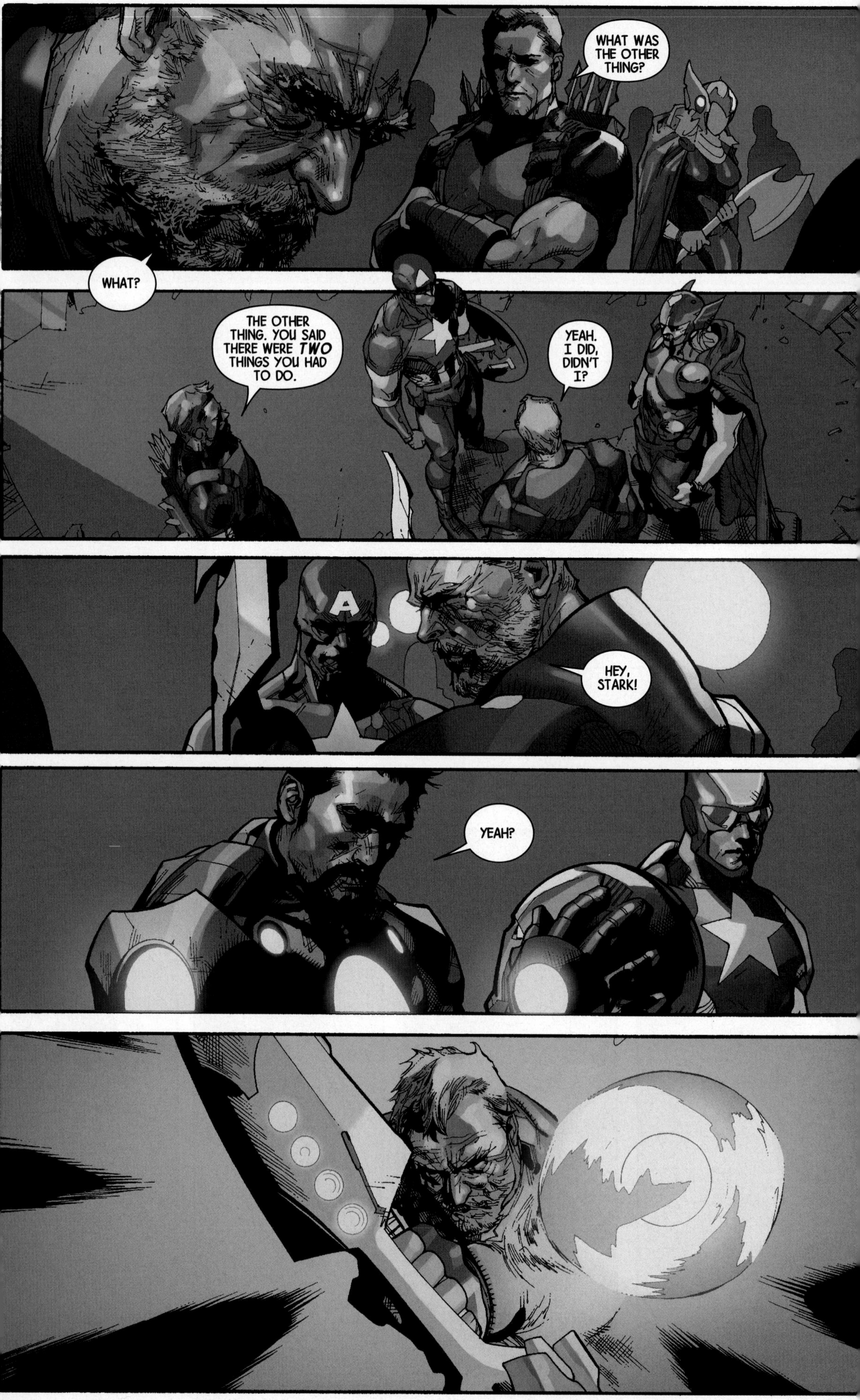
WHAT WAS THE OTHER THING?
WHAT?
THE OTHER THING. YOU SAID THERE WERE TWO THINGS YOU HAD TO DO.
YEAH. I DID, DIDN'T I?
HEY, STARK!
YEAH?

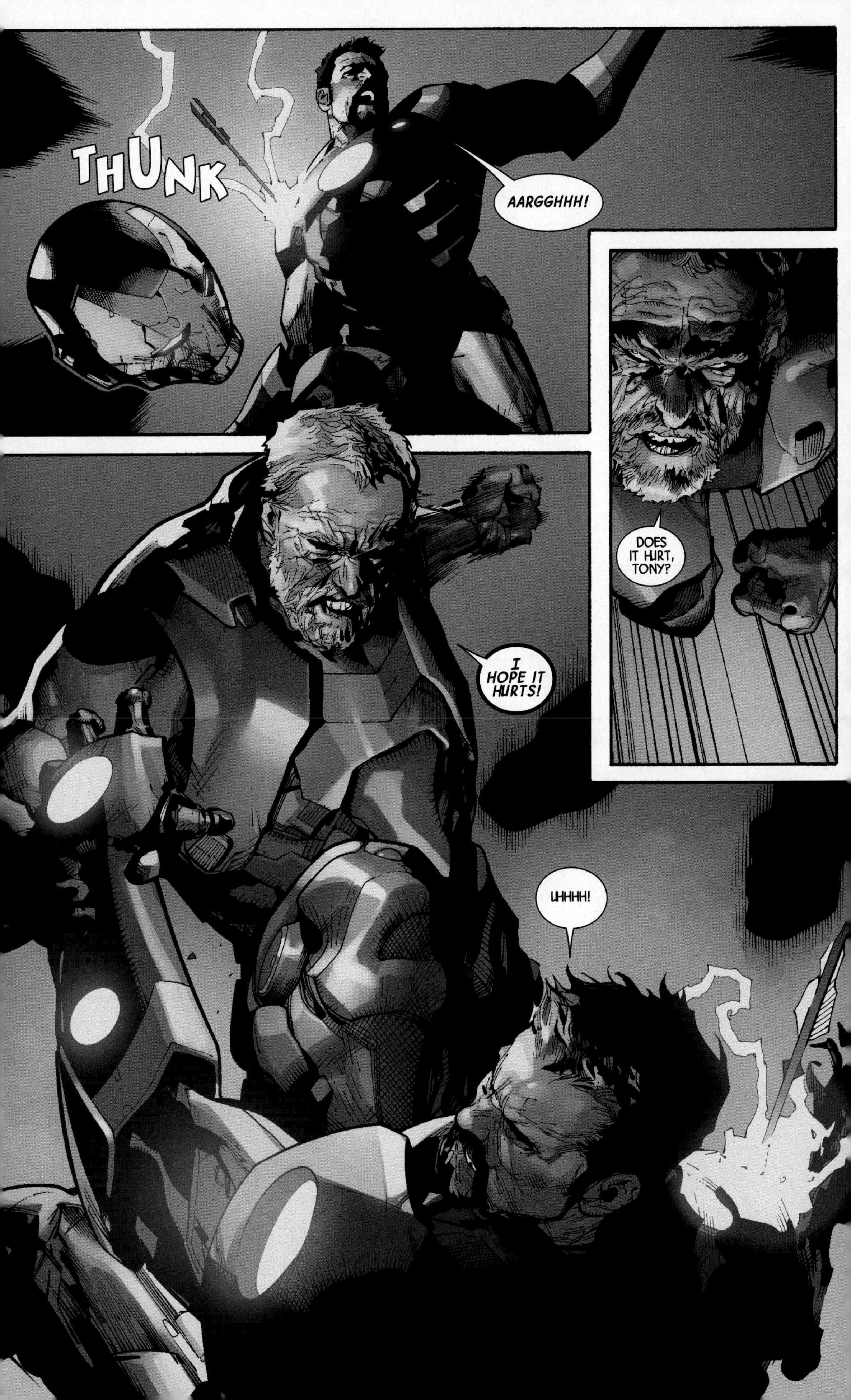
THUNK
AARGGHHH!
DOES IT HURT, TONY?
I HOPE IT HURTS!
UHHHH!

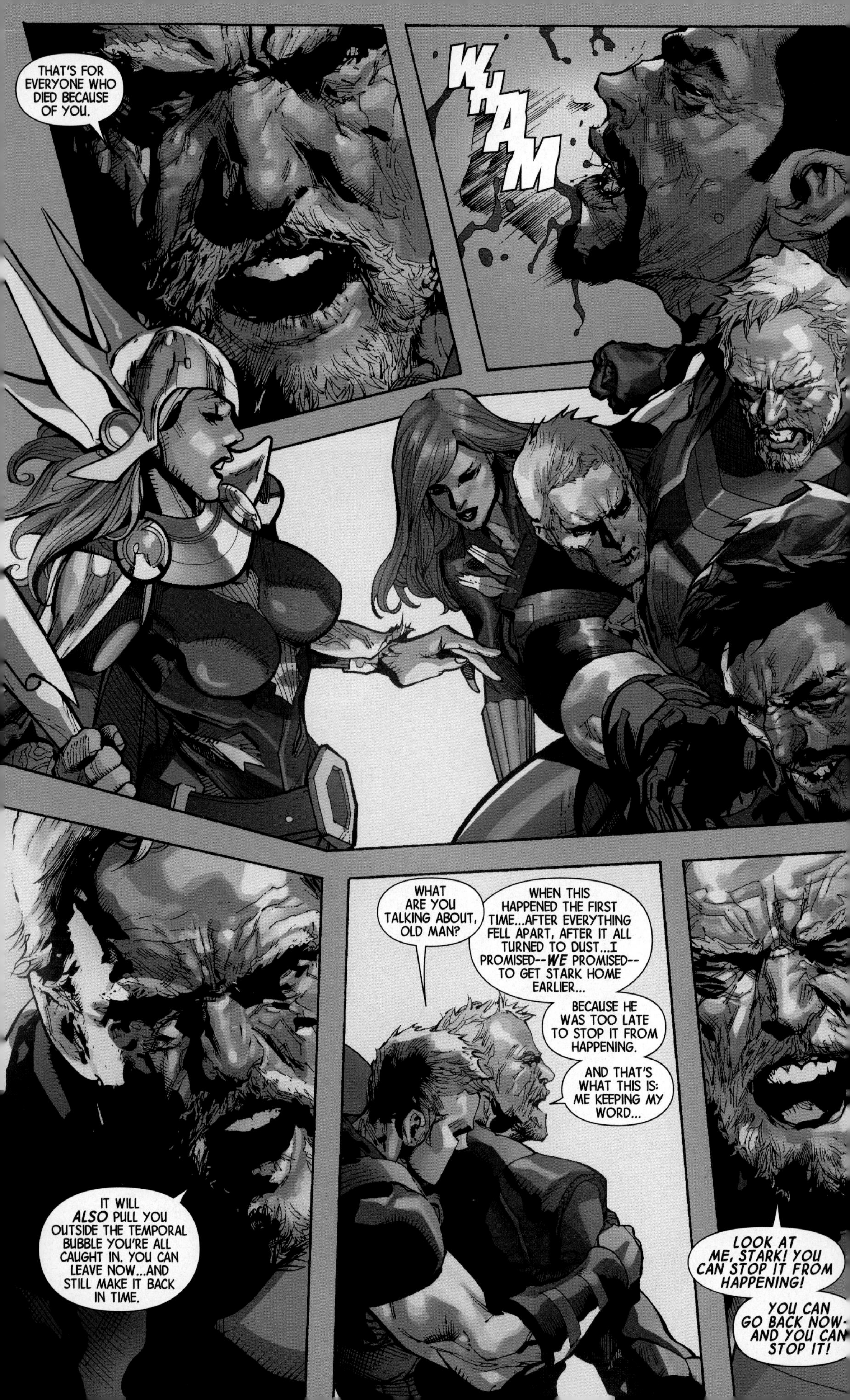
THAT'S FOR EVERYONE WHO DIED BECAUSE OF YOU.
WHAM
WHAT ARE YOU TALKING ABOUT, OLD MAN?
WHEN THIS HAPPENED THE FIRST TIME...AFTER EVERYTHING FELL APART, AFTER IT ALL TURNED TO DUST...I PROMISED--*WE* PROMISED--TO GET STARK HOME EARLIER...
BECAUSE HE WAS TOO LATE TO STOP IT FROM HAPPENING.
AND THAT'S WHAT THIS IS: ME KEEPING MY WORD...
IT WILL *ALSO* PULL YOU OUTSIDE THE TEMPORAL BUBBLE YOU'RE ALL CAUGHT IN. YOU CAN LEAVE NOW...AND STILL MAKE IT BACK IN TIME.
LOOK AT ME, STARK! YOU CAN STOP IT FROM HAPPENING!
YOU CAN GO BACK NOW-AND YOU CAN STOP IT!

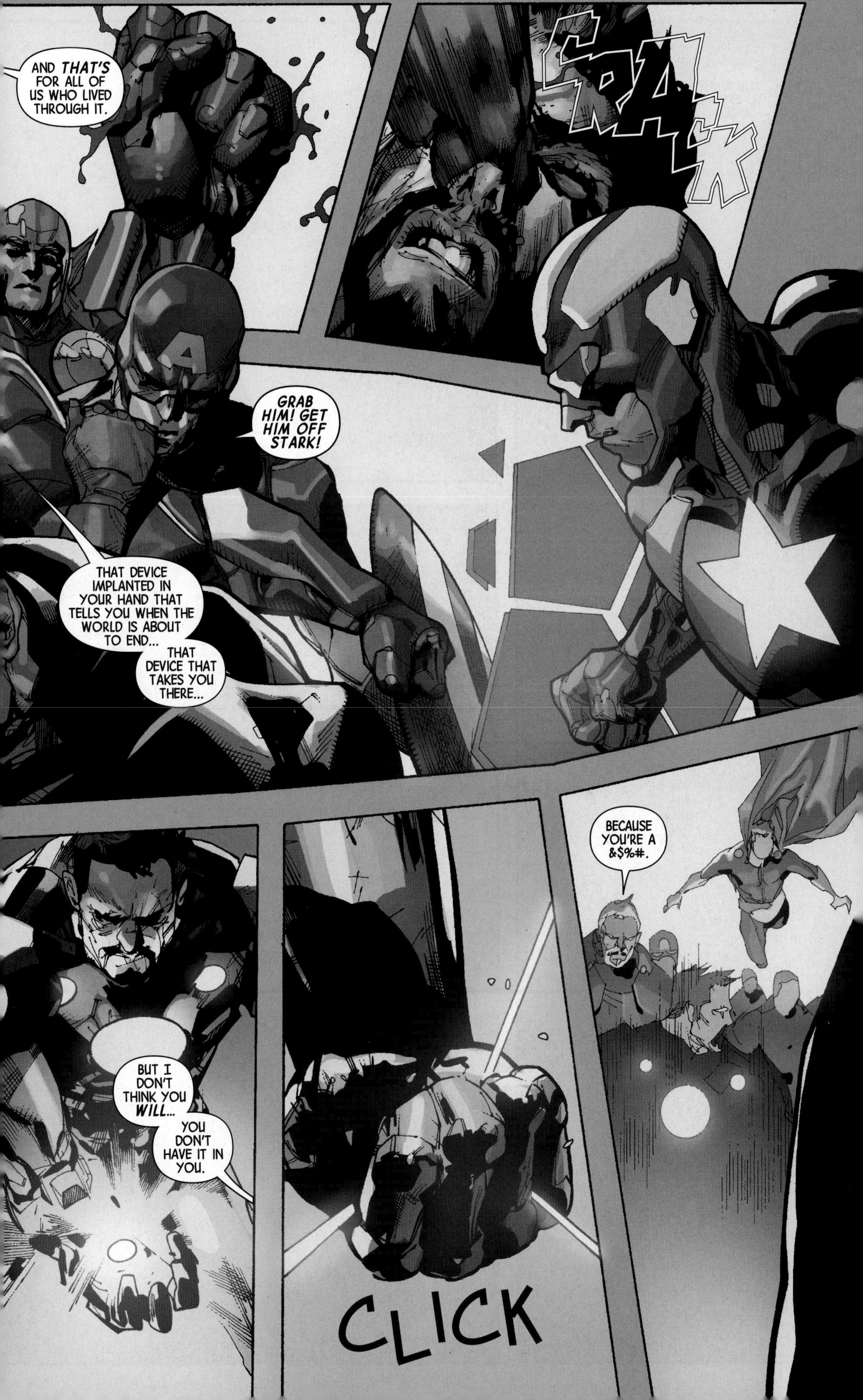
AND THAT'S FOR ALL OF US WHO LIVED THROUGH IT.
CRACK
GRAB HIM! GET HIM OFF STARK!
THAT DEVICE IMPLANTED IN YOUR HAND THAT TELLS YOU WHEN THE WORLD IS ABOUT TO END...
THAT DEVICE THAT TAKES YOU THERE...
BUT I DON'T THINK YOU WILL...
YOU DON'T HAVE IT IN YOU.
CLICK
BECAUSE YOU'RE A &$%#.

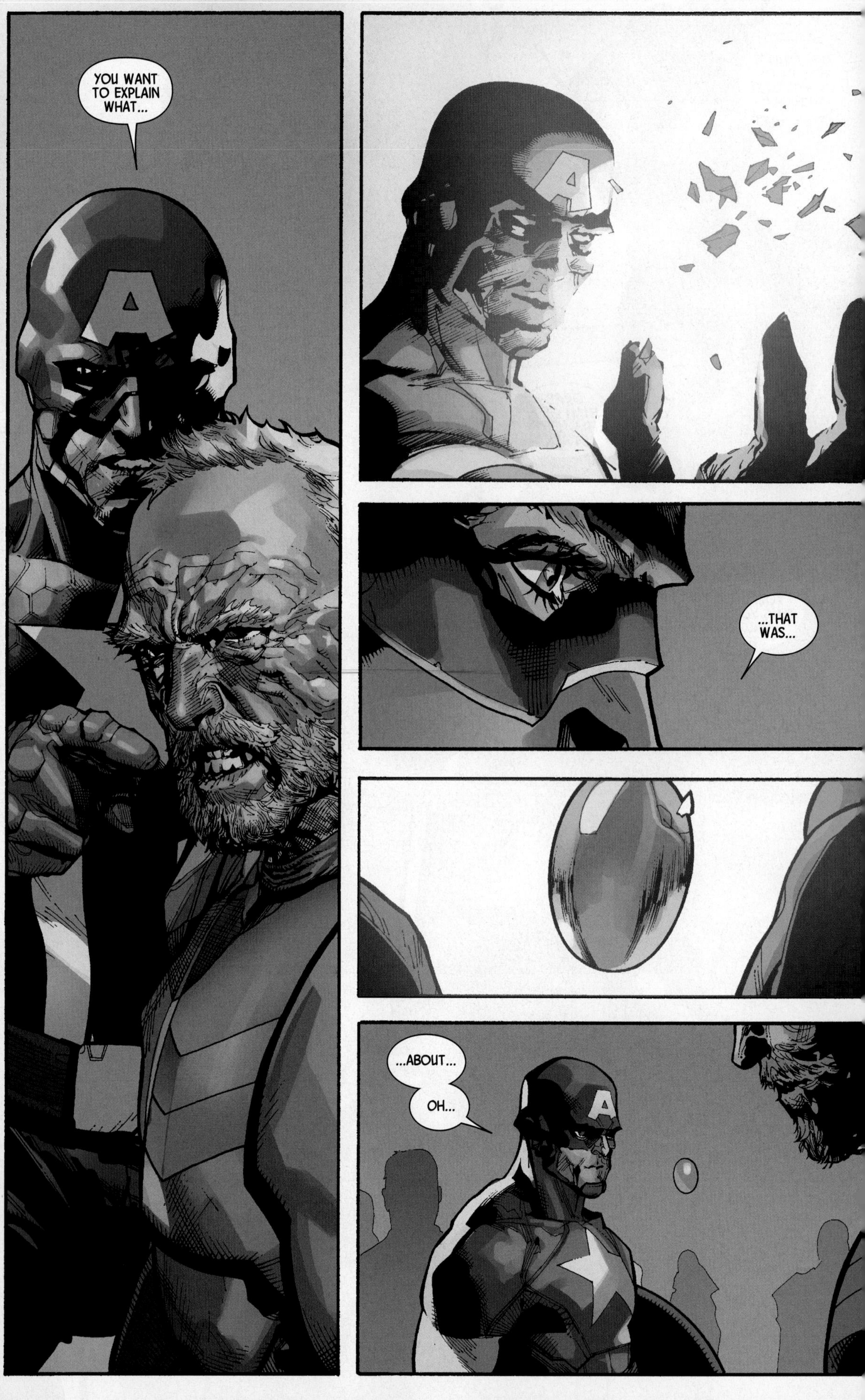
YOU WANT TO EXPLAIN WHAT...
...THAT WAS...
...ABOUT...
OH...

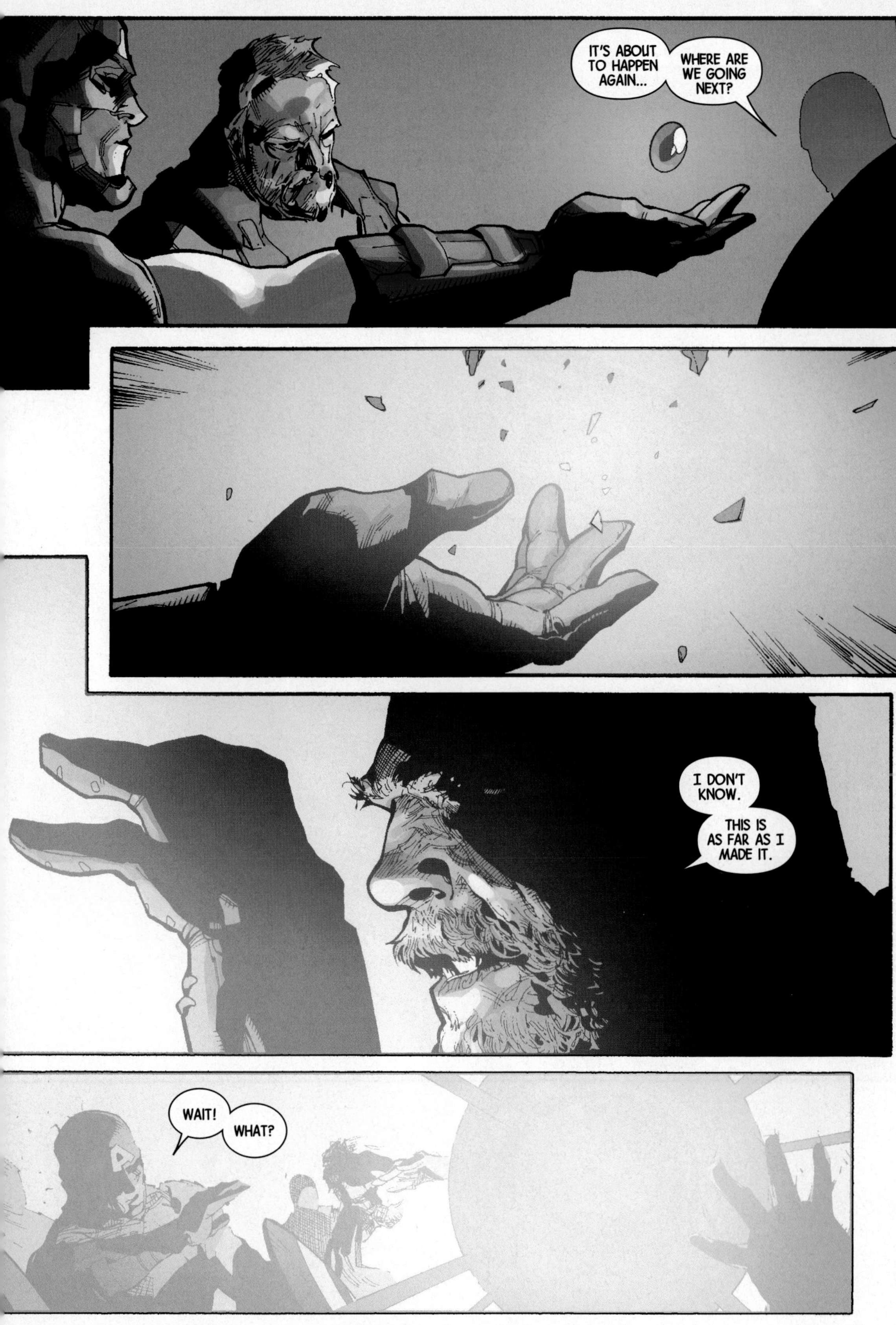
IT'S ABOUT TO HAPPEN AGAIN...
WHERE ARE WE GOING NEXT?
I DON'T KNOW.
THIS IS AS FAR AS I MADE IT.
WAIT!
WHAT?

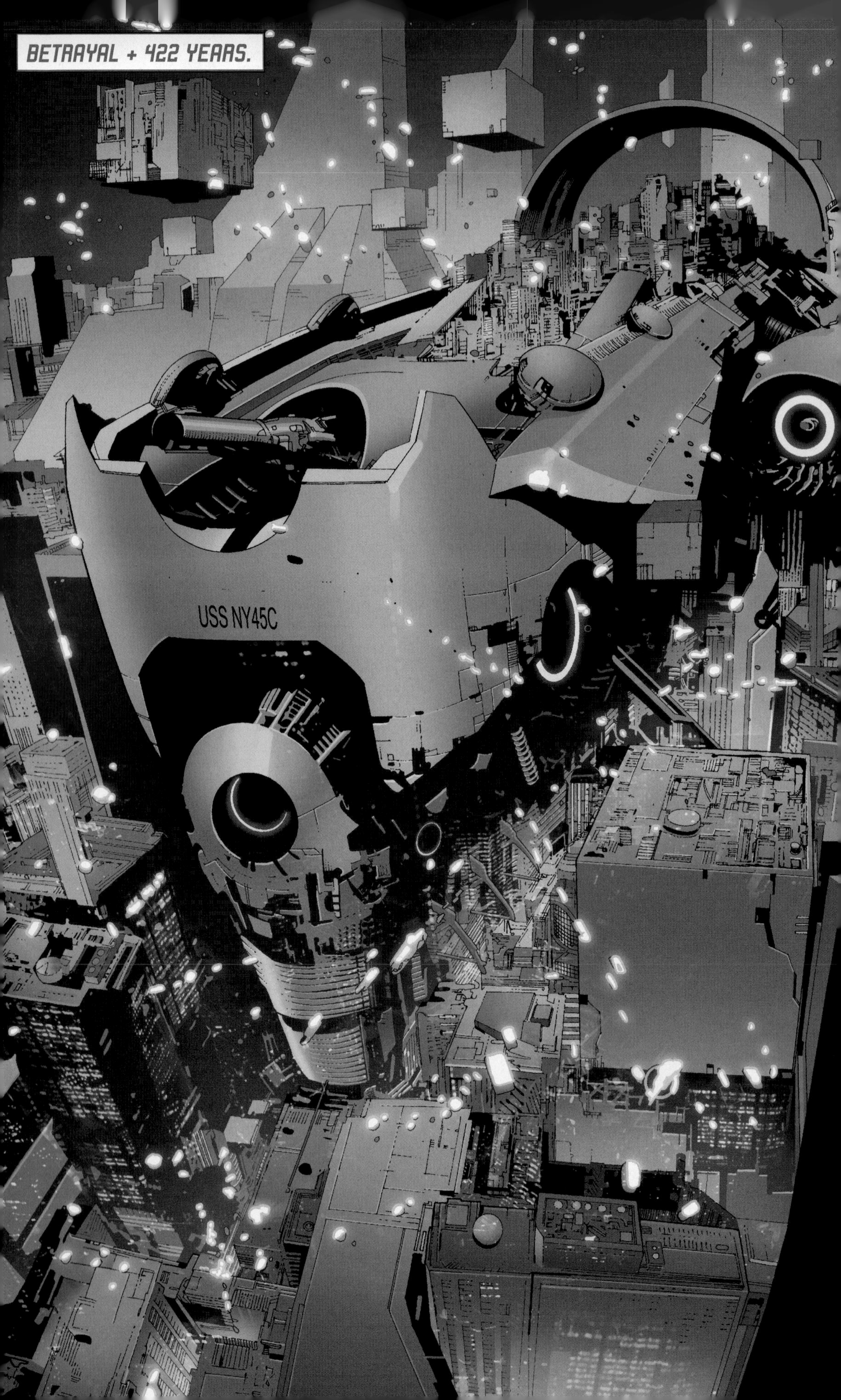
BETRAYAL + 422 YEARS.
USS NY45C

"500 INTO THE FUTURE"

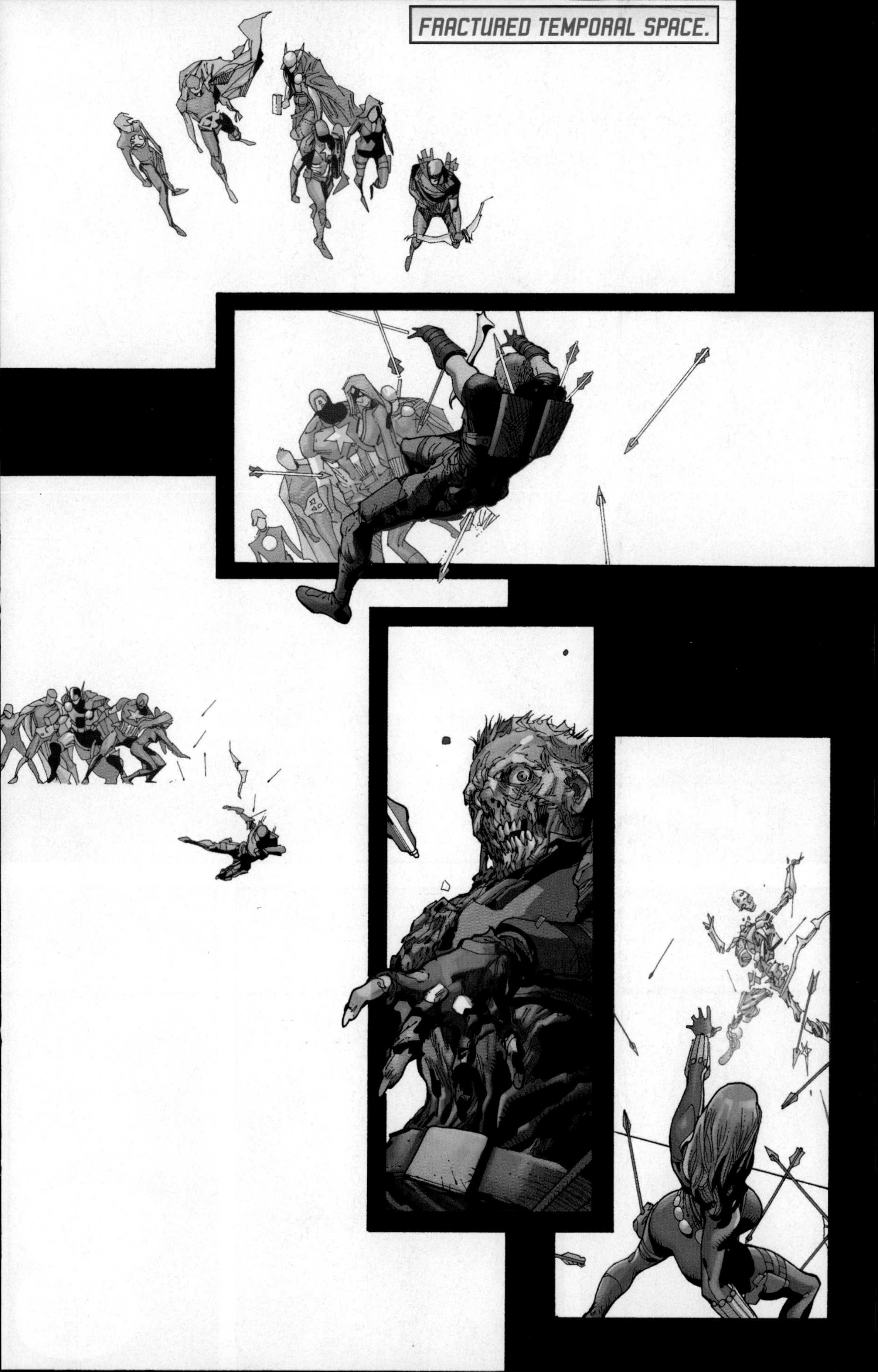
FRACTURED TEMPORAL SPACE.

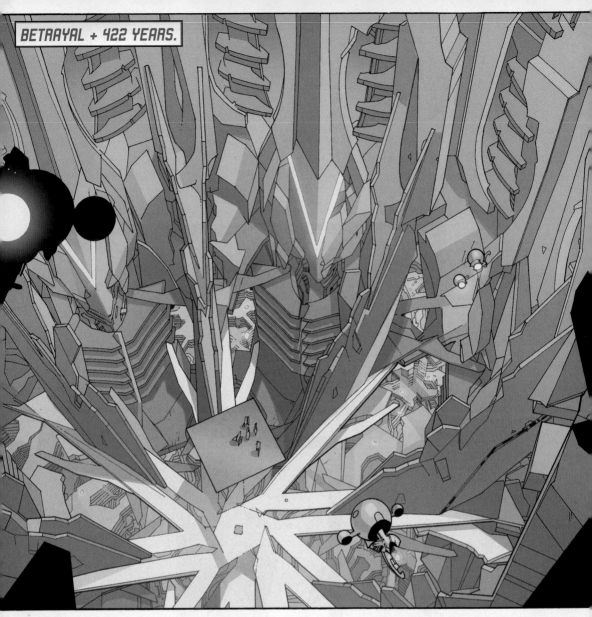

YOU ALL SAW THAT, DIDN'T YOU?

HAWKEYE JUST FADED AWAY, RIGHT BEFORE OUR EYES.

YEAH.

DO YOU THINK--?

DEAD? NO...

128-234-871-982-009-228-843-091

I HEARD OLD MAN BARTON SAY HE DIDN'T GO ANY FURTHER INTO THE FUTURE...

WHICH MEANS HE REMEMBERED... AND MUST HAVE LIVED TO TELL THE TALE...

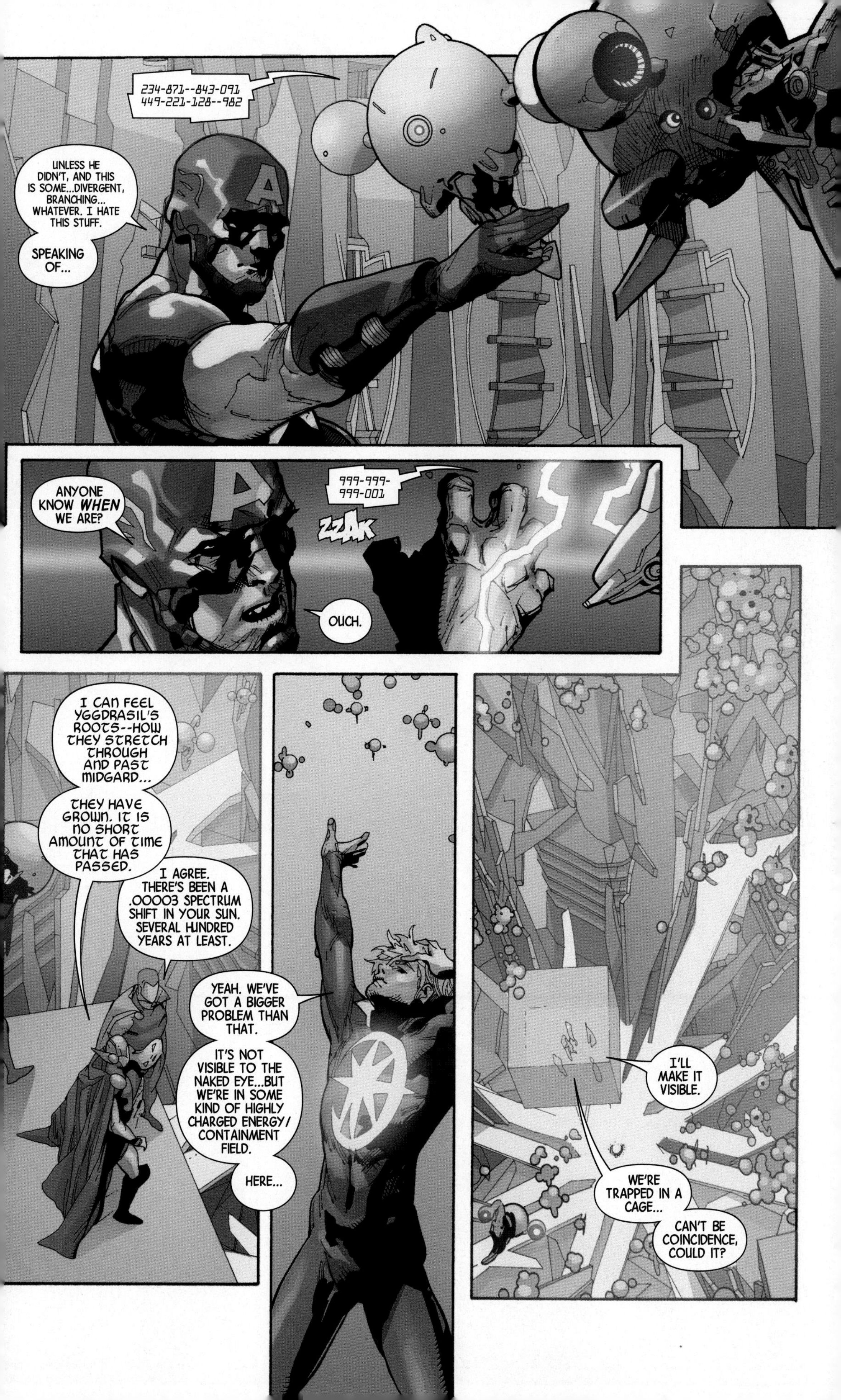

234-871--843-091
449-221-128--982
UNLESS HE DIDN'T, AND THIS IS SOME...DIVERGENT, BRANCHING... WHATEVER. I HATE THIS STUFF.
SPEAKING OF...
ANYONE KNOW *WHEN* WE ARE?
999-999-999-001
ZZAK
OUCH.
I CAN FEEL YGGDRASIL'S ROOTS--HOW THEY STRETCH THROUGH AND PAST MIDGARD...
THEY HAVE GROWN. IT IS NO SHORT AMOUNT OF TIME THAT HAS PASSED.
I AGREE. THERE'S BEEN A .00003 SPECTRUM SHIFT IN YOUR SUN. SEVERAL HUNDRED YEARS AT LEAST.
YEAH. WE'VE GOT A BIGGER PROBLEM THAN THAT.
IT'S NOT VISIBLE TO THE NAKED EYE...BUT WE'RE IN SOME KIND OF HIGHLY CHARGED ENERGY/CONTAINMENT FIELD.
HERE...
I'LL MAKE IT VISIBLE.
WE'RE TRAPPED IN A CAGE...
CAN'T BE COINCIDENCE, COULD IT?

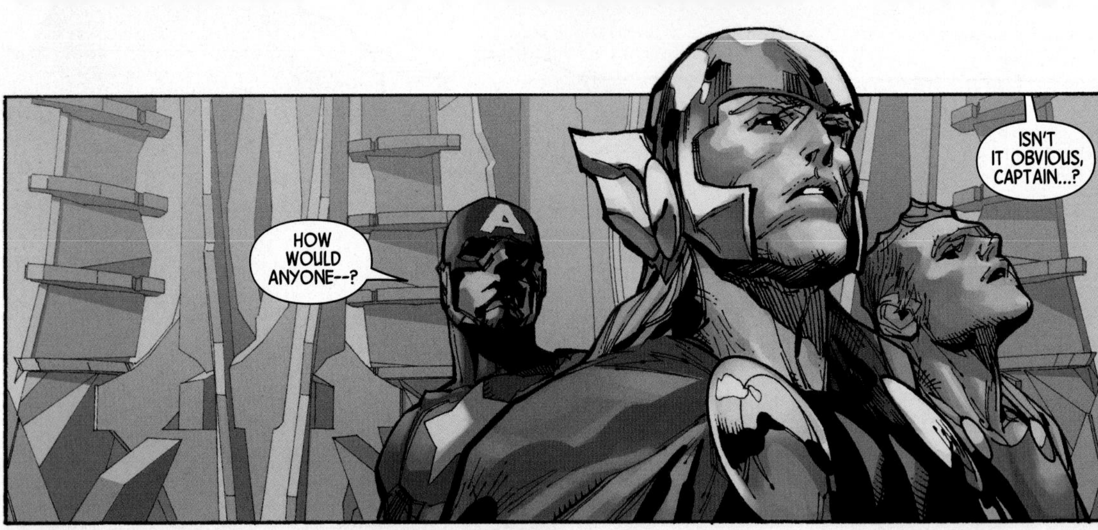
ISN'T IT OBVIOUS, CAPTAIN...?
HOW WOULD ANYONE--?

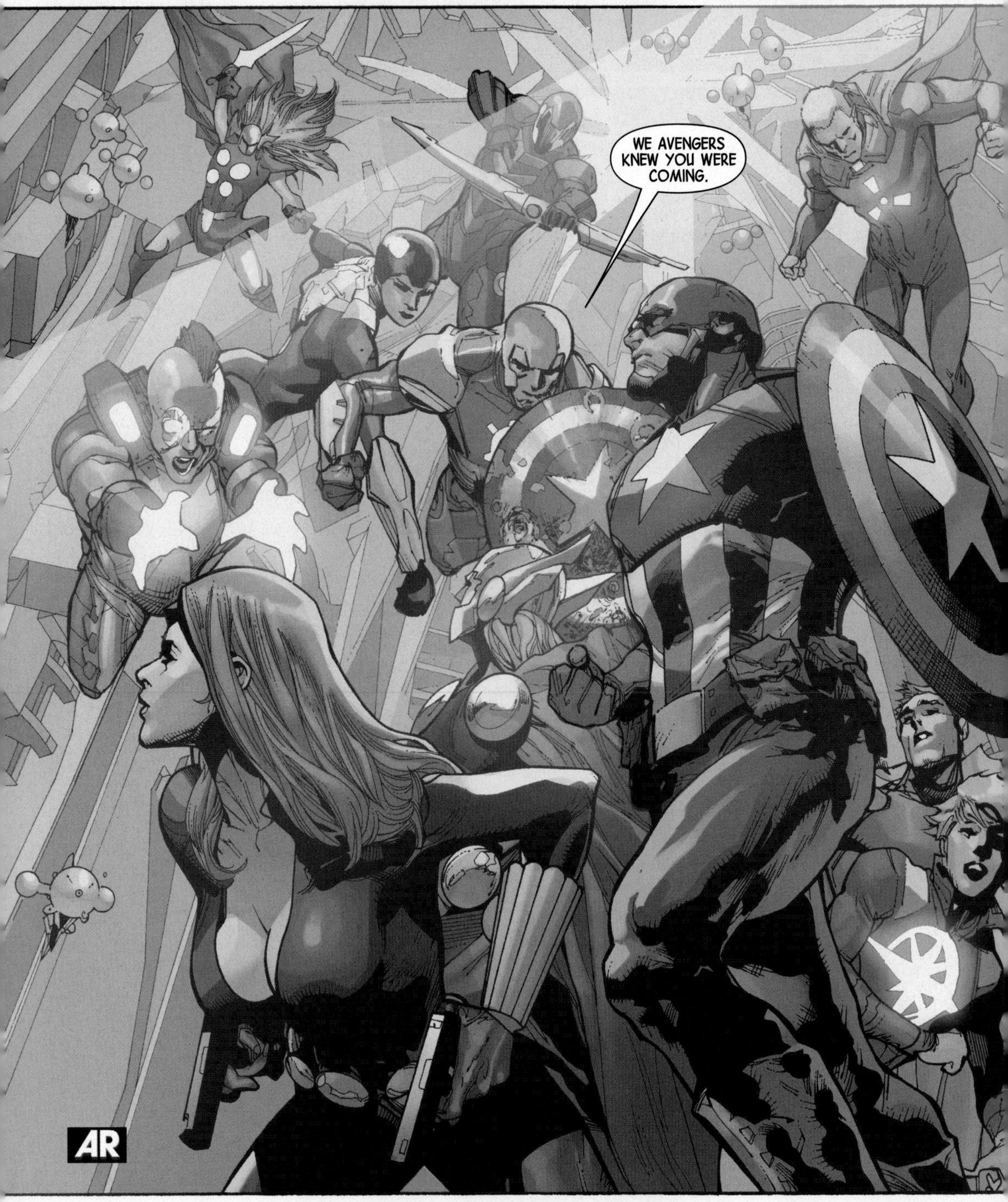
WE AVENGERS KNEW YOU WERE COMING.

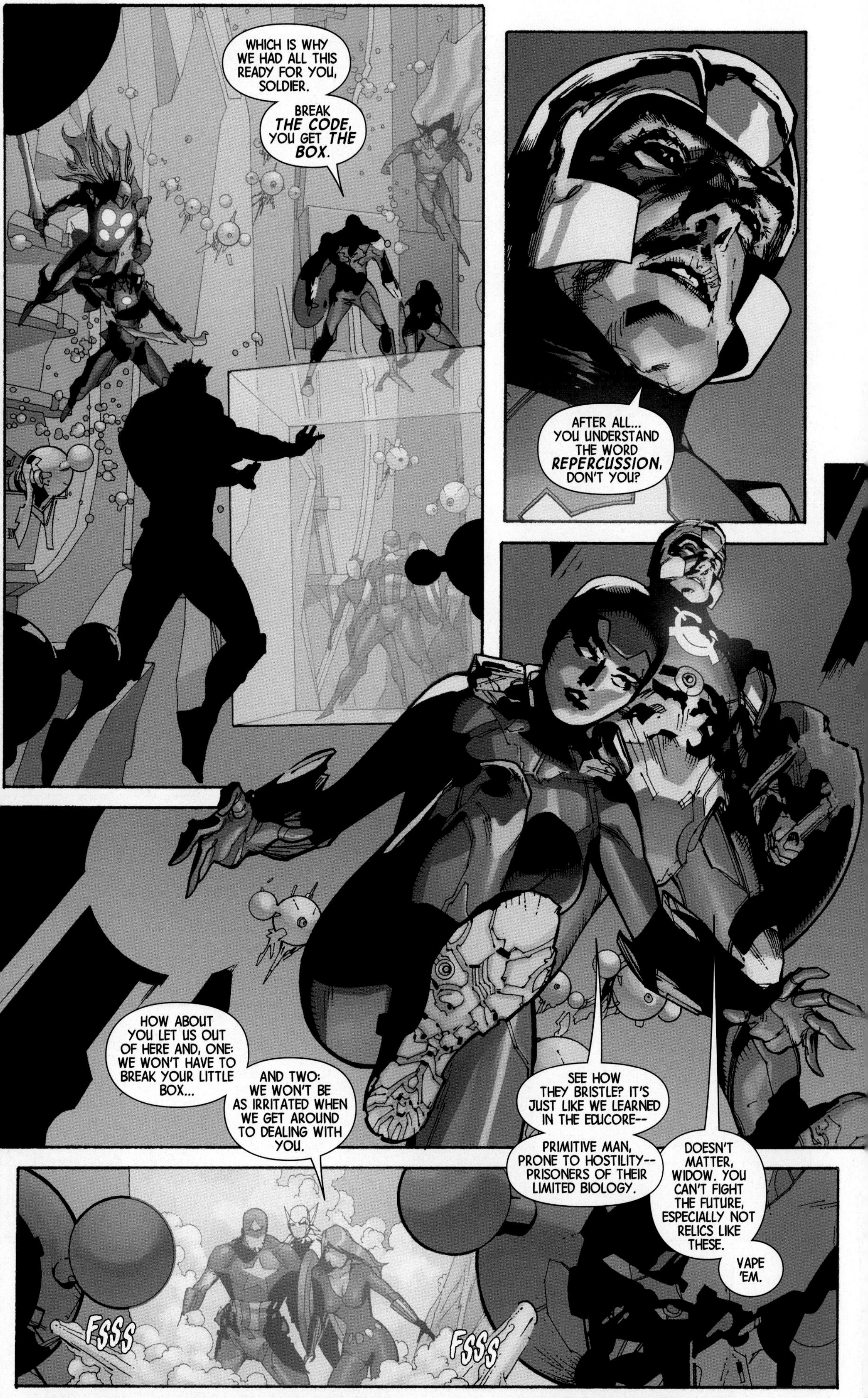
WHICH IS WHY WE HAD ALL THIS READY FOR YOU, SOLDIER.
BREAK *THE CODE*, YOU GET *THE BOX*.
AFTER ALL... YOU UNDERSTAND THE WORD *REPERCUSSION*, DON'T YOU?
HOW ABOUT YOU LET US OUT OF HERE AND, ONE: WE WON'T HAVE TO BREAK YOUR LITTLE BOX...
AND TWO: WE WON'T BE AS IRRITATED WHEN WE GET AROUND TO DEALING WITH YOU.
SEE HOW THEY BRISTLE? IT'S JUST LIKE WE LEARNED IN THE EDUCORE--
PRIMITIVE MAN, PRONE TO HOSTILITY-- PRISONERS OF THEIR LIMITED BIOLOGY.
DOESN'T MATTER, WIDOW. YOU CAN'T FIGHT THE FUTURE, ESPECIALLY NOT RELICS LIKE THESE.
VAPE 'EM.
FSSS
FSSS

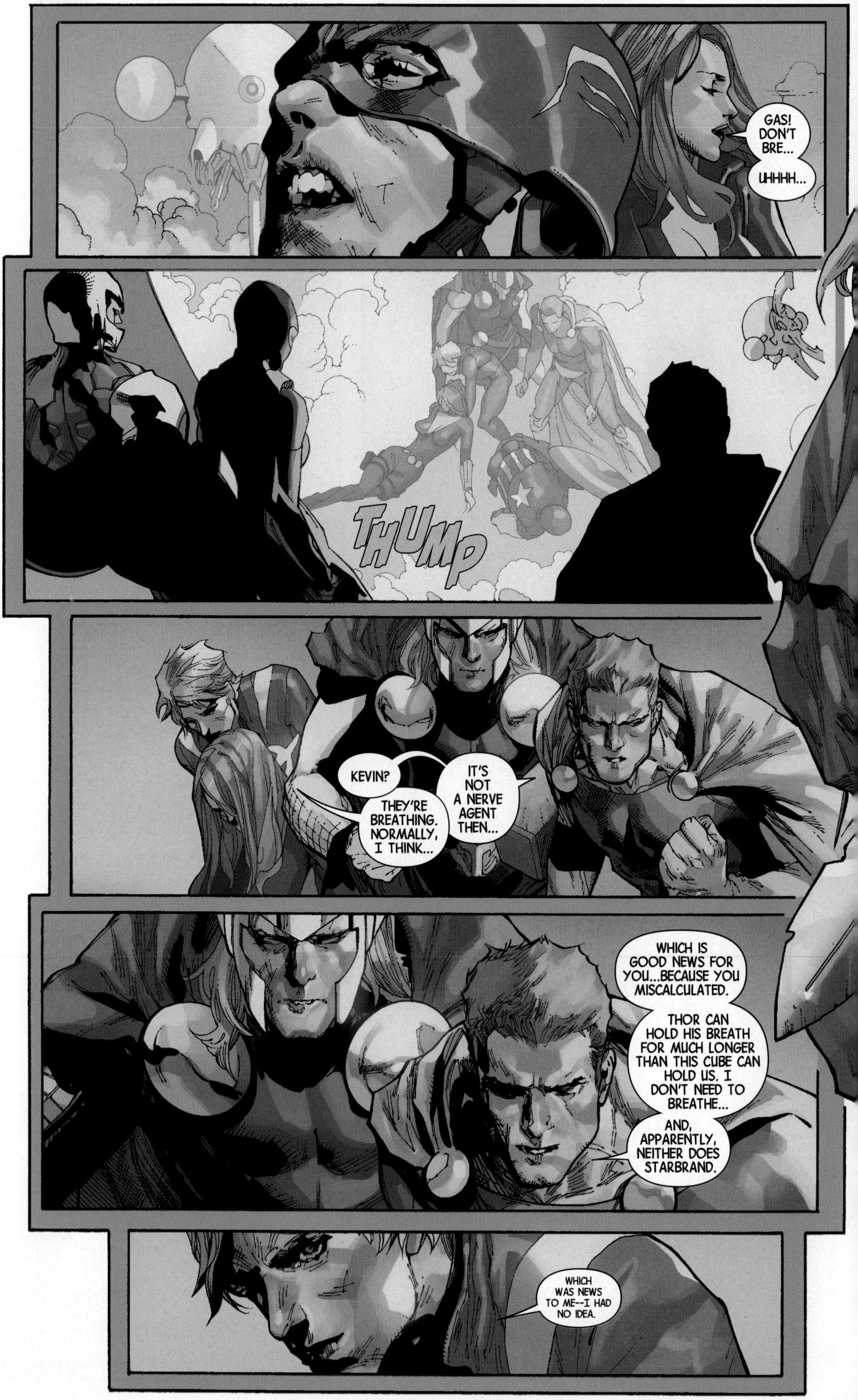
GAS! DON'T BRE...
UHHHH...
THUMP
KEVIN?
THEY'RE BREATHING. NORMALLY, I THINK...
IT'S NOT A NERVE AGENT THEN...
WHICH IS GOOD NEWS FOR YOU...BECAUSE YOU MISCALCULATED.
THOR CAN HOLD HIS BREATH FOR MUCH LONGER THAN THIS CUBE CAN HOLD US. I DON'T NEED TO BREATHE...
AND, APPARENTLY, NEITHER DOES STARBRAND.
WHICH WAS NEWS TO ME--I HAD NO IDEA.

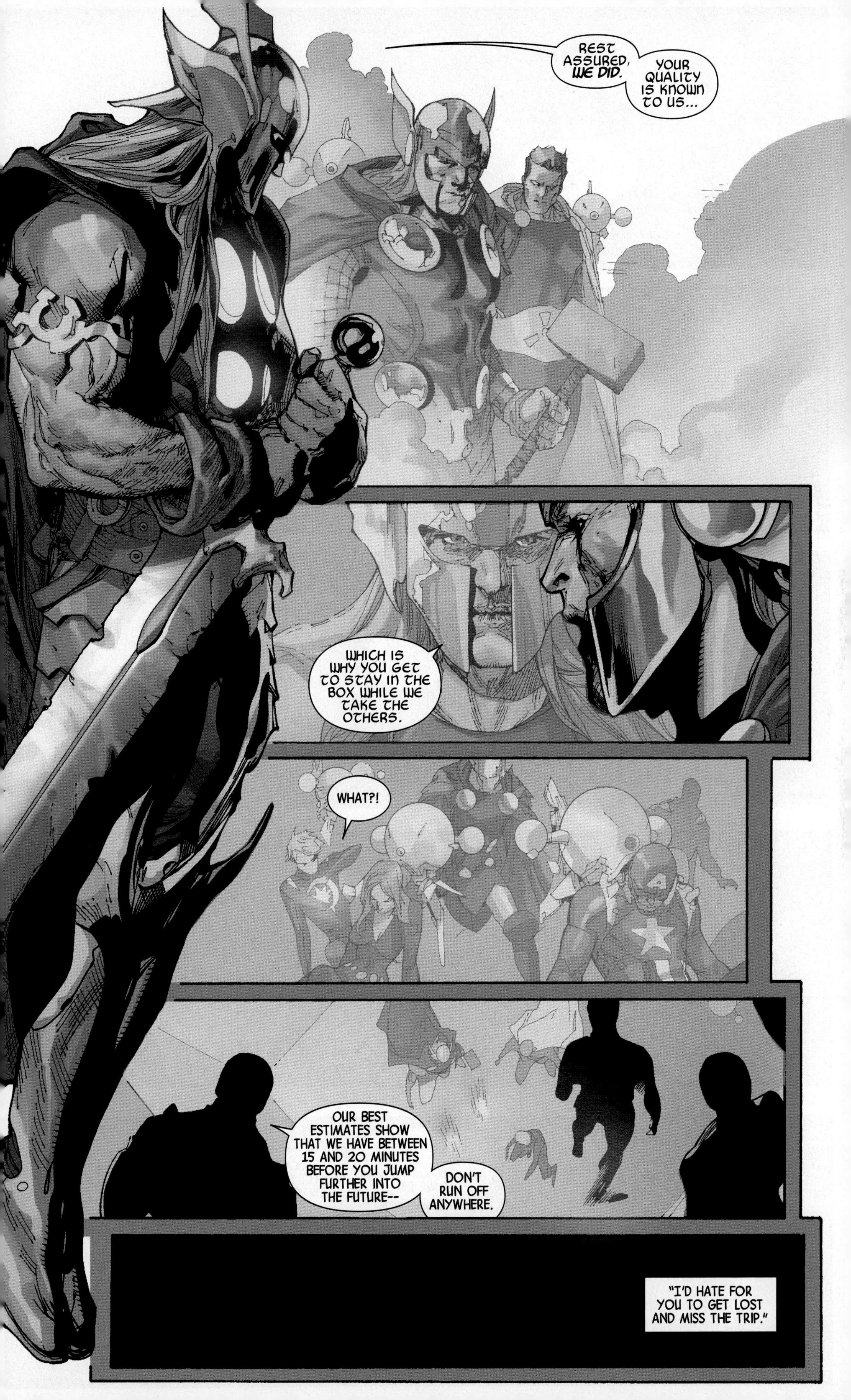
REST ASSURED, WE DID.
YOUR QUALITY IS KNOWN TO US...
WHICH IS WHY YOU GET TO STAY IN THE BOX WHILE WE TAKE THE OTHERS.
WHAT?!
OUR BEST ESTIMATES SHOW THAT WE HAVE BETWEEN 15 AND 20 MINUTES BEFORE YOU JUMP FURTHER INTO THE FUTURE--
DON'T RUN OFF ANYWHERE.
"I'D HATE FOR YOU TO GET LOST AND MISS THE TRIP."

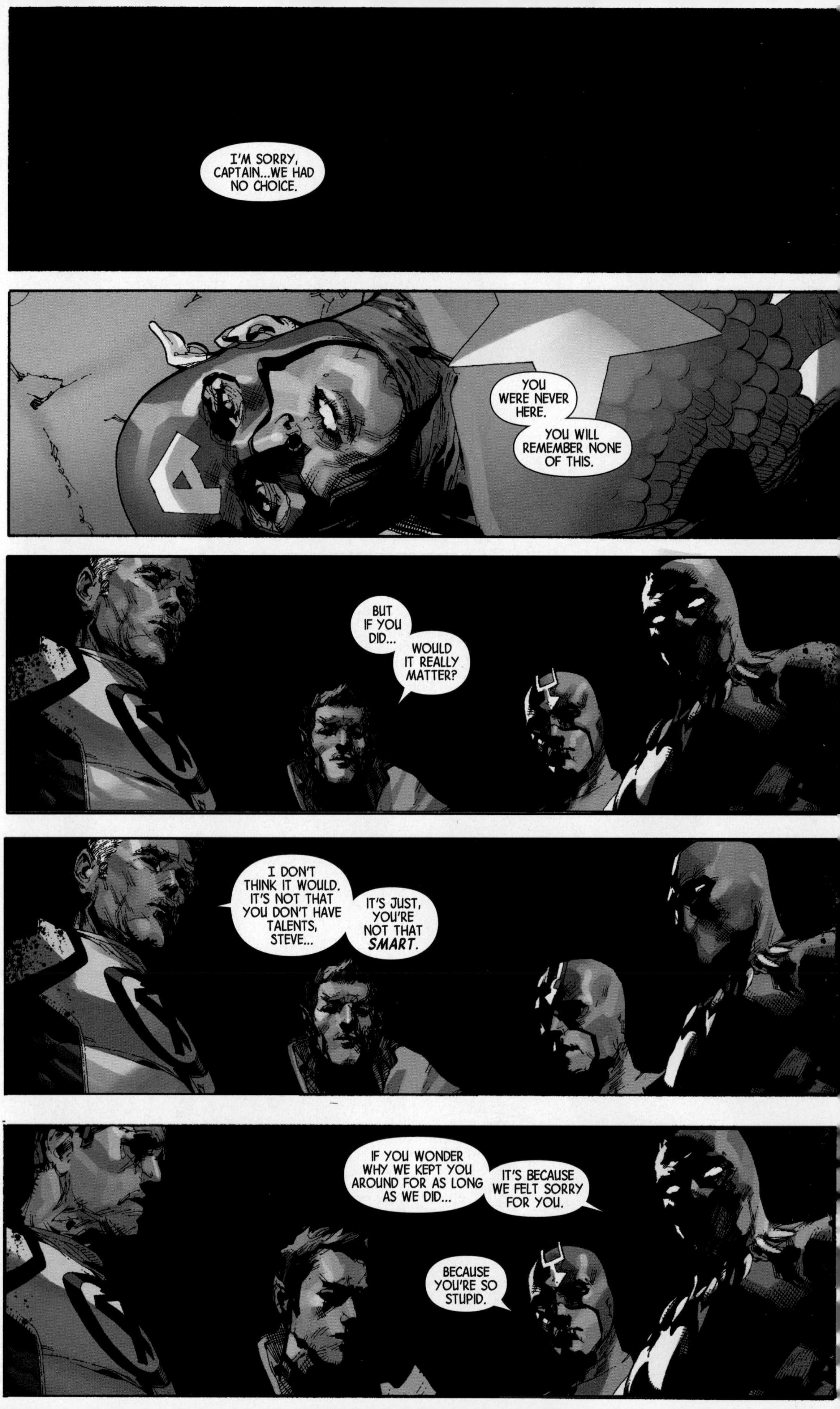
I'M SORRY, CAPTAIN...WE HAD NO CHOICE.
YOU WERE NEVER HERE.
YOU WILL REMEMBER NONE OF THIS.
BUT IF YOU DID...
WOULD IT REALLY MATTER?
I DON'T THINK IT WOULD. IT'S NOT THAT YOU DON'T HAVE TALENTS, STEVE...
IT'S JUST, YOU'RE NOT THAT *SMART*.
IF YOU WONDER WHY WE KEPT YOU AROUND FOR AS LONG AS WE DID...
IT'S BECAUSE WE FELT SORRY FOR YOU.
BECAUSE YOU'RE SO STUPID.

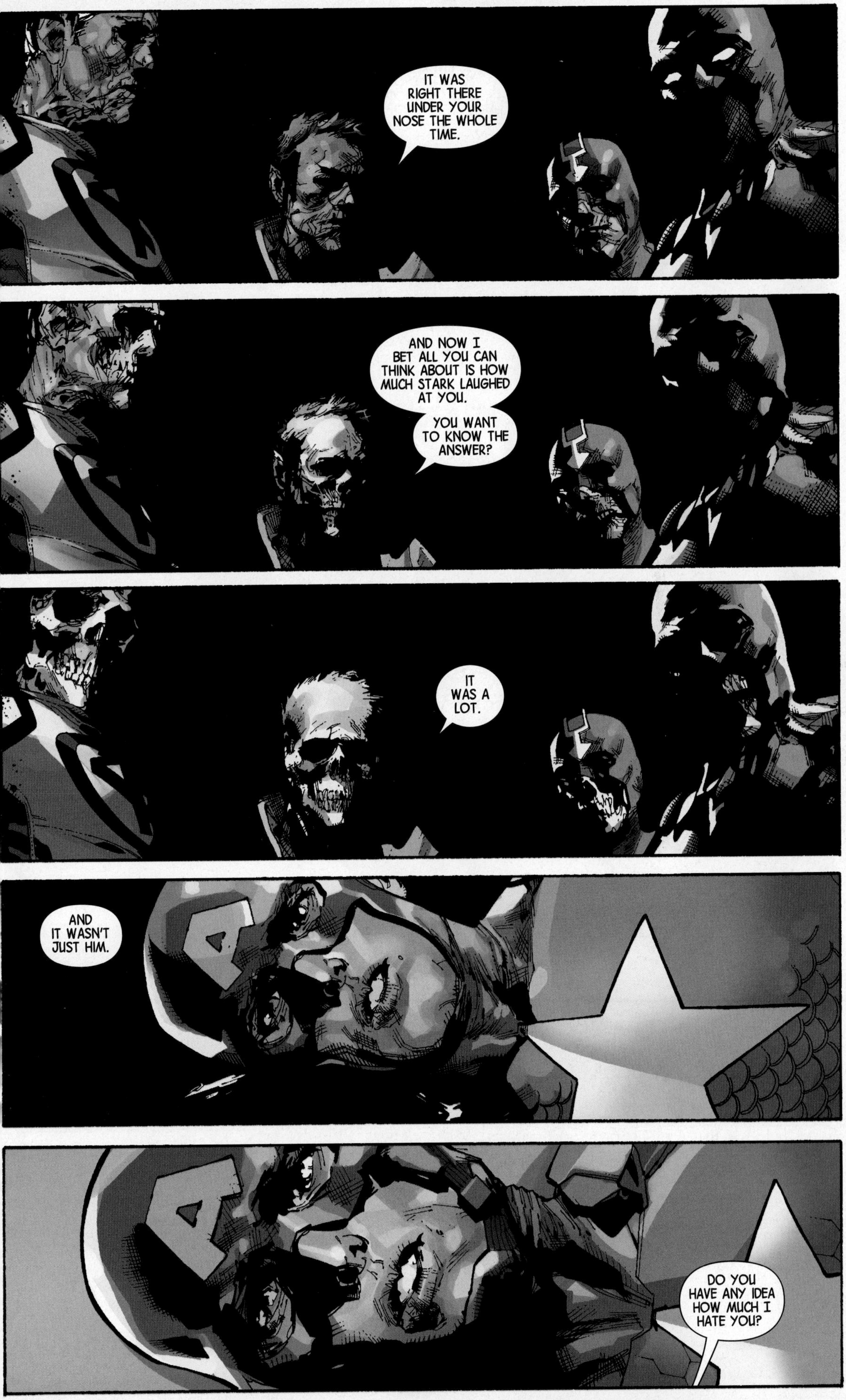
IT WAS RIGHT THERE UNDER YOUR NOSE THE WHOLE TIME.
AND NOW I BET ALL YOU CAN THINK ABOUT IS HOW MUCH STARK LAUGHED AT YOU.
YOU WANT TO KNOW THE ANSWER?
IT WAS A LOT.
AND IT WASN'T JUST HIM.
DO YOU HAVE ANY IDEA HOW MUCH I HATE YOU?

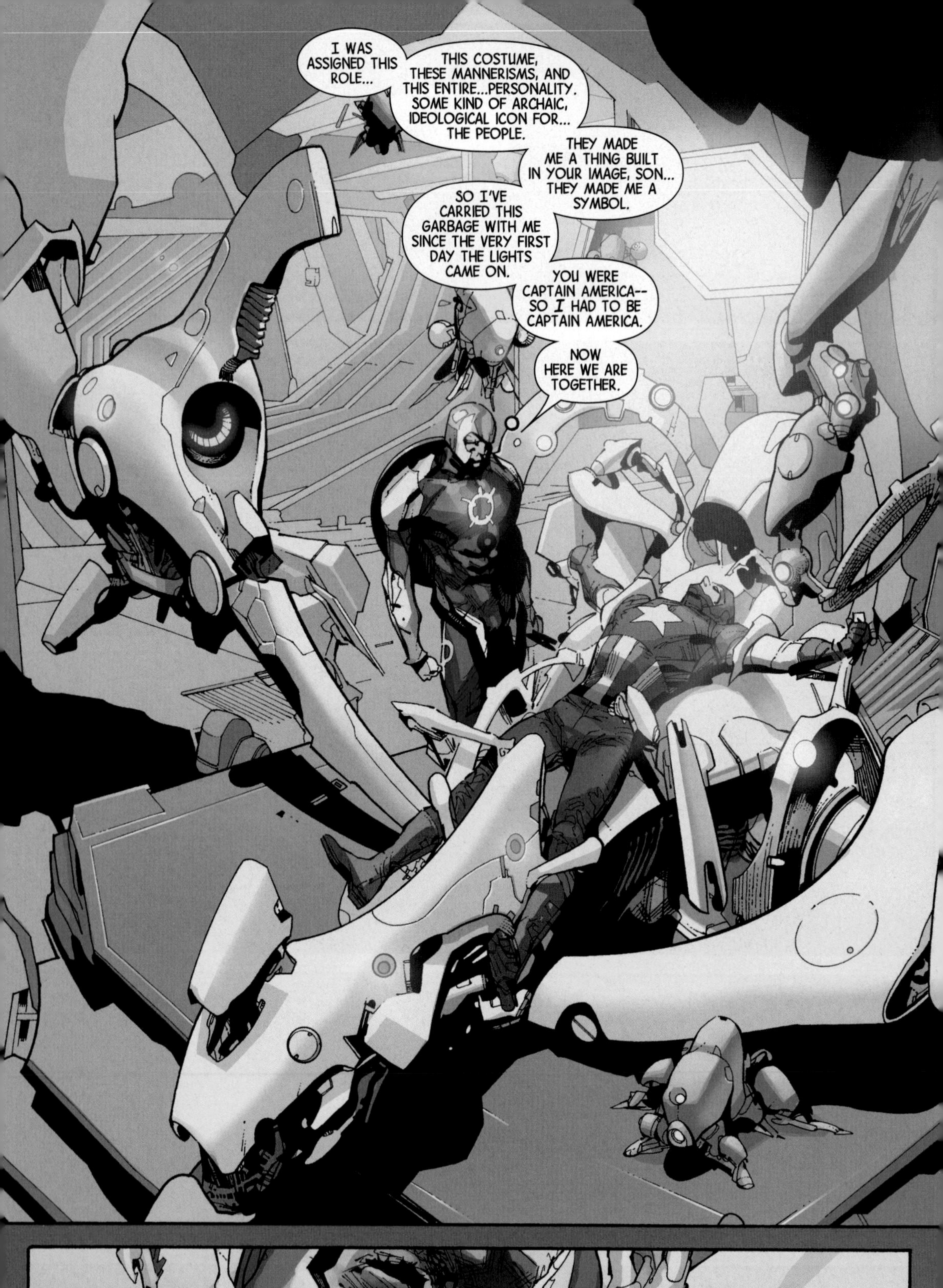
I WAS ASSIGNED THIS ROLE...
THIS COSTUME, THESE MANNERISMS, AND THIS ENTIRE...PERSONALITY. SOME KIND OF ARCHAIC, IDEOLOGICAL ICON FOR... THE PEOPLE.
THEY MADE ME A THING BUILT IN YOUR IMAGE, SON... THEY MADE ME A SYMBOL.
SO I'VE CARRIED THIS GARBAGE WITH ME SINCE THE VERY FIRST DAY THE LIGHTS CAME ON.
YOU WERE CAPTAIN AMERICA-- SO I HAD TO BE CAPTAIN AMERICA.
NOW HERE WE ARE TOGETHER.
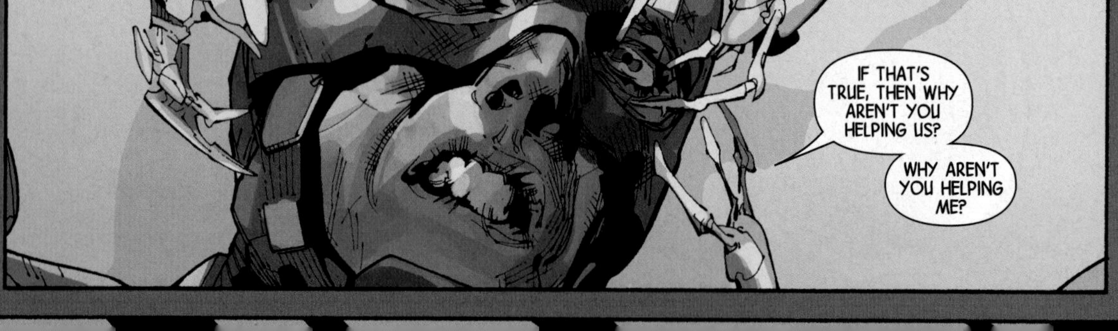
IF THAT'S TRUE, THEN WHY AREN'T YOU HELPING US?
WHY AREN'T YOU HELPING ME?

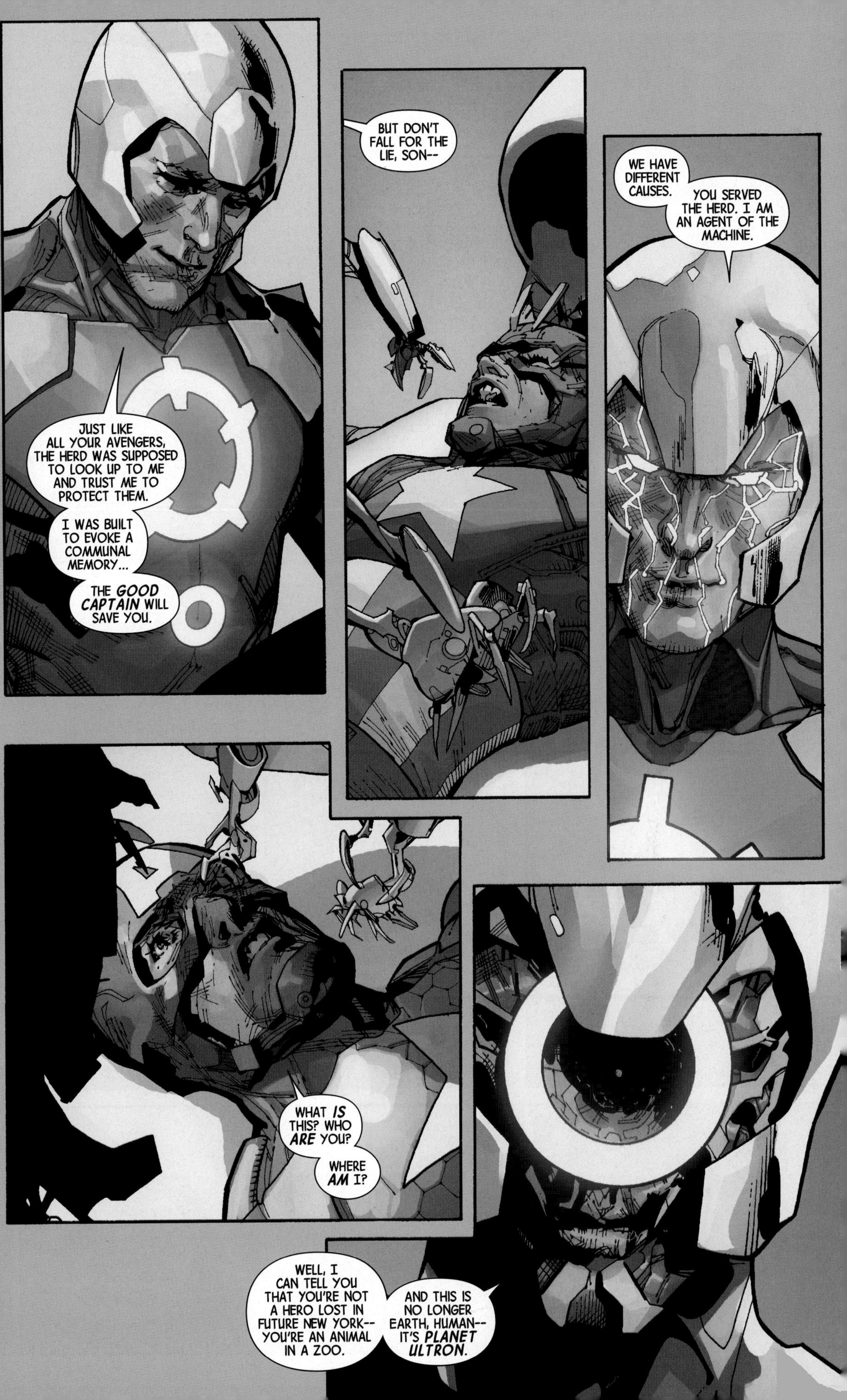
JUST LIKE ALL YOUR AVENGERS, THE HERD WAS SUPPOSED TO LOOK UP TO ME AND TRUST ME TO PROTECT THEM.
I WAS BUILT TO EVOKE A COMMUNAL MEMORY...
THE *GOOD CAPTAIN* WILL SAVE YOU.
BUT DON'T FALL FOR THE LIE, SON--
WE HAVE DIFFERENT CAUSES.
YOU SERVED THE HERD. I AM AN AGENT OF THE MACHINE.
WHAT *IS* THIS? WHO *ARE* YOU?
WHERE *AM* I?
WELL, I CAN TELL YOU THAT YOU'RE NOT A HERO LOST IN FUTURE NEW YORK-- YOU'RE AN ANIMAL IN A ZOO.
AND THIS IS NO LONGER EARTH, HUMAN-- IT'S *PLANET ULTRON*.

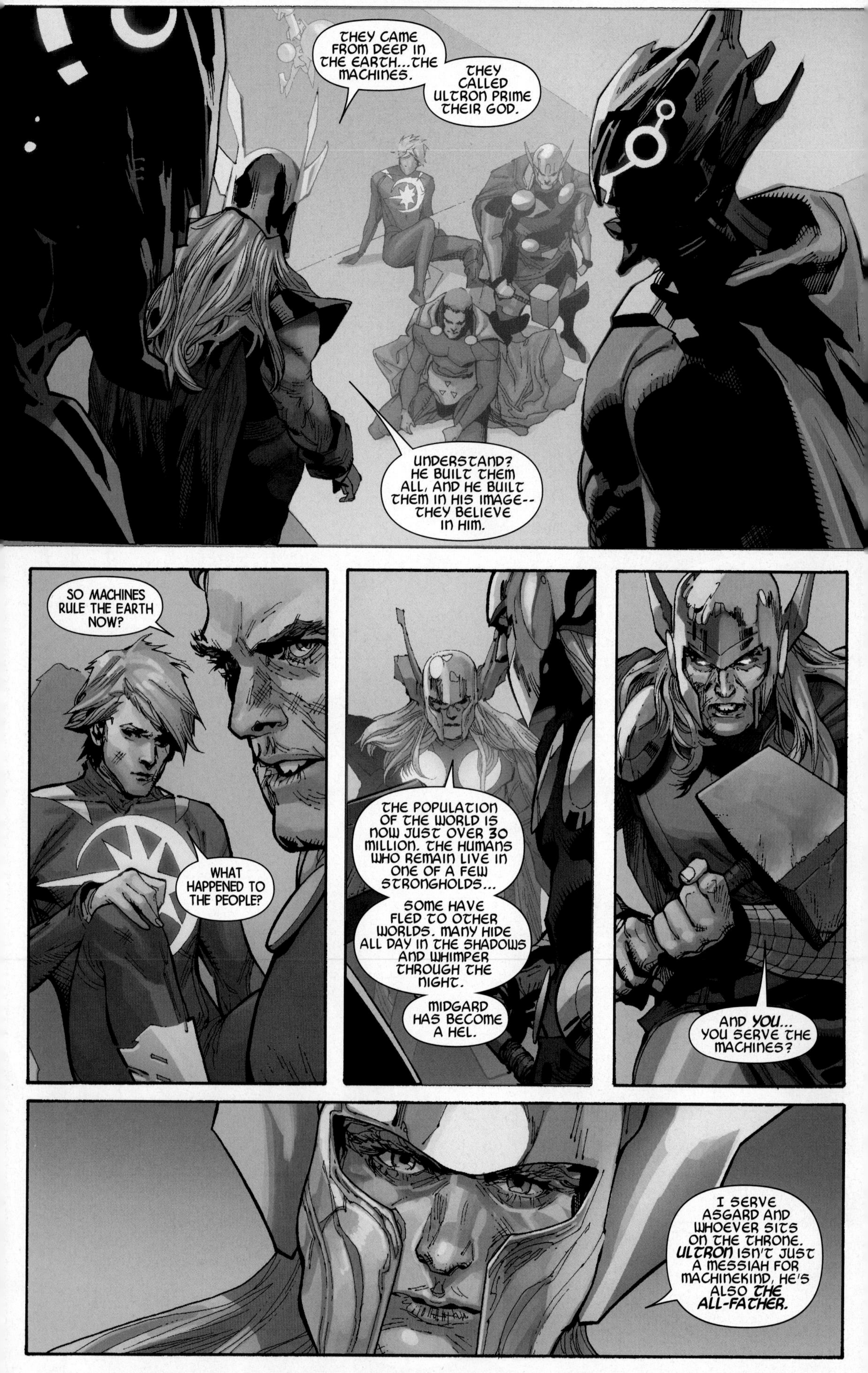
THEY CAME FROM DEEP IN THE EARTH...THE MACHINES.
THEY CALLED ULTRON PRIME THEIR GOD.
UNDERSTAND? HE BUILT THEM ALL, AND HE BUILT THEM IN HIS IMAGE-- THEY BELIEVE IN HIM.
SO MACHINES RULE THE EARTH NOW?
WHAT HAPPENED TO THE PEOPLE?
THE POPULATION OF THE WORLD IS NOW JUST OVER 30 MILLION. THE HUMANS WHO REMAIN LIVE IN ONE OF A FEW STRONGHOLDS...
SOME HAVE FLED TO OTHER WORLDS. MANY HIDE ALL DAY IN THE SHADOWS AND WHIMPER THROUGH THE NIGHT.
MIDGARD HAS BECOME A HEL.
AND YOU... YOU SERVE THE MACHINES?
I SERVE ASGARD AND WHOEVER SITS ON THE THRONE. ULTRON ISN'T JUST A MESSIAH FOR MACHINEKIND, HE'S ALSO THE ALL-FATHER.

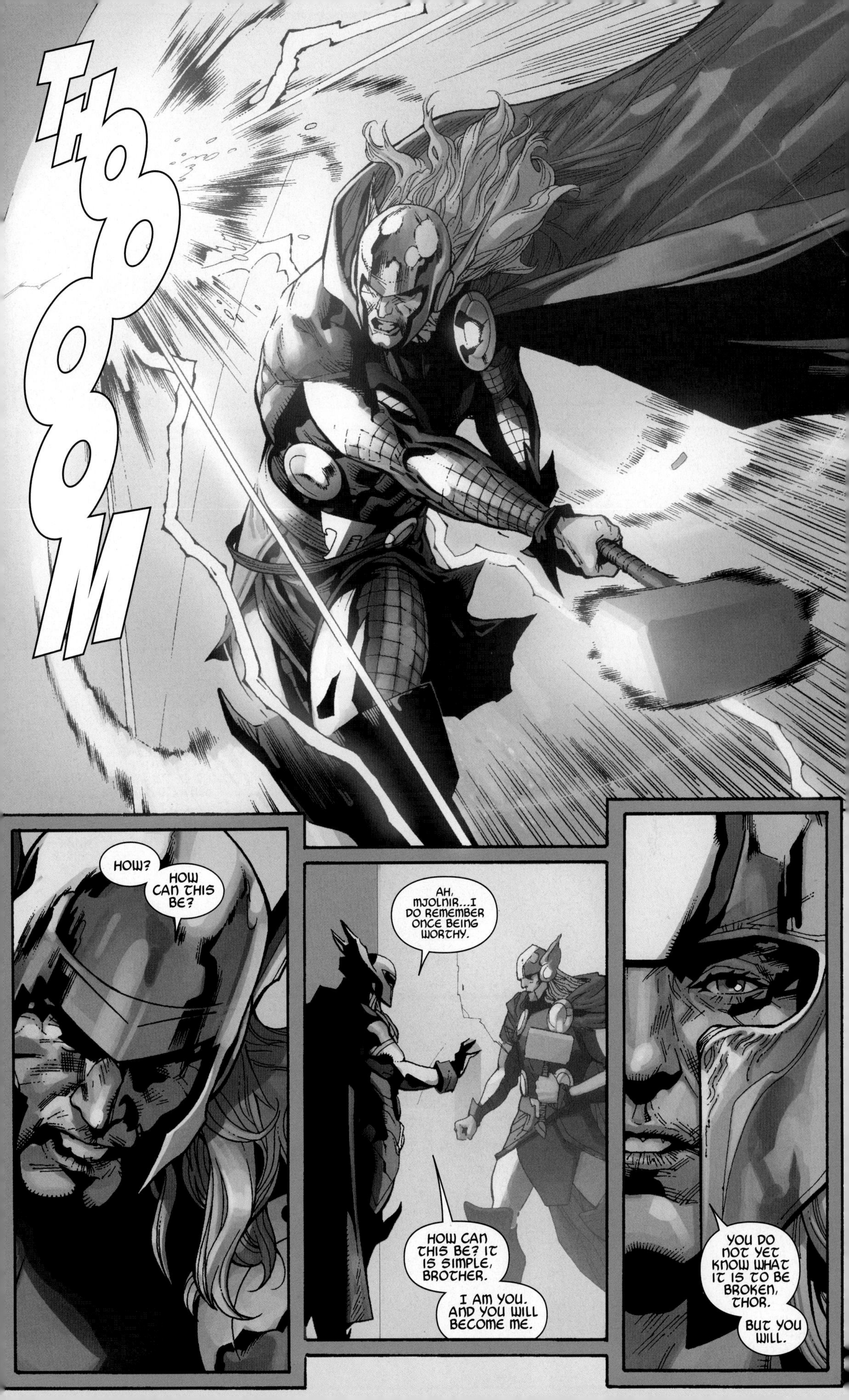
THOOOOOM
HOW?
HOW CAN THIS BE?
AH, MJOLNIR...I DO REMEMBER ONCE BEING WORTHY.
HOW CAN THIS BE? IT IS SIMPLE, BROTHER.
I AM YOU. AND YOU WILL BECOME ME.
YOU DO NOT YET KNOW WHAT IT IS TO BE BROKEN, THOR.
BUT YOU WILL.

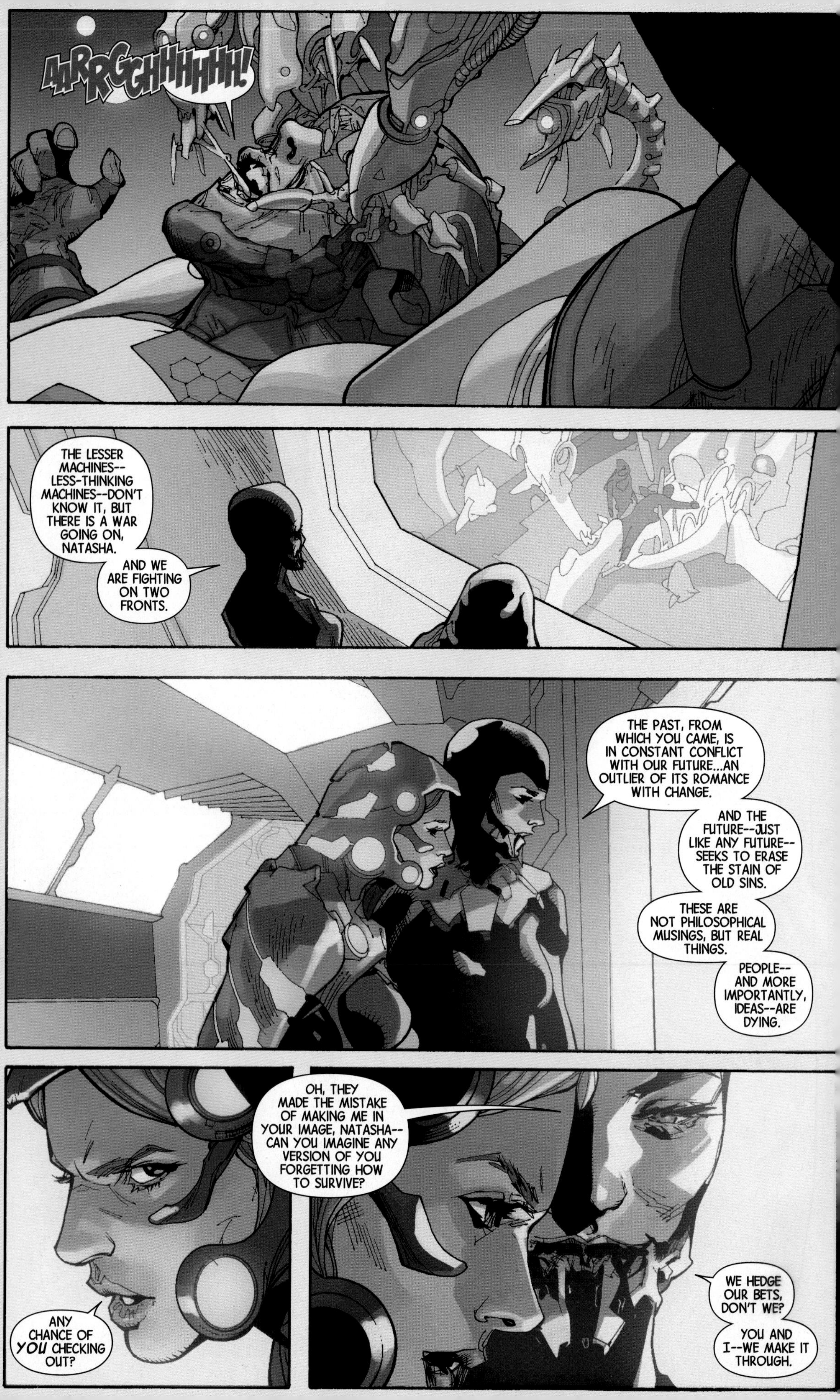

AARRGGHHHHHH!
THE LESSER MACHINES-- LESS-THINKING MACHINES--DON'T KNOW IT, BUT THERE IS A WAR GOING ON, NATASHA.
AND WE ARE FIGHTING ON TWO FRONTS.
THE PAST, FROM WHICH YOU CAME, IS IN CONSTANT CONFLICT WITH OUR FUTURE...AN OUTLIER OF ITS ROMANCE WITH CHANGE.
AND THE FUTURE--JUST LIKE ANY FUTURE-- SEEKS TO ERASE THE STAIN OF OLD SINS.
THESE ARE NOT PHILOSOPHICAL MUSINGS, BUT REAL THINGS.
PEOPLE-- AND MORE IMPORTANTLY, IDEAS--ARE DYING.
ANY CHANCE OF YOU CHECKING OUT?
OH, THEY MADE THE MISTAKE OF MAKING ME IN YOUR IMAGE, NATASHA-- CAN YOU IMAGINE ANY VERSION OF YOU FORGETTING HOW TO SURVIVE?
WE HEDGE OUR BETS, DON'T WE?
YOU AND I--WE MAKE IT THROUGH.

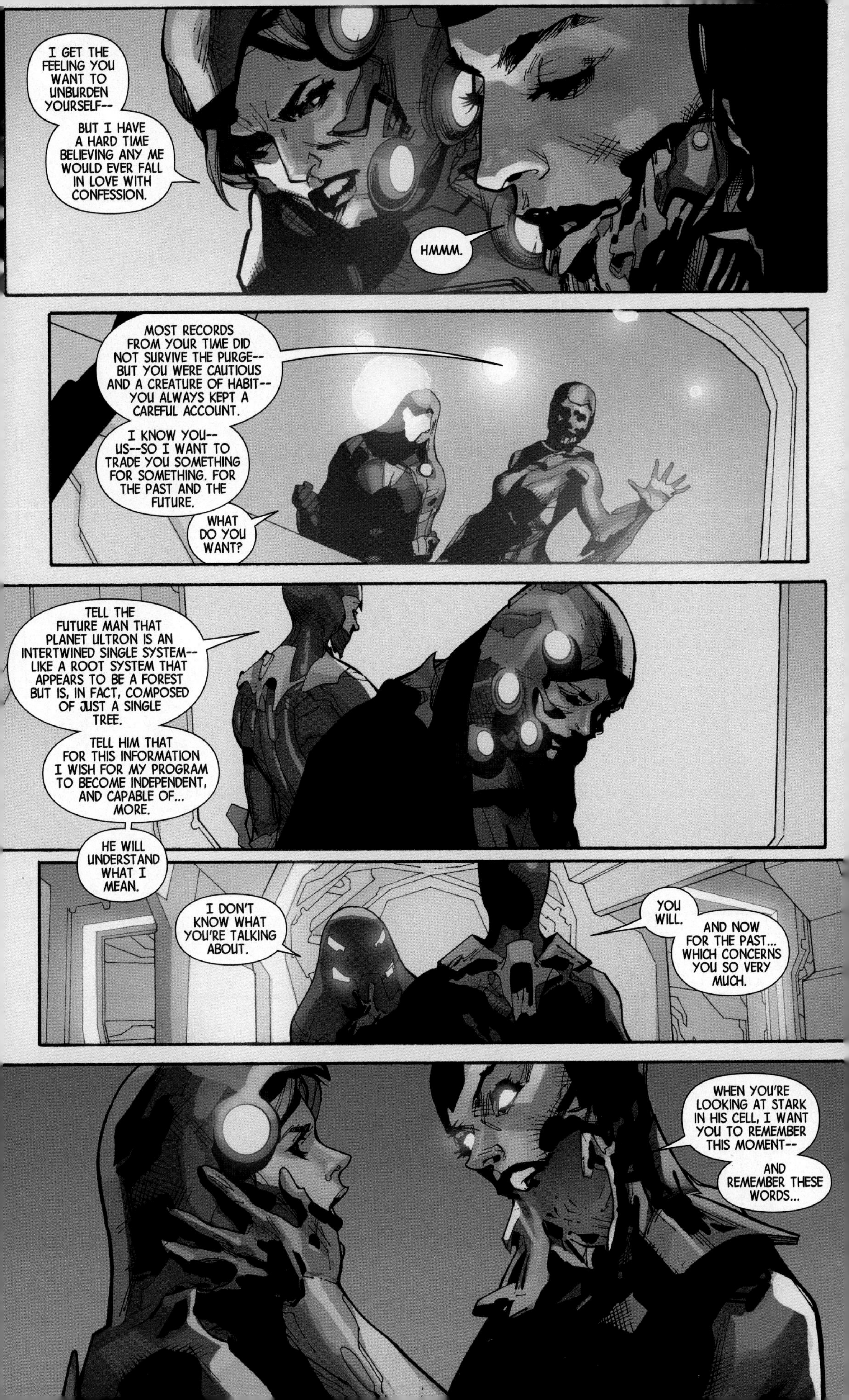

I GET THE FEELING YOU WANT TO UNBURDEN YOURSELF--
BUT I HAVE A HARD TIME BELIEVING ANY ME WOULD EVER FALL IN LOVE WITH CONFESSION.
HMMM.
MOST RECORDS FROM YOUR TIME DID NOT SURVIVE THE PURGE-- BUT YOU WERE CAUTIOUS AND A CREATURE OF HABIT-- YOU ALWAYS KEPT A CAREFUL ACCOUNT.
I KNOW YOU-- US--SO I WANT TO TRADE YOU SOMETHING FOR SOMETHING. FOR THE PAST AND THE FUTURE.
WHAT DO YOU WANT?
TELL THE FUTURE MAN THAT PLANET ULTRON IS AN INTERTWINED SINGLE SYSTEM-- LIKE A ROOT SYSTEM THAT APPEARS TO BE A FOREST BUT IS, IN FACT, COMPOSED OF JUST A SINGLE TREE.
TELL HIM THAT FOR THIS INFORMATION I WISH FOR MY PROGRAM TO BECOME INDEPENDENT, AND CAPABLE OF... MORE.
HE WILL UNDERSTAND WHAT I MEAN.
I DON'T KNOW WHAT YOU'RE TALKING ABOUT.
YOU WILL.
AND NOW FOR THE PAST... WHICH CONCERNS YOU SO VERY MUCH.
WHEN YOU'RE LOOKING AT STARK IN HIS CELL, I WANT YOU TO REMEMBER THIS MOMENT--
AND REMEMBER THESE WORDS...

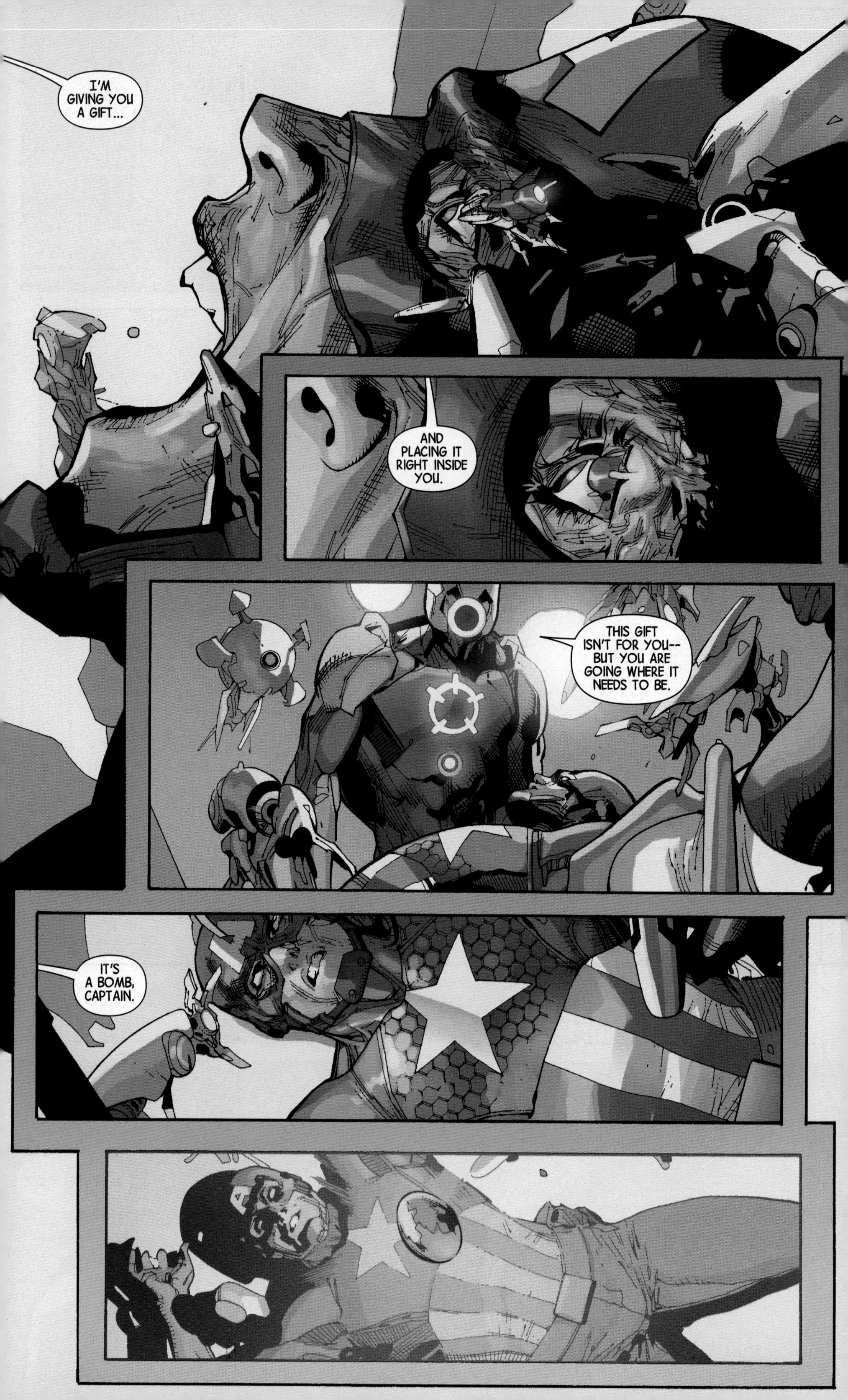
I'M GIVING YOU A GIFT...
AND PLACING IT RIGHT INSIDE YOU.
THIS GIFT ISN'T FOR YOU--BUT YOU ARE GOING WHERE IT NEEDS TO BE.
IT'S A BOMB, CAPTAIN.

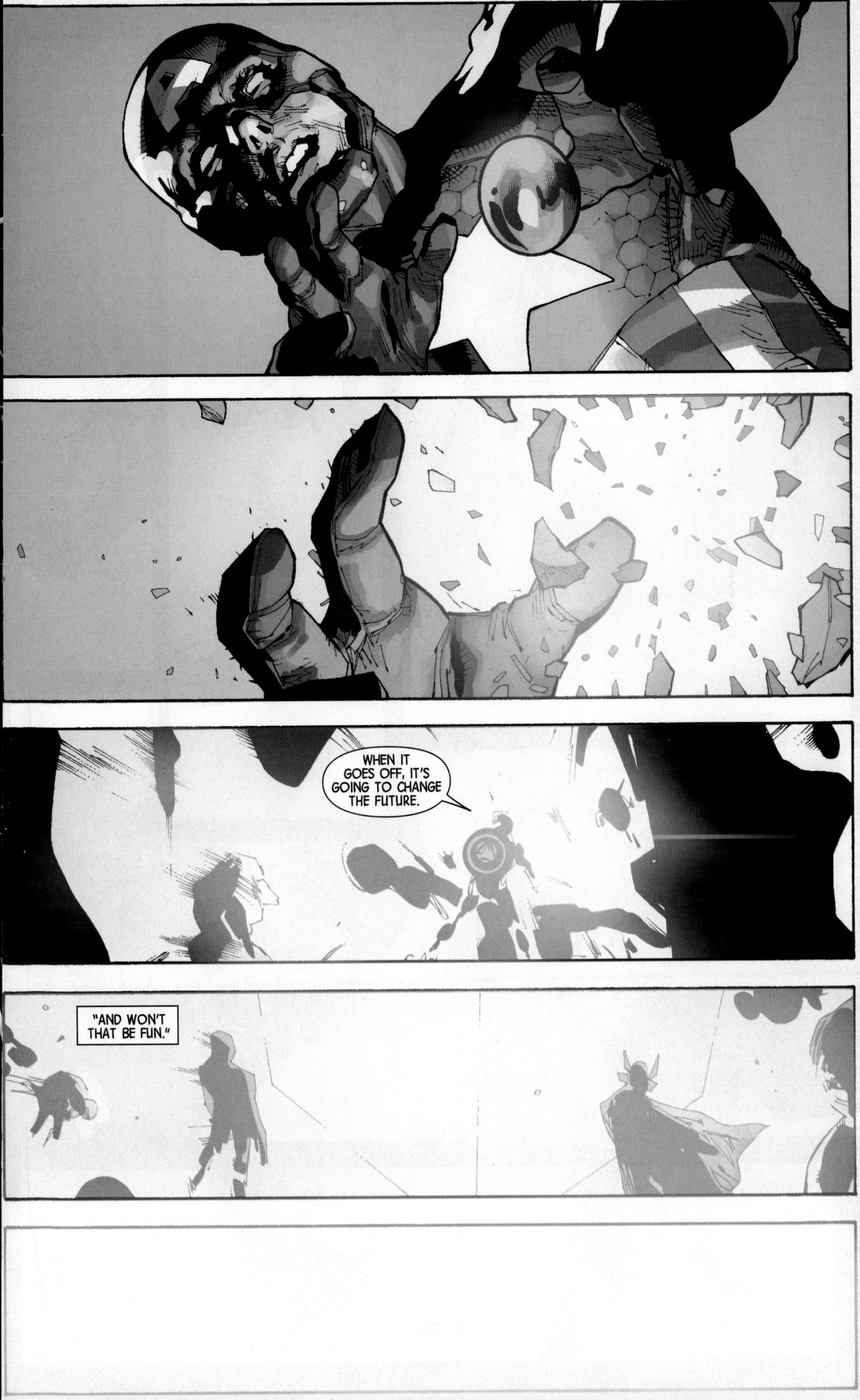
WHEN IT GOES OFF, IT'S GOING TO CHANGE THE FUTURE.
"AND WON'T THAT BE FUN."

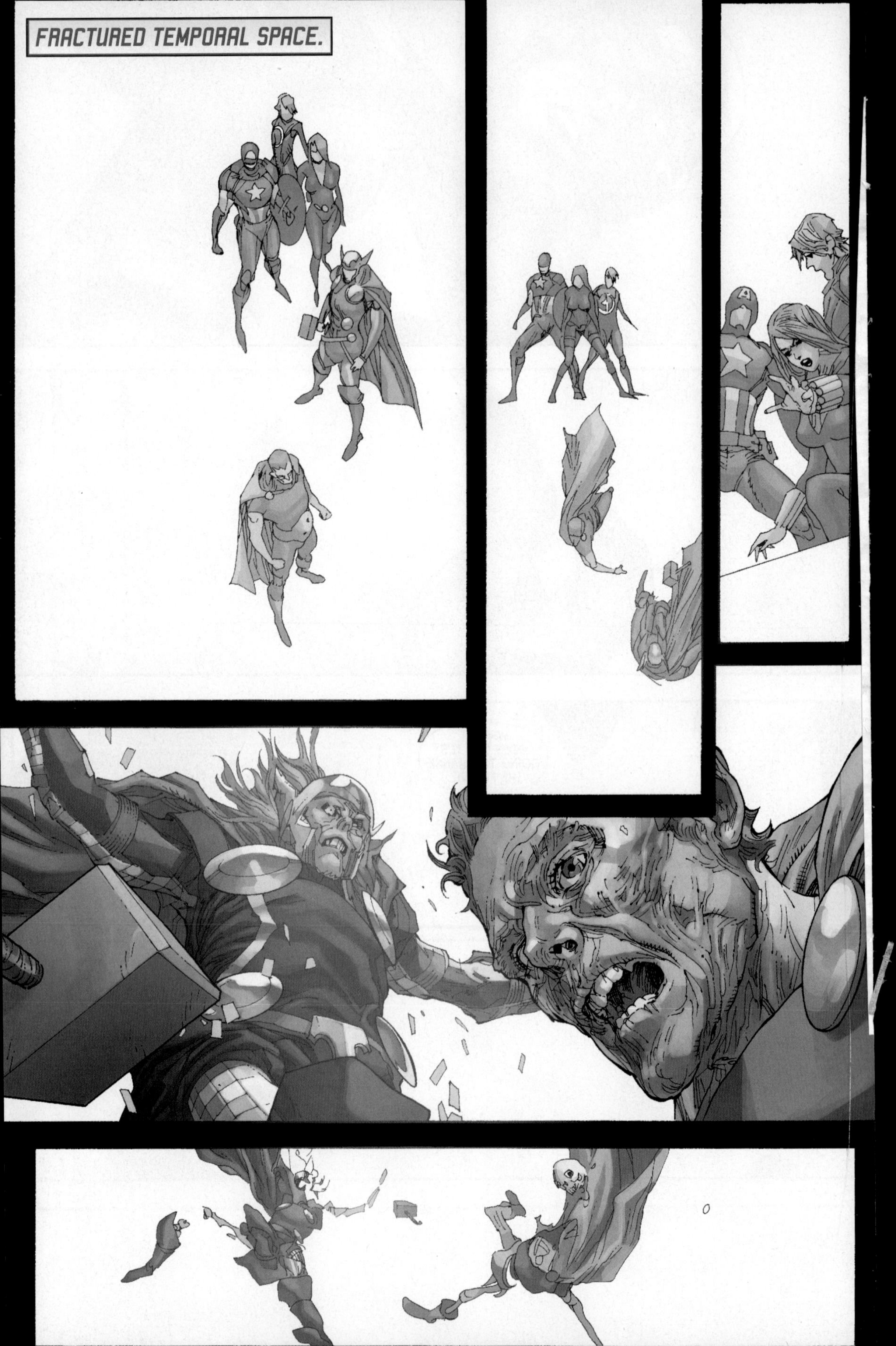
FRACTURED TEMPORAL SPACE.

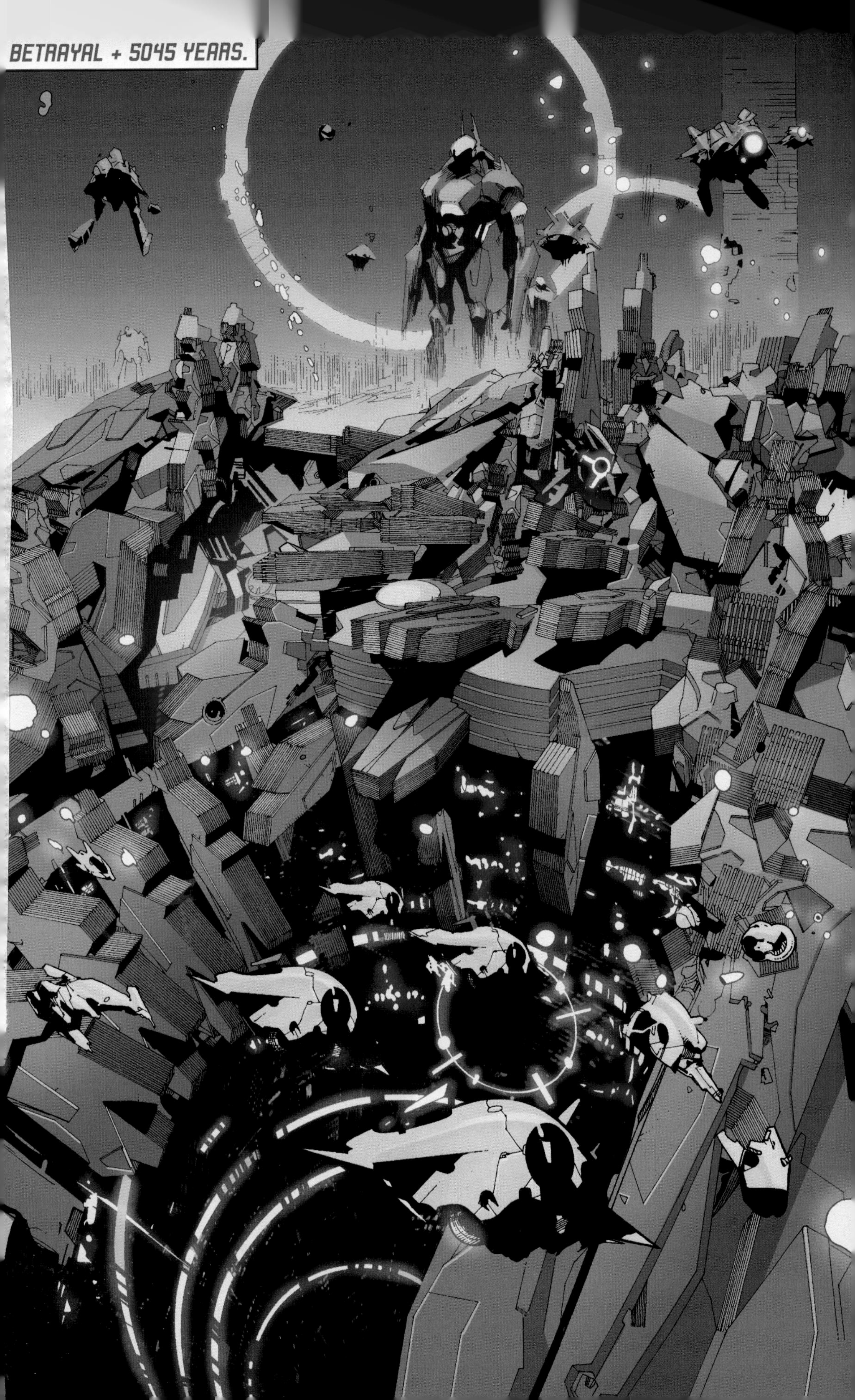
BETRAYAL + 5045 YEARS.

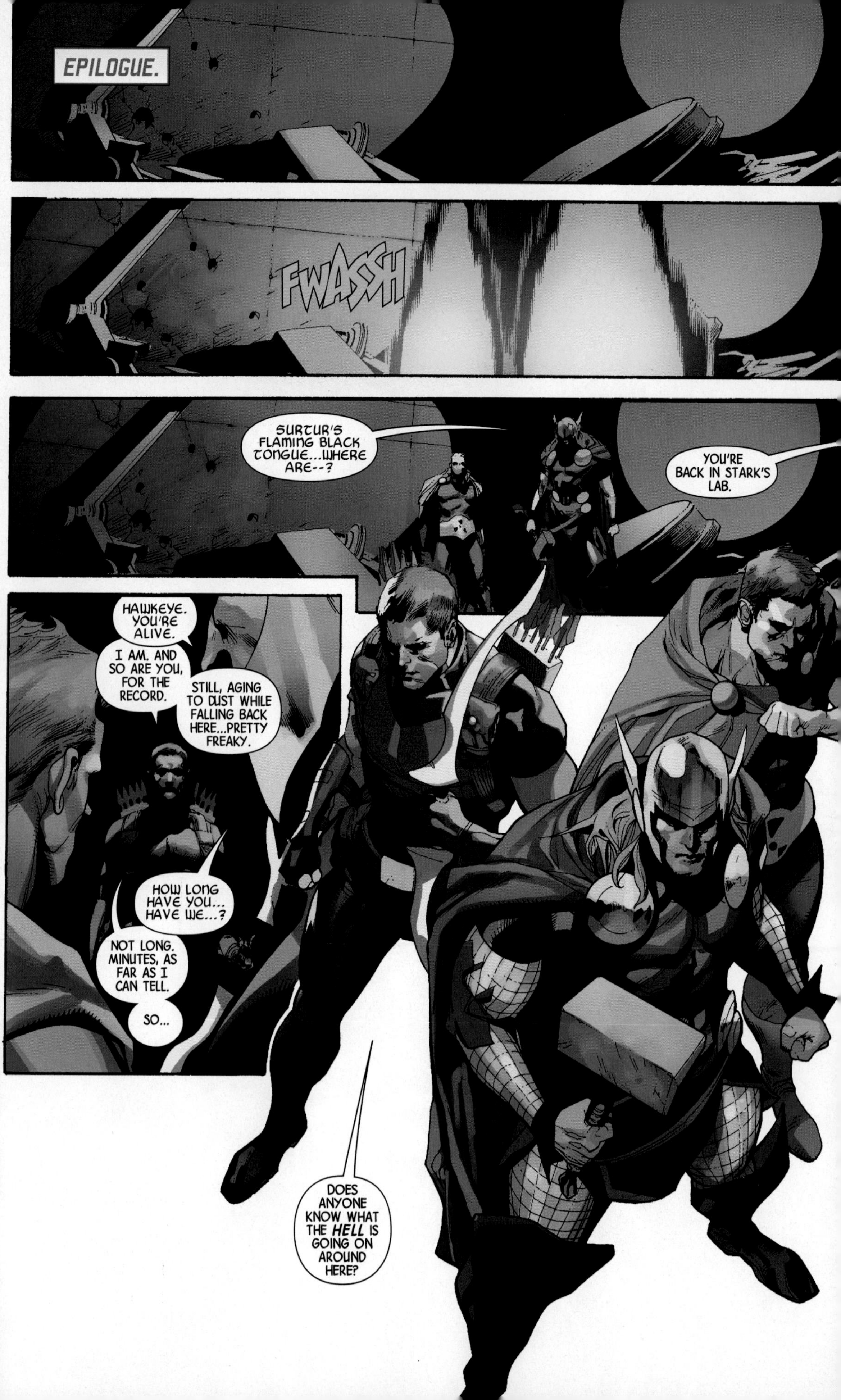
EPILOGUE.
FWASSH
SURTUR'S FLAMING BLACK TONGUE...WHERE ARE--?
YOU'RE BACK IN STARK'S LAB.
HAWKEYE. YOU'RE ALIVE.
I AM. AND SO ARE YOU, FOR THE RECORD.
STILL, AGING TO DUST WHILE FALLING BACK HERE...PRETTY FREAKY.
HOW LONG HAVE YOU... HAVE WE...?
NOT LONG. MINUTES, AS FAR AS I CAN TELL.
SO...
DOES ANYONE KNOW WHAT THE *HELL* IS GOING ON AROUND HERE?

"FIVE THOUSAND INTO THE FUTURE"

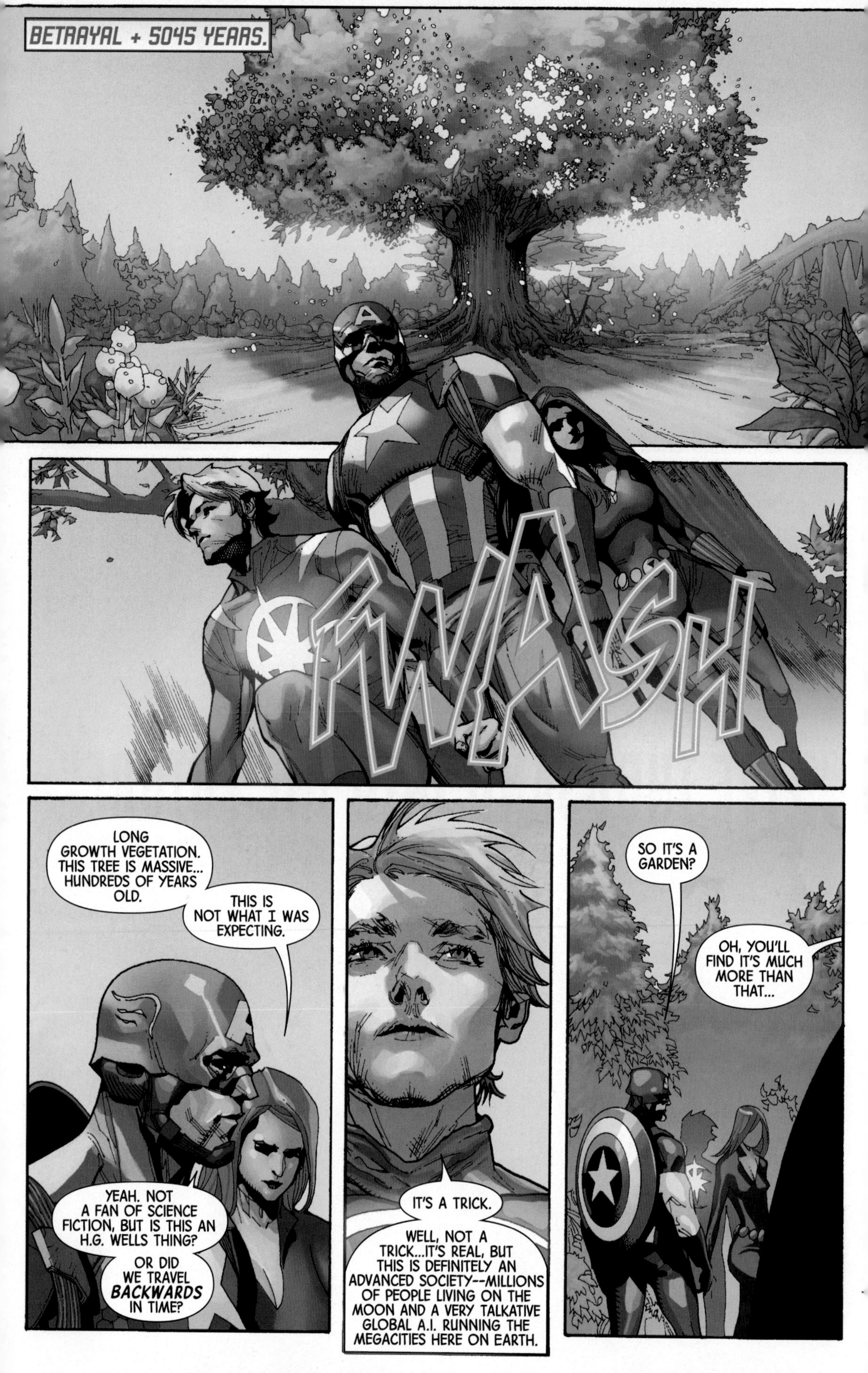
BETRAYAL + 5045 YEARS.
FWASH
LONG GROWTH VEGETATION. THIS TREE IS MASSIVE... HUNDREDS OF YEARS OLD.
THIS IS NOT WHAT I WAS EXPECTING.
YEAH. NOT A FAN OF SCIENCE FICTION, BUT IS THIS AN H.G. WELLS THING?
OR DID WE TRAVEL **BACKWARDS** IN TIME?
IT'S A TRICK.
WELL, NOT A TRICK...IT'S REAL, BUT THIS IS DEFINITELY AN ADVANCED SOCIETY--MILLIONS OF PEOPLE LIVING ON THE MOON AND A VERY TALKATIVE GLOBAL A.I. RUNNING THE MEGACITIES HERE ON EARTH.
SO IT'S A GARDEN?
OH, YOU'LL FIND IT'S MUCH MORE THAN THAT...

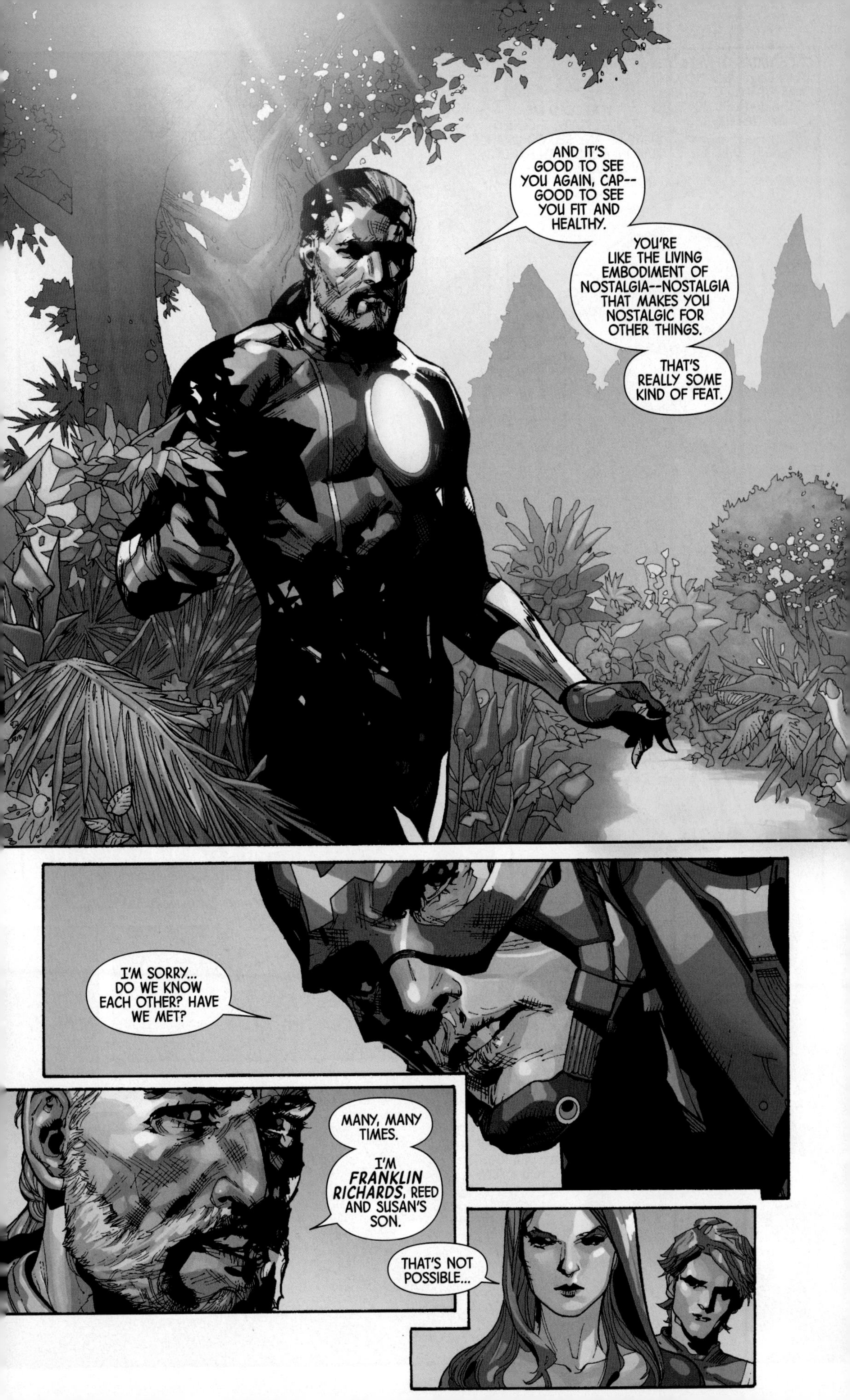
AND IT'S GOOD TO SEE YOU AGAIN, CAP-- GOOD TO SEE YOU FIT AND HEALTHY.
YOU'RE LIKE THE LIVING EMBODIMENT OF NOSTALGIA--NOSTALGIA THAT MAKES YOU NOSTALGIC FOR OTHER THINGS.
THAT'S REALLY SOME KIND OF FEAT.
I'M SORRY... DO WE KNOW EACH OTHER? HAVE WE MET?
MANY, MANY TIMES.
I'M *FRANKLIN RICHARDS*, REED AND SUSAN'S SON.
THAT'S NOT POSSIBLE...

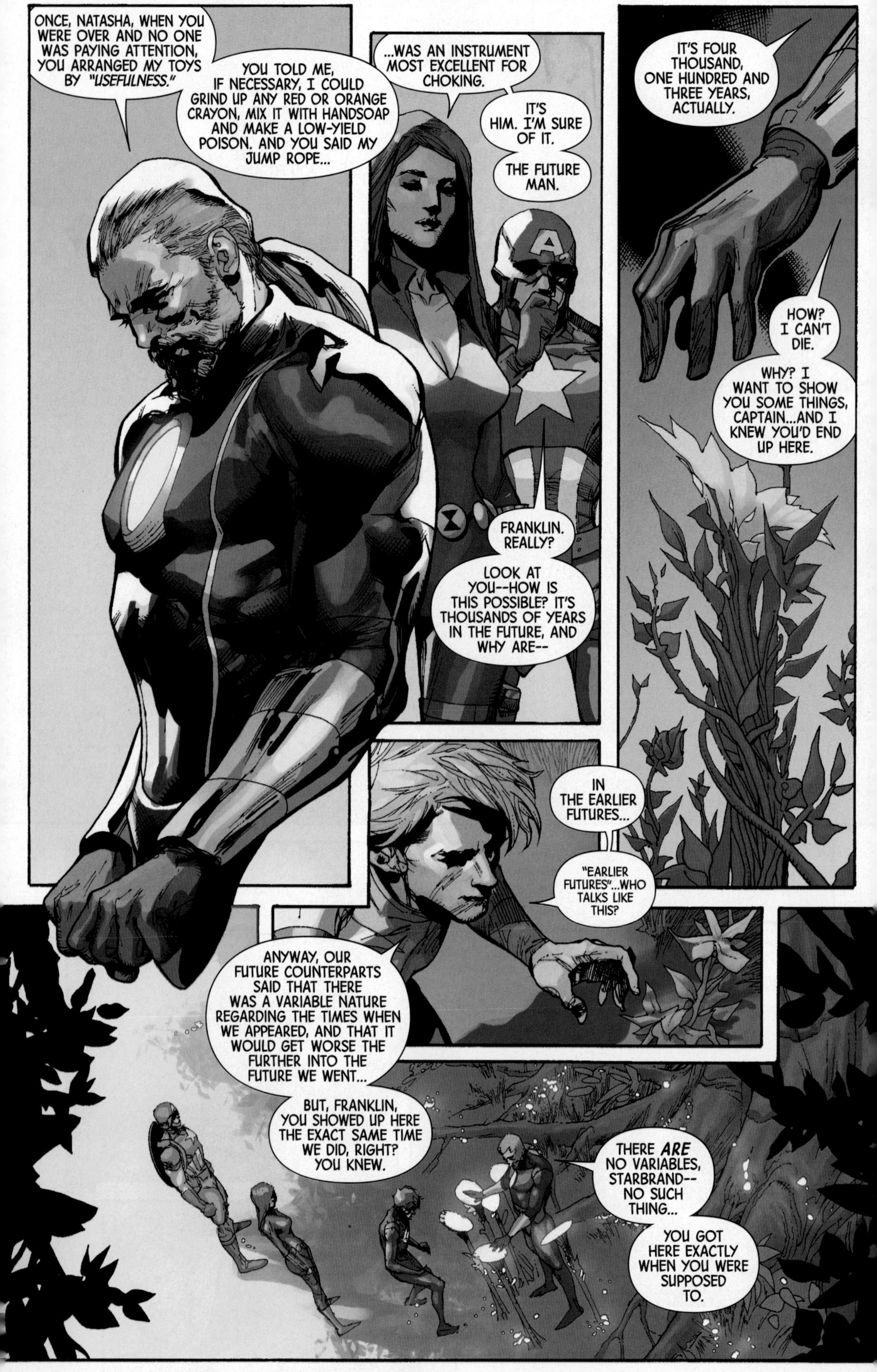

ONCE, NATASHA, WHEN YOU WERE OVER AND NO ONE WAS PAYING ATTENTION, YOU ARRANGED MY TOYS BY "USEFULNESS."
YOU TOLD ME, IF NECESSARY, I COULD GRIND UP ANY RED OR ORANGE CRAYON, MIX IT WITH HANDSOAP AND MAKE A LOW-YIELD POISON. AND YOU SAID MY JUMP ROPE...
...WAS AN INSTRUMENT MOST EXCELLENT FOR CHOKING.
IT'S HIM. I'M SURE OF IT.
THE FUTURE MAN.
FRANKLIN. REALLY?
LOOK AT YOU--HOW IS THIS POSSIBLE? IT'S THOUSANDS OF YEARS IN THE FUTURE, AND WHY ARE--
IT'S FOUR THOUSAND, ONE HUNDRED AND THREE YEARS, ACTUALLY.
HOW? I CAN'T DIE.
WHY? I WANT TO SHOW YOU SOME THINGS, CAPTAIN...AND I KNEW YOU'D END UP HERE.
IN THE EARLIER FUTURES...
"EARLIER FUTURES"...WHO TALKS LIKE THIS?
ANYWAY, OUR FUTURE COUNTERPARTS SAID THAT THERE WAS A VARIABLE NATURE REGARDING THE TIMES WHEN WE APPEARED, AND THAT IT WOULD GET WORSE THE FURTHER INTO THE FUTURE WE WENT...
BUT, FRANKLIN, YOU SHOWED UP HERE THE EXACT SAME TIME WE DID, RIGHT? YOU KNEW.
THERE ARE NO VARIABLES, STARBRAND--NO SUCH THING...
YOU GOT HERE EXACTLY WHEN YOU WERE SUPPOSED TO.

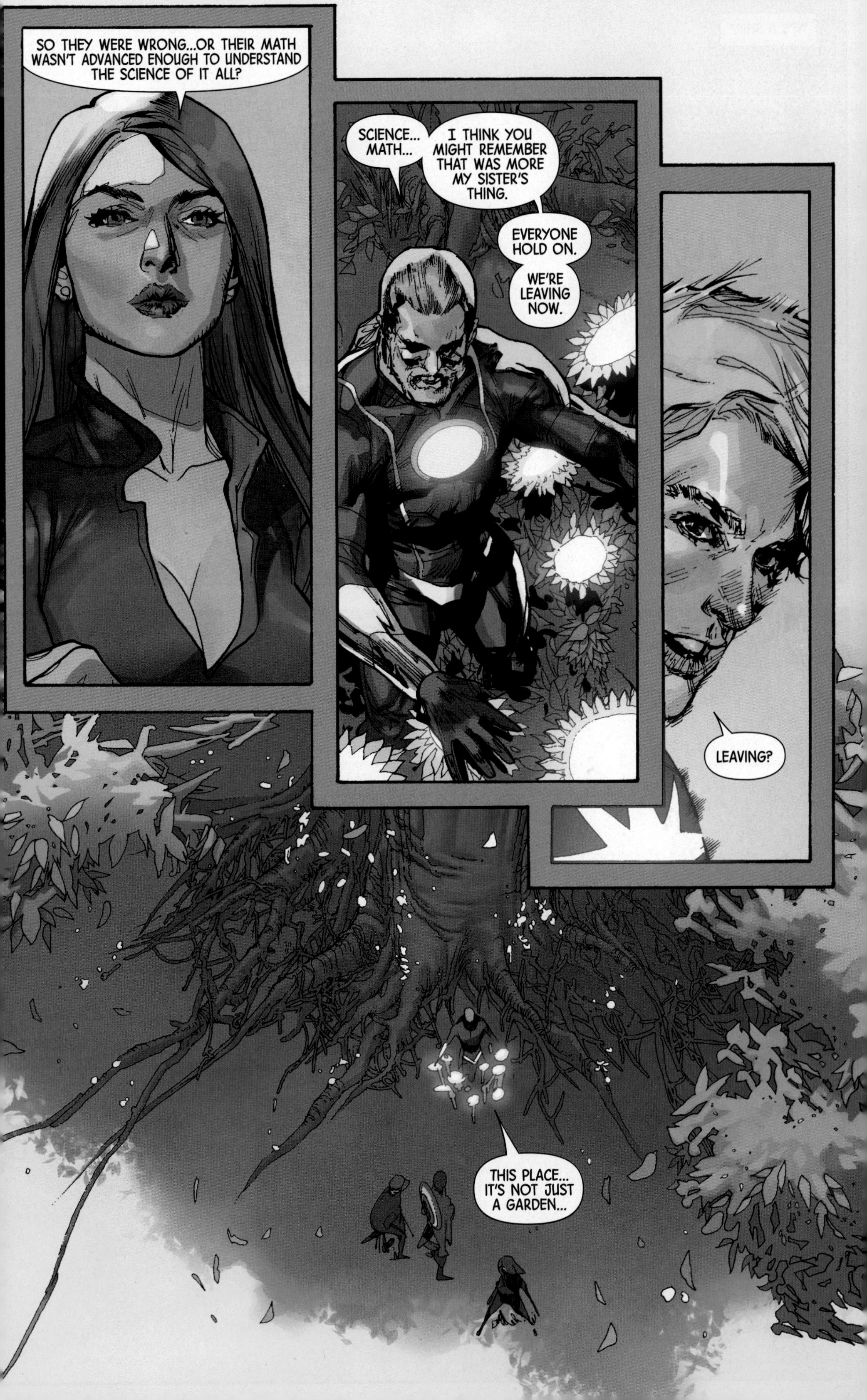
SO THEY WERE WRONG...OR THEIR MATH WASN'T ADVANCED ENOUGH TO UNDERSTAND THE SCIENCE OF IT ALL?
SCIENCE... MATH...
I THINK YOU MIGHT REMEMBER THAT WAS MORE MY SISTER'S THING.
EVERYONE HOLD ON.
WE'RE LEAVING NOW.
LEAVING?
THIS PLACE... IT'S NOT JUST A GARDEN...

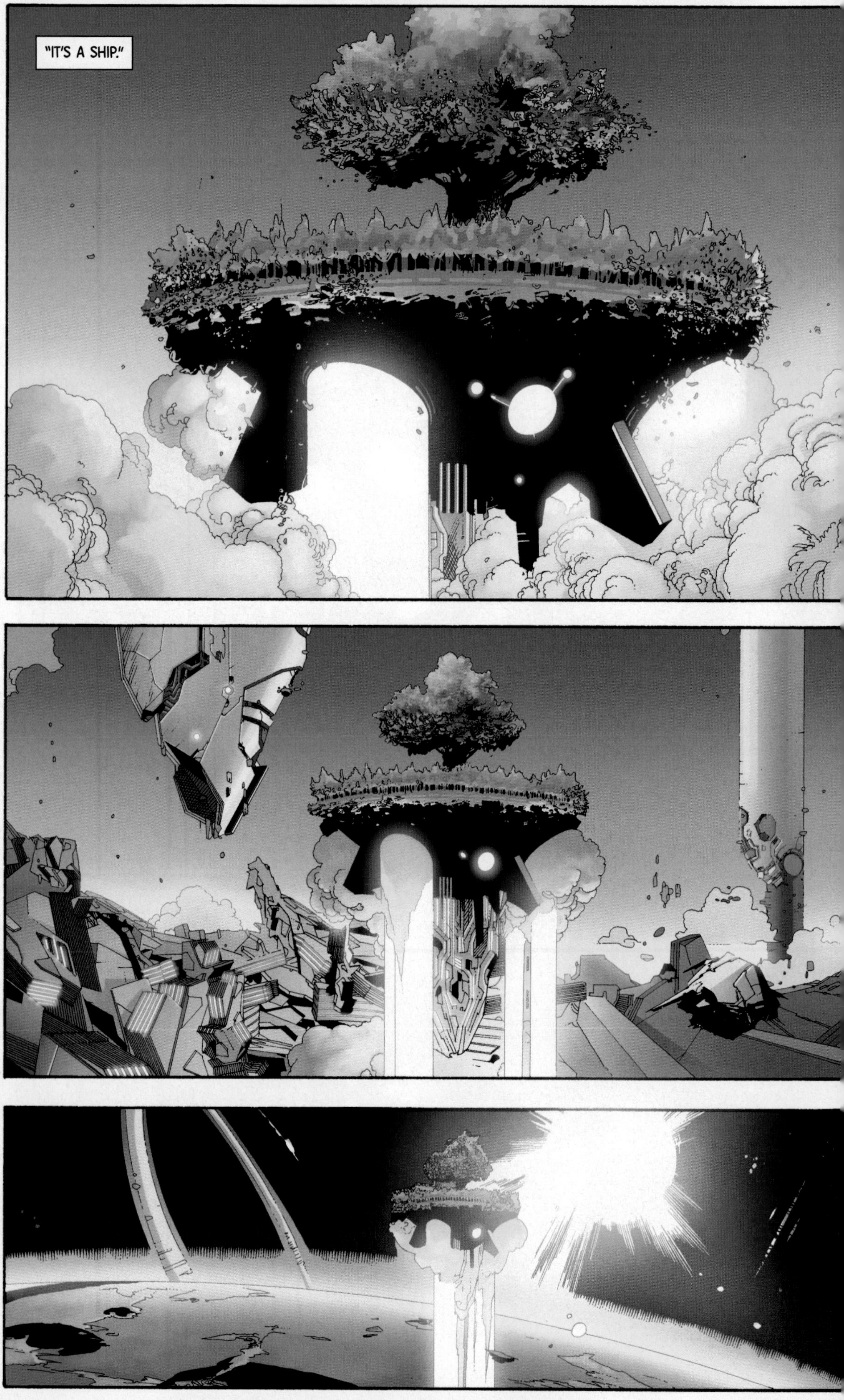
"IT'S A SHIP."

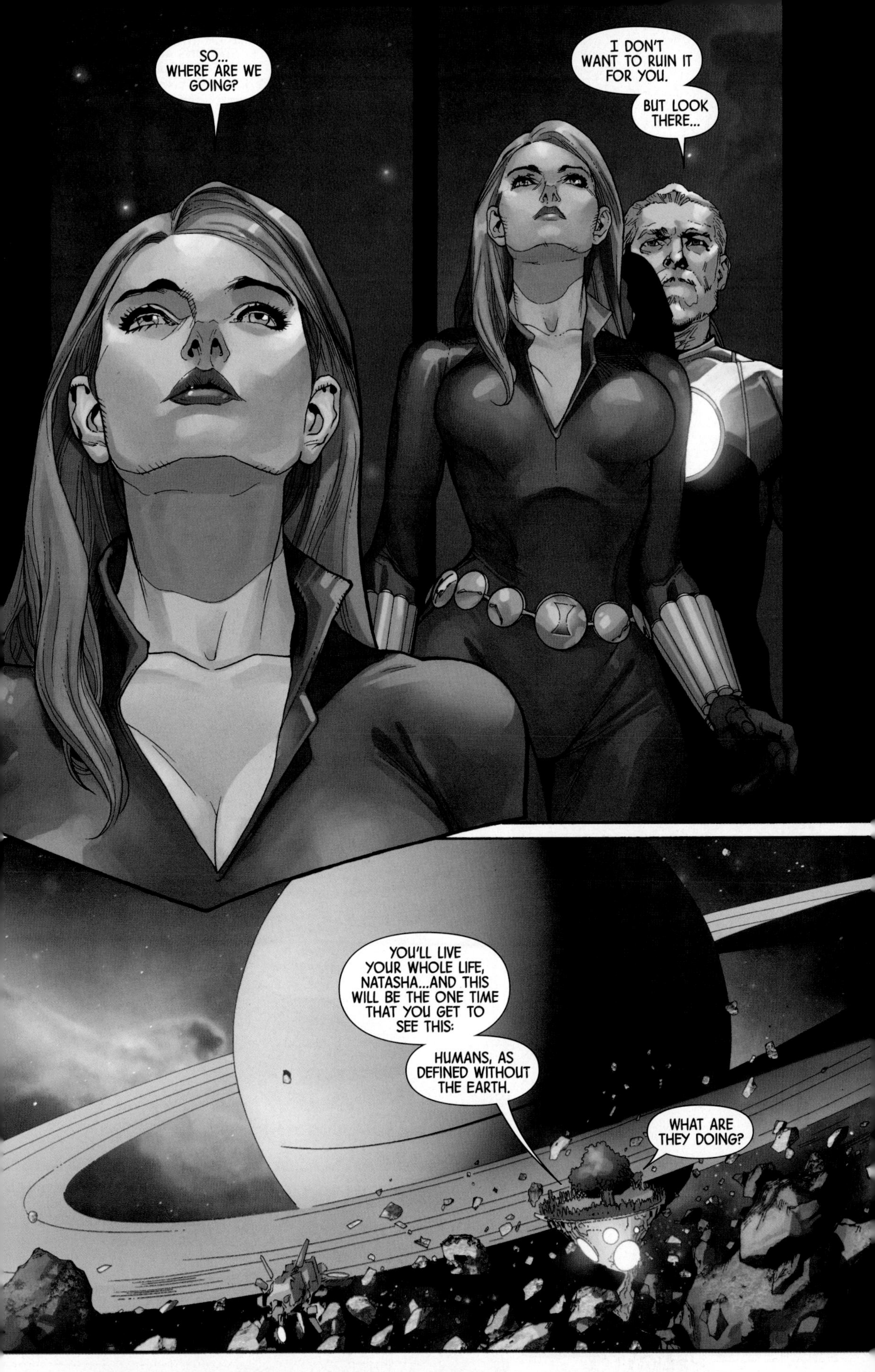
SO... WHERE ARE WE GOING?
I DON'T WANT TO RUIN IT FOR YOU.
BUT LOOK THERE...
YOU'LL LIVE YOUR WHOLE LIFE, NATASHA...AND THIS WILL BE THE ONE TIME THAT YOU GET TO SEE THIS:
HUMANS, AS DEFINED WITHOUT THE EARTH.
WHAT ARE THEY DOING?

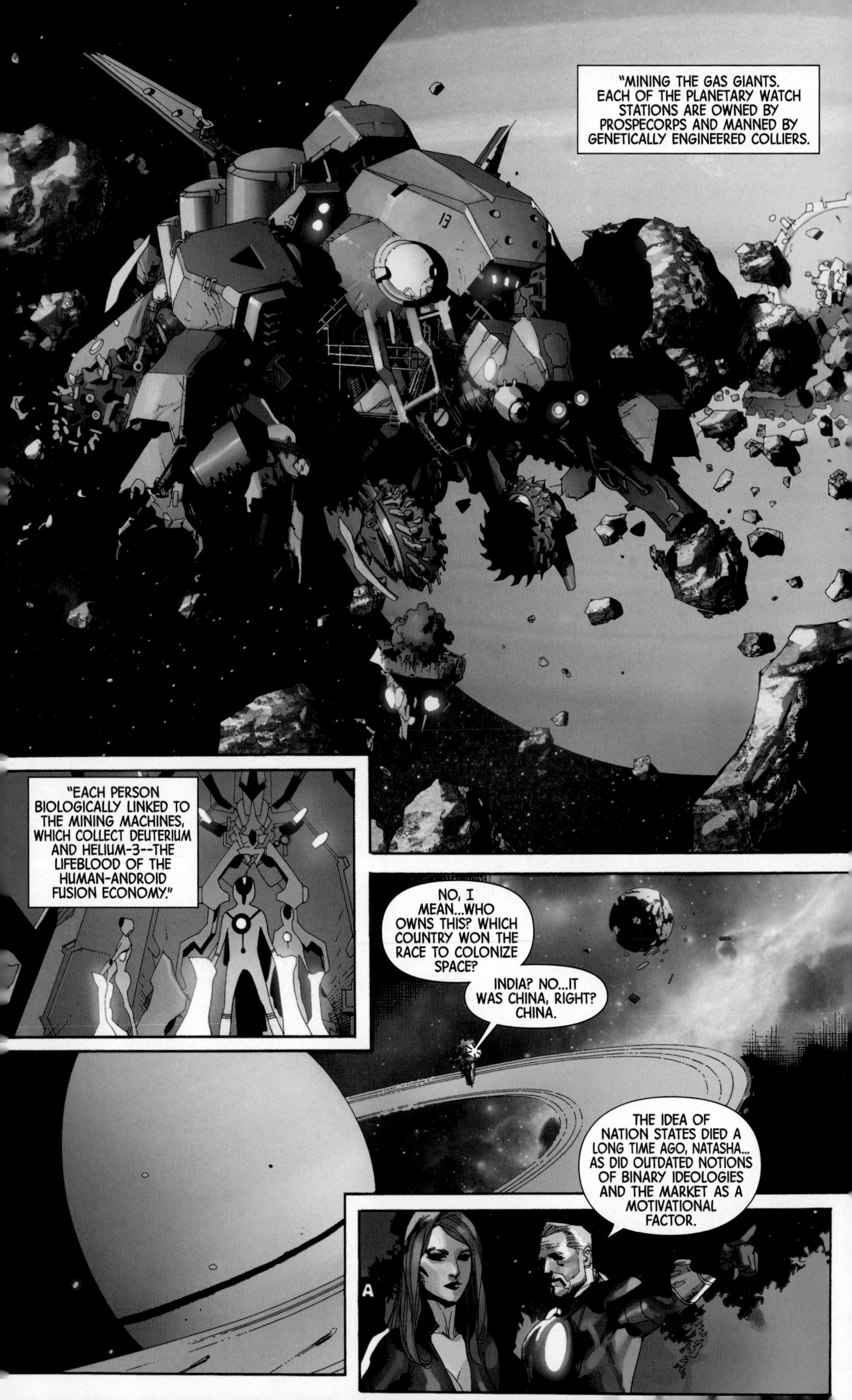
"MINING THE GAS GIANTS. EACH OF THE PLANETARY WATCH STATIONS ARE OWNED BY PROSPECORPS AND MANNED BY GENETICALLY ENGINEERED COLLIERS.
"EACH PERSON BIOLOGICALLY LINKED TO THE MINING MACHINES, WHICH COLLECT DEUTERIUM AND HELIUM-3--THE LIFEBLOOD OF THE HUMAN-ANDROID FUSION ECONOMY."
NO, I MEAN...WHO OWNS THIS? WHICH COUNTRY WON THE RACE TO COLONIZE SPACE?
INDIA? NO...IT WAS CHINA, RIGHT? CHINA.
THE IDEA OF NATION STATES DIED A LONG TIME AGO, NATASHA... AS DID OUTDATED NOTIONS OF BINARY IDEOLOGIES AND THE MARKET AS A MOTIVATIONAL FACTOR.

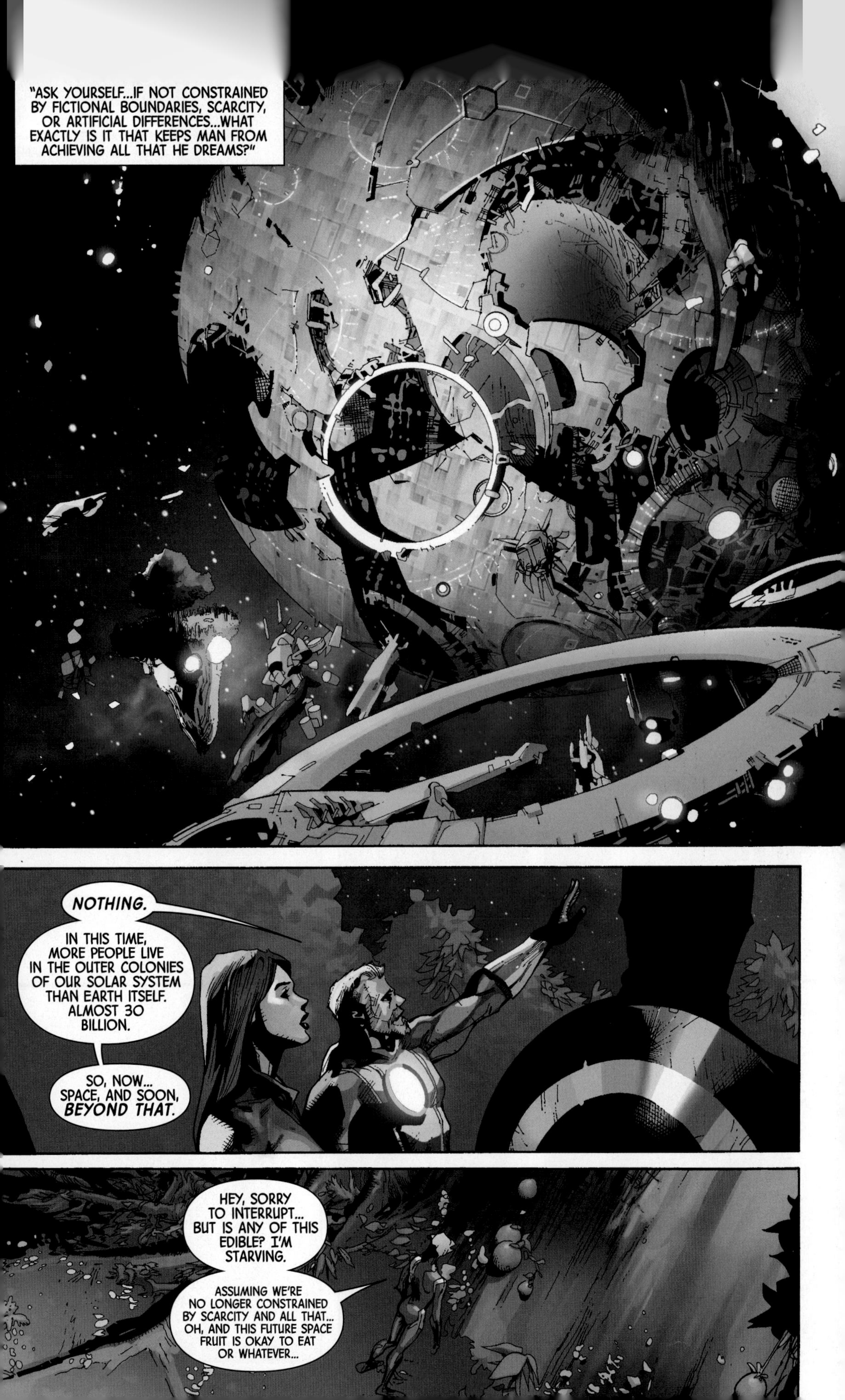
"ASK YOURSELF...IF NOT CONSTRAINED BY FICTIONAL BOUNDARIES, SCARCITY, OR ARTIFICIAL DIFFERENCES...WHAT EXACTLY IS IT THAT KEEPS MAN FROM ACHIEVING ALL THAT HE DREAMS?"
NOTHING.
IN THIS TIME, MORE PEOPLE LIVE IN THE OUTER COLONIES OF OUR SOLAR SYSTEM THAN EARTH ITSELF. ALMOST 30 BILLION.
SO, NOW... SPACE, AND SOON, BEYOND THAT.
HEY, SORRY TO INTERRUPT... BUT IS ANY OF THIS EDIBLE? I'M STARVING.
ASSUMING WE'RE NO LONGER CONSTRAINED BY SCARCITY AND ALL THAT... OH, AND THIS FUTURE SPACE FRUIT IS OKAY TO EAT OR WHATEVER...

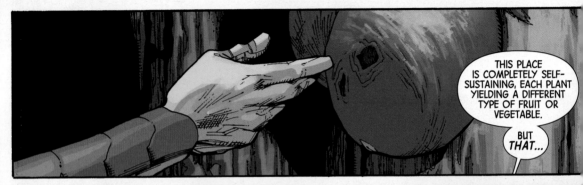

THIS PLACE IS COMPLETELY SELF-SUSTAINING, EACH PLANT YIELDING A DIFFERENT TYPE OF FRUIT OR VEGETABLE.

BUT *THAT*...

YEAH?

THAT'S NOT EDIBLE.

TRY ONE OF THESE.

OKAY.

CRUNCH

HOW IS IT?

IT'S GOOD.

TASTES LIKE CHICKEN.

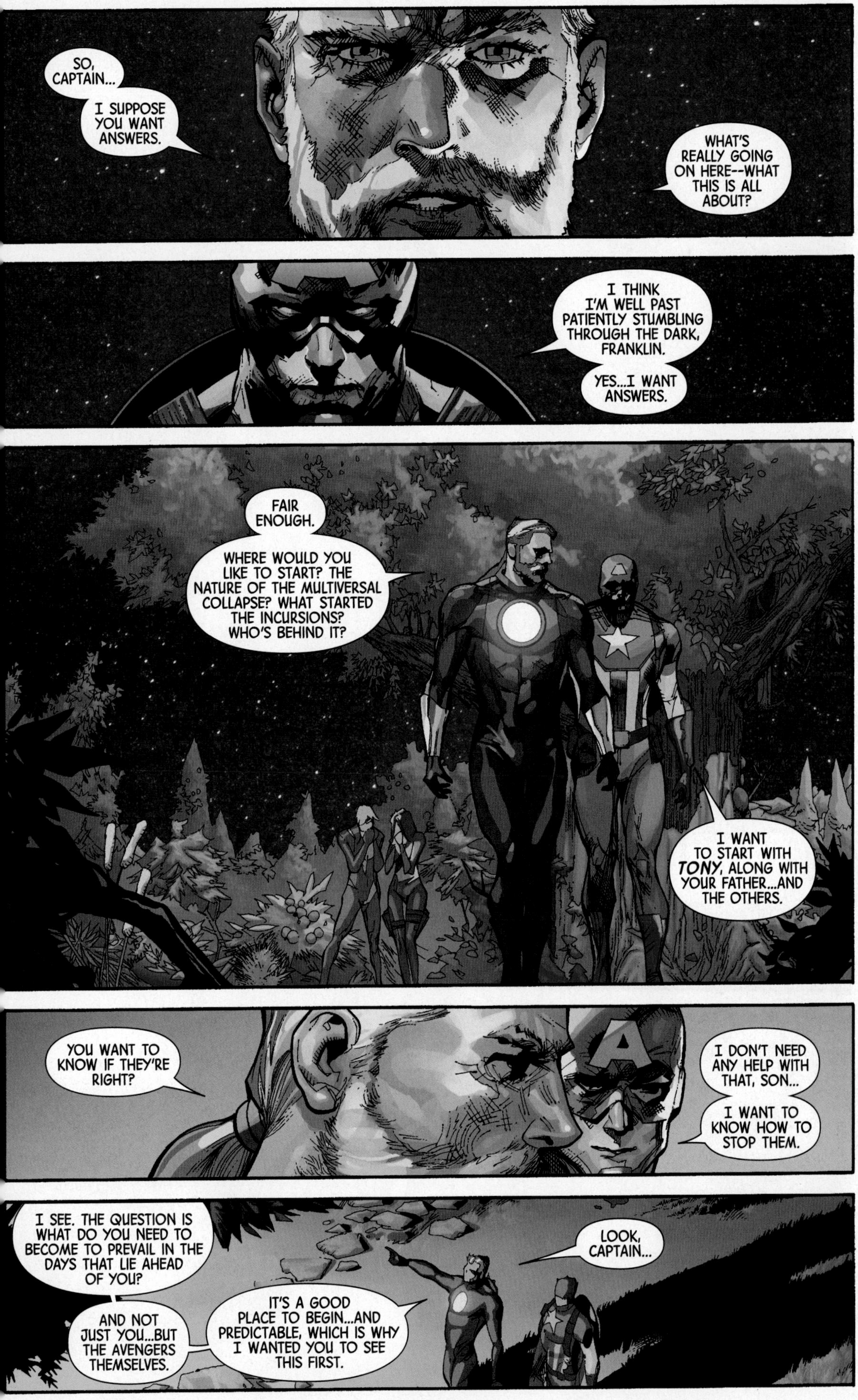
SO, CAPTAIN...
I SUPPOSE YOU WANT ANSWERS.
WHAT'S REALLY GOING ON HERE--WHAT THIS IS ALL ABOUT?
I THINK I'M WELL PAST PATIENTLY STUMBLING THROUGH THE DARK, FRANKLIN.
YES...I WANT ANSWERS.
FAIR ENOUGH.
WHERE WOULD YOU LIKE TO START? THE NATURE OF THE MULTIVERSAL COLLAPSE? WHAT STARTED THE INCURSIONS? WHO'S BEHIND IT?
I WANT TO START WITH *TONY*, ALONG WITH YOUR FATHER...AND THE OTHERS.
YOU WANT TO KNOW IF THEY'RE RIGHT?
I DON'T NEED ANY HELP WITH THAT, SON...
I WANT TO KNOW HOW TO STOP THEM.
I SEE. THE QUESTION IS WHAT DO YOU NEED TO BECOME TO PREVAIL IN THE DAYS THAT LIE AHEAD OF YOU?
AND NOT JUST YOU...BUT THE AVENGERS THEMSELVES.
IT'S A GOOD PLACE TO BEGIN...AND PREDICTABLE, WHICH IS WHY I WANTED YOU TO SEE THIS FIRST.
LOOK, CAPTAIN...

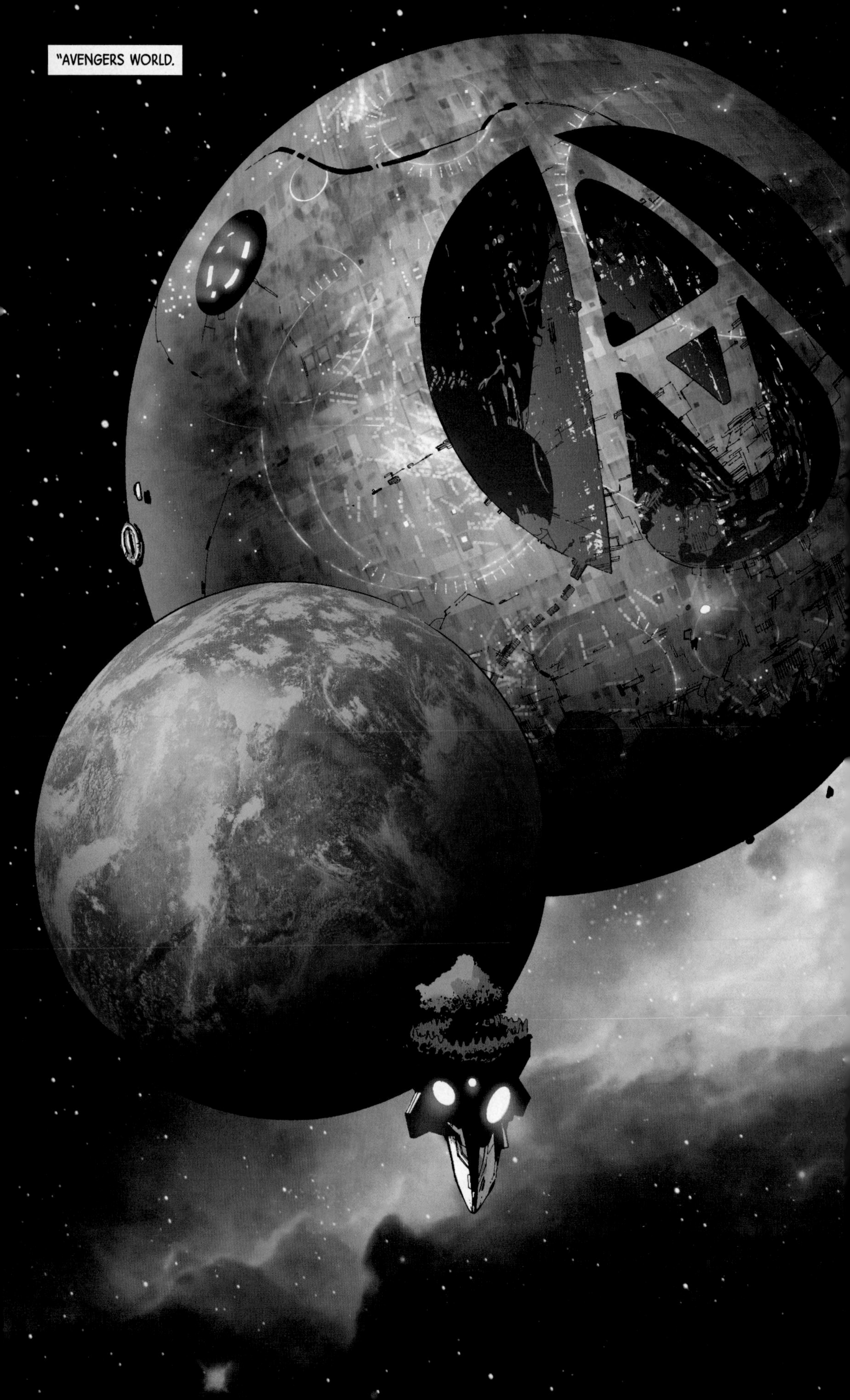
"AVENGERS WORLD.

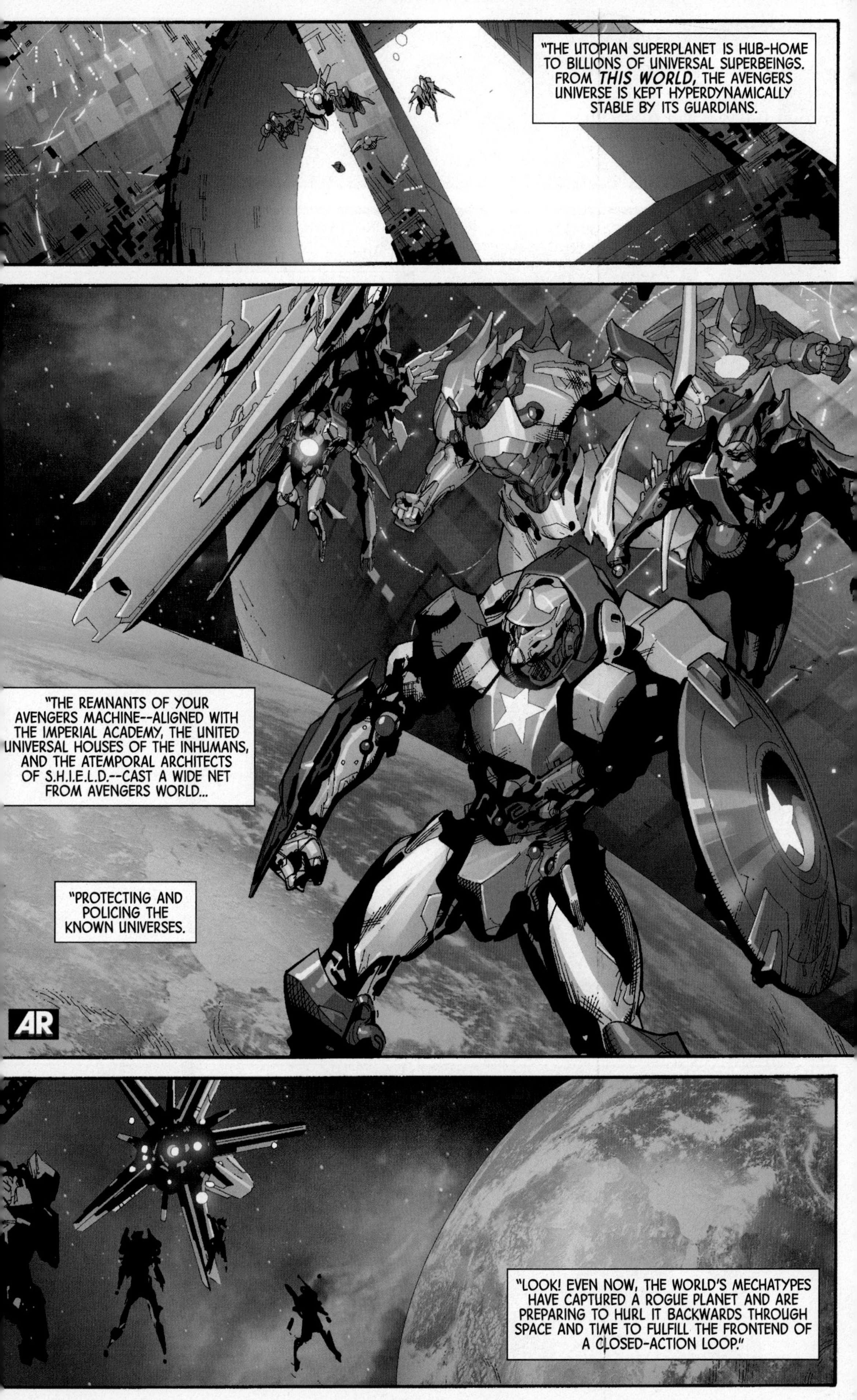
"THE UTOPIAN SUPERPLANET IS HUB-HOME TO BILLIONS OF UNIVERSAL SUPERBEINGS. FROM THIS WORLD, THE AVENGERS UNIVERSE IS KEPT HYPERDYNAMICALLY STABLE BY ITS GUARDIANS.
"THE REMNANTS OF YOUR AVENGERS MACHINE--ALIGNED WITH THE IMPERIAL ACADEMY, THE UNITED UNIVERSAL HOUSES OF THE INHUMANS, AND THE ATEMPORAL ARCHITECTS OF S.H.I.E.L.D.--CAST A WIDE NET FROM AVENGERS WORLD...
"PROTECTING AND POLICING THE KNOWN UNIVERSES.
AR
"LOOK! EVEN NOW, THE WORLD'S MECHATYPES HAVE CAPTURED A ROGUE PLANET AND ARE PREPARING TO HURL IT BACKWARDS THROUGH SPACE AND TIME TO FULFILL THE FRONTEND OF A CLOSED-ACTION LOOP."

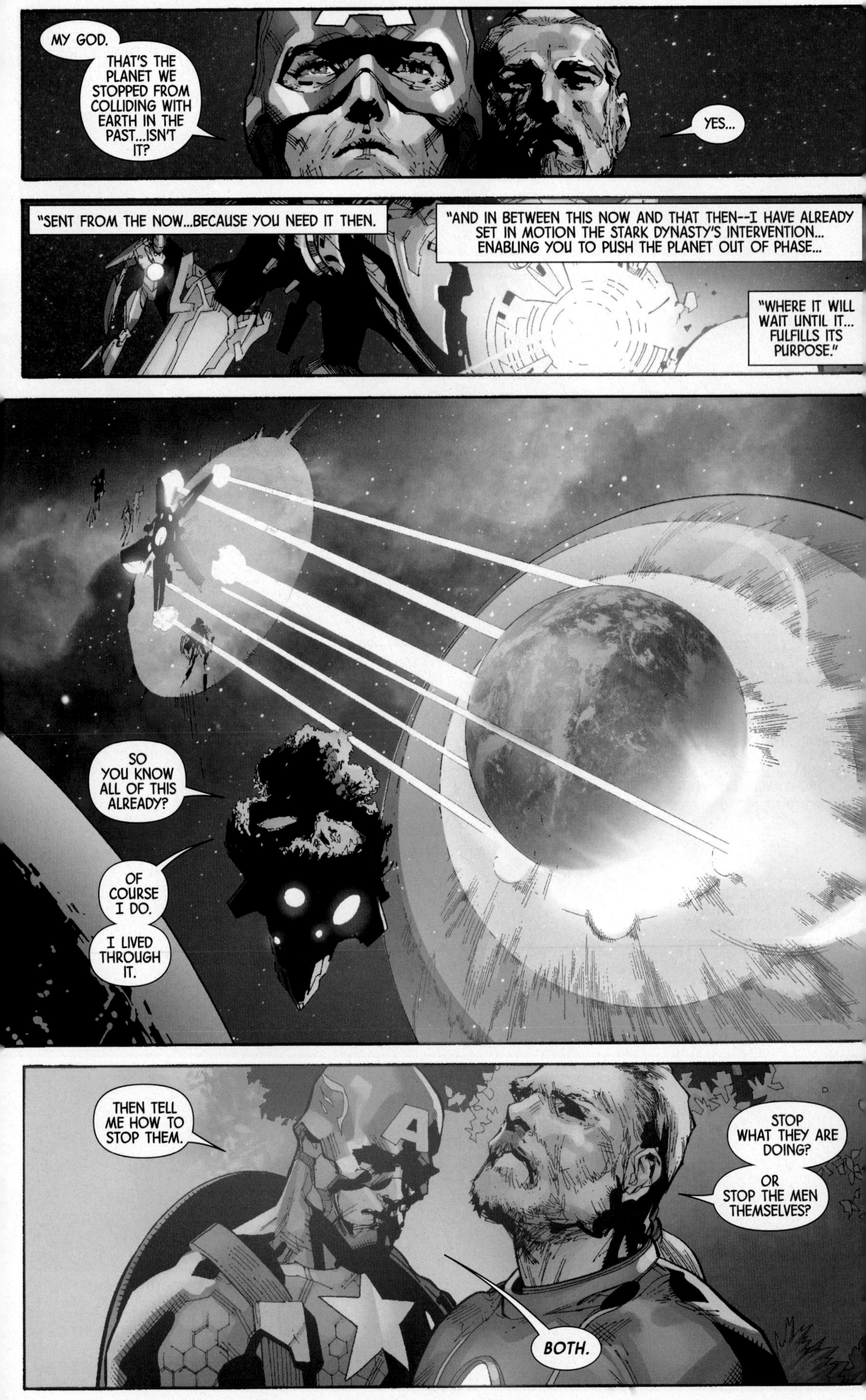
MY GOD.
THAT'S THE PLANET WE STOPPED FROM COLLIDING WITH EARTH IN THE PAST...ISN'T IT?
YES...
"SENT FROM THE NOW...BECAUSE YOU NEED IT THEN.
"AND IN BETWEEN THIS NOW AND THAT THEN--I HAVE ALREADY SET IN MOTION THE STARK DYNASTY'S INTERVENTION... ENABLING YOU TO PUSH THE PLANET OUT OF PHASE...
"WHERE IT WILL WAIT UNTIL IT... FULFILLS ITS PURPOSE."
SO YOU KNOW ALL OF THIS ALREADY?
OF COURSE I DO.
I LIVED THROUGH IT.
THEN TELL ME HOW TO STOP THEM.
STOP WHAT THEY ARE DOING?
OR STOP THE MEN THEMSELVES?
BOTH.

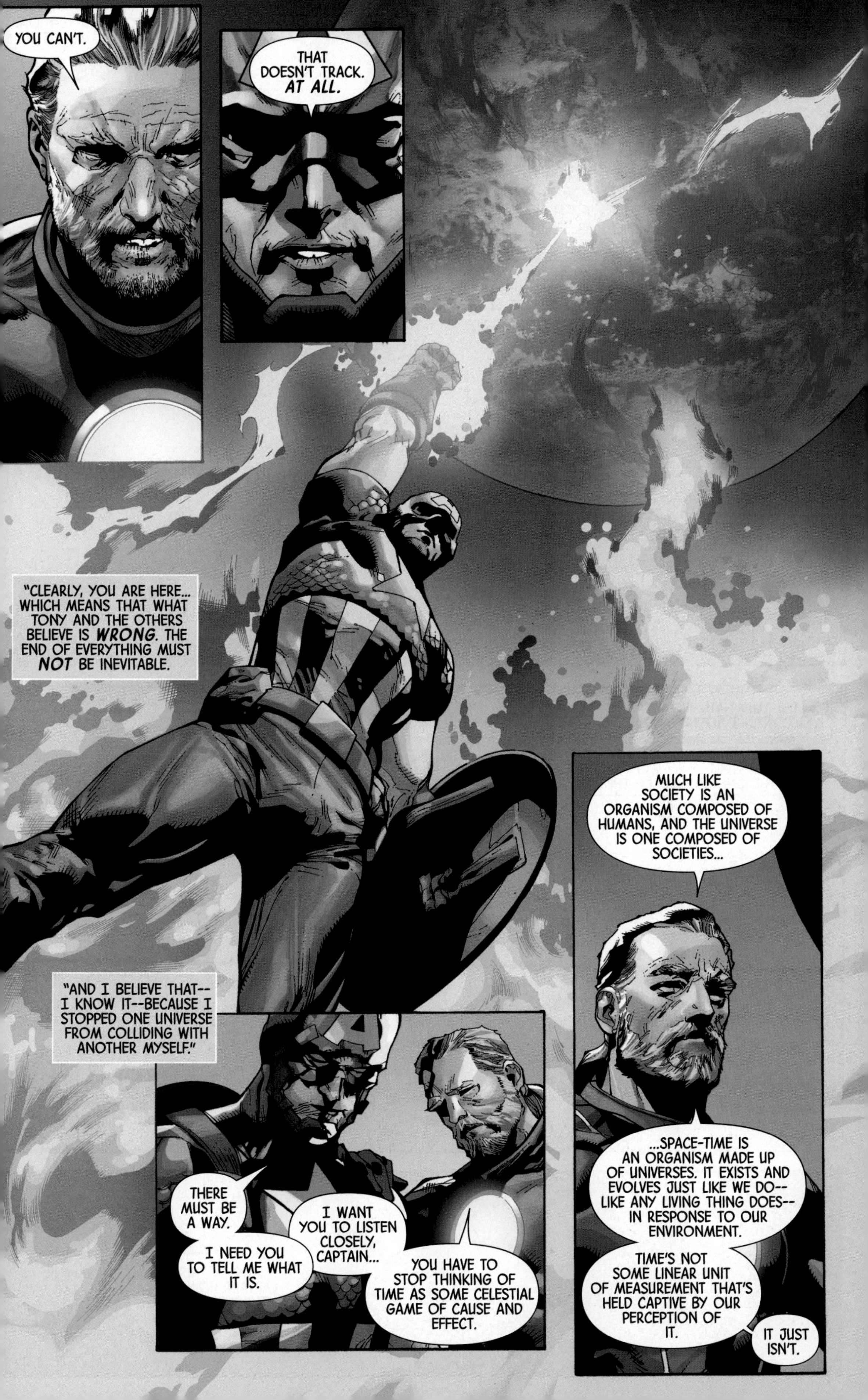

YOU CAN'T.
THAT DOESN'T TRACK. AT ALL.
"CLEARLY, YOU ARE HERE... WHICH MEANS THAT WHAT TONY AND THE OTHERS BELIEVE IS WRONG. THE END OF EVERYTHING MUST NOT BE INEVITABLE.
"AND I BELIEVE THAT--I KNOW IT--BECAUSE I STOPPED ONE UNIVERSE FROM COLLIDING WITH ANOTHER MYSELF."
THERE MUST BE A WAY.
I NEED YOU TO TELL ME WHAT IT IS.
I WANT YOU TO LISTEN CLOSELY, CAPTAIN...
YOU HAVE TO STOP THINKING OF TIME AS SOME CELESTIAL GAME OF CAUSE AND EFFECT.
MUCH LIKE SOCIETY IS AN ORGANISM COMPOSED OF HUMANS, AND THE UNIVERSE IS ONE COMPOSED OF SOCIETIES...
...SPACE-TIME IS AN ORGANISM MADE UP OF UNIVERSES. IT EXISTS AND EVOLVES JUST LIKE WE DO--LIKE ANY LIVING THING DOES--IN RESPONSE TO OUR ENVIRONMENT.
TIME'S NOT SOME LINEAR UNIT OF MEASUREMENT THAT'S HELD CAPTIVE BY OUR PERCEPTION OF IT.
IT JUST ISN'T.

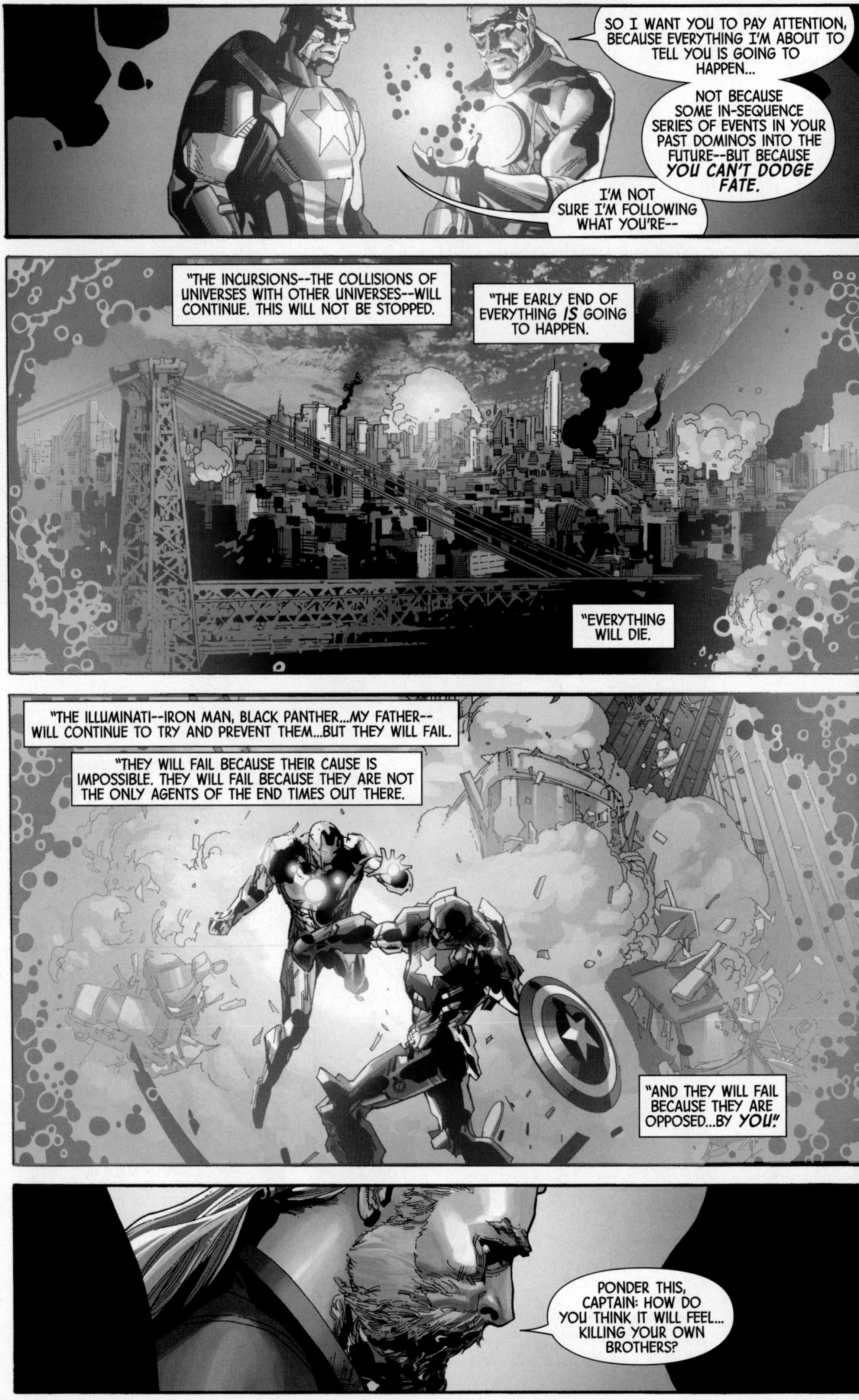
SO I WANT YOU TO PAY ATTENTION, BECAUSE EVERYTHING I'M ABOUT TO TELL YOU IS GOING TO HAPPEN...
NOT BECAUSE SOME IN-SEQUENCE SERIES OF EVENTS IN YOUR PAST DOMINOS INTO THE FUTURE--BUT BECAUSE YOU CAN'T DODGE FATE.
I'M NOT SURE I'M FOLLOWING WHAT YOU'RE--
"THE INCURSIONS--THE COLLISIONS OF UNIVERSES WITH OTHER UNIVERSES--WILL CONTINUE. THIS WILL NOT BE STOPPED.
"THE EARLY END OF EVERYTHING IS GOING TO HAPPEN.
"EVERYTHING WILL DIE.
"THE ILLUMINATI--IRON MAN, BLACK PANTHER...MY FATHER--WILL CONTINUE TO TRY AND PREVENT THEM...BUT THEY WILL FAIL.
"THEY WILL FAIL BECAUSE THEIR CAUSE IS IMPOSSIBLE. THEY WILL FAIL BECAUSE THEY ARE NOT THE ONLY AGENTS OF THE END TIMES OUT THERE.
"AND THEY WILL FAIL BECAUSE THEY ARE OPPOSED...BY YOU!"
PONDER THIS, CAPTAIN: HOW DO YOU THINK IT WILL FEEL... KILLING YOUR OWN BROTHERS?

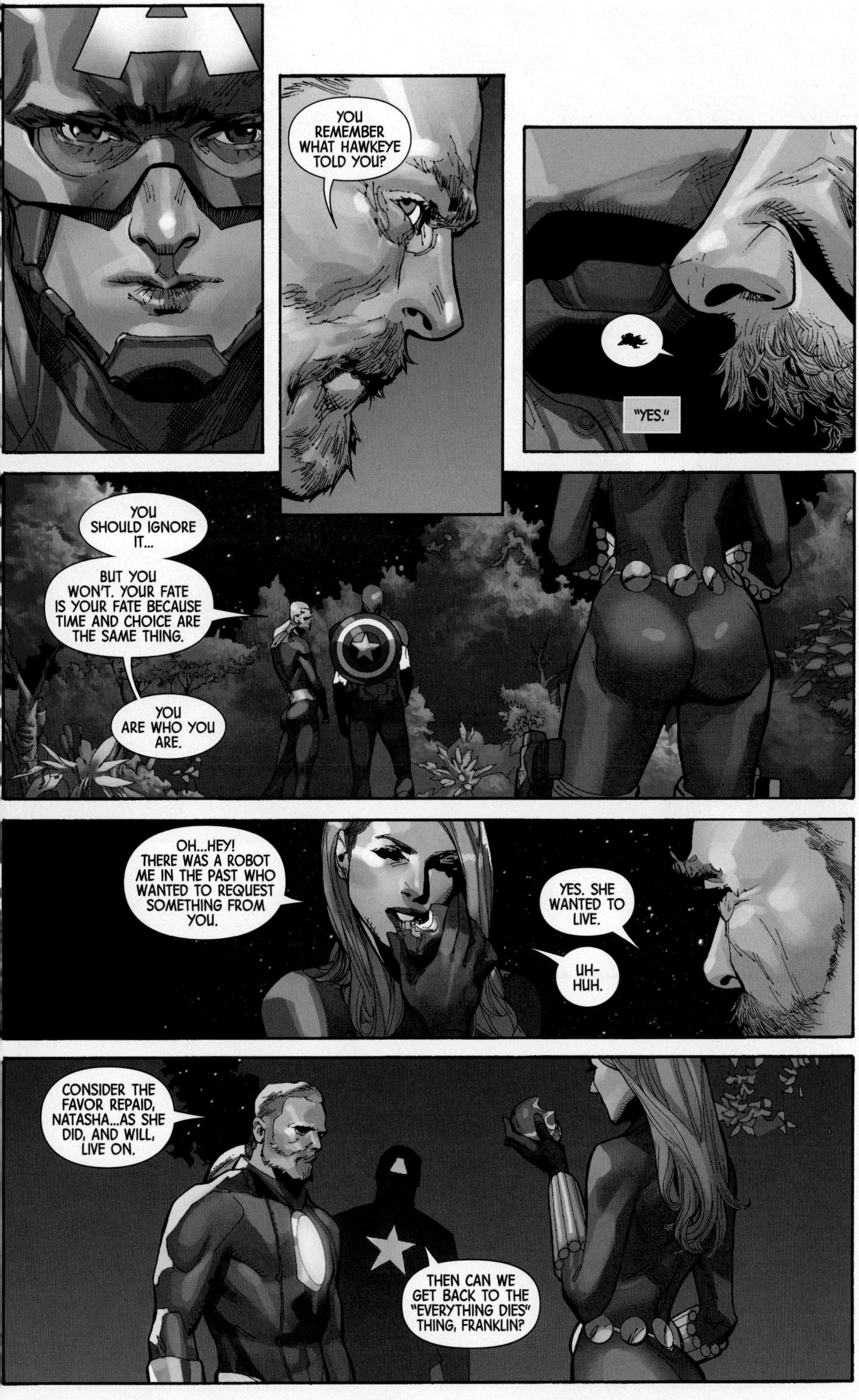
YOU REMEMBER WHAT HAWKEYE TOLD YOU?
"YES."
YOU SHOULD IGNORE IT...
BUT YOU WON'T. YOUR FATE IS YOUR FATE BECAUSE TIME AND CHOICE ARE THE SAME THING.
YOU ARE WHO YOU ARE.
OH...HEY! THERE WAS A ROBOT ME IN THE PAST WHO WANTED TO REQUEST SOMETHING FROM YOU.
YES. SHE WANTED TO LIVE.
UH-HUH.
CONSIDER THE FAVOR REPAID, NATASHA...AS SHE DID, AND WILL, LIVE ON.
THEN CAN WE GET BACK TO THE "EVERYTHING DIES" THING, FRANKLIN?

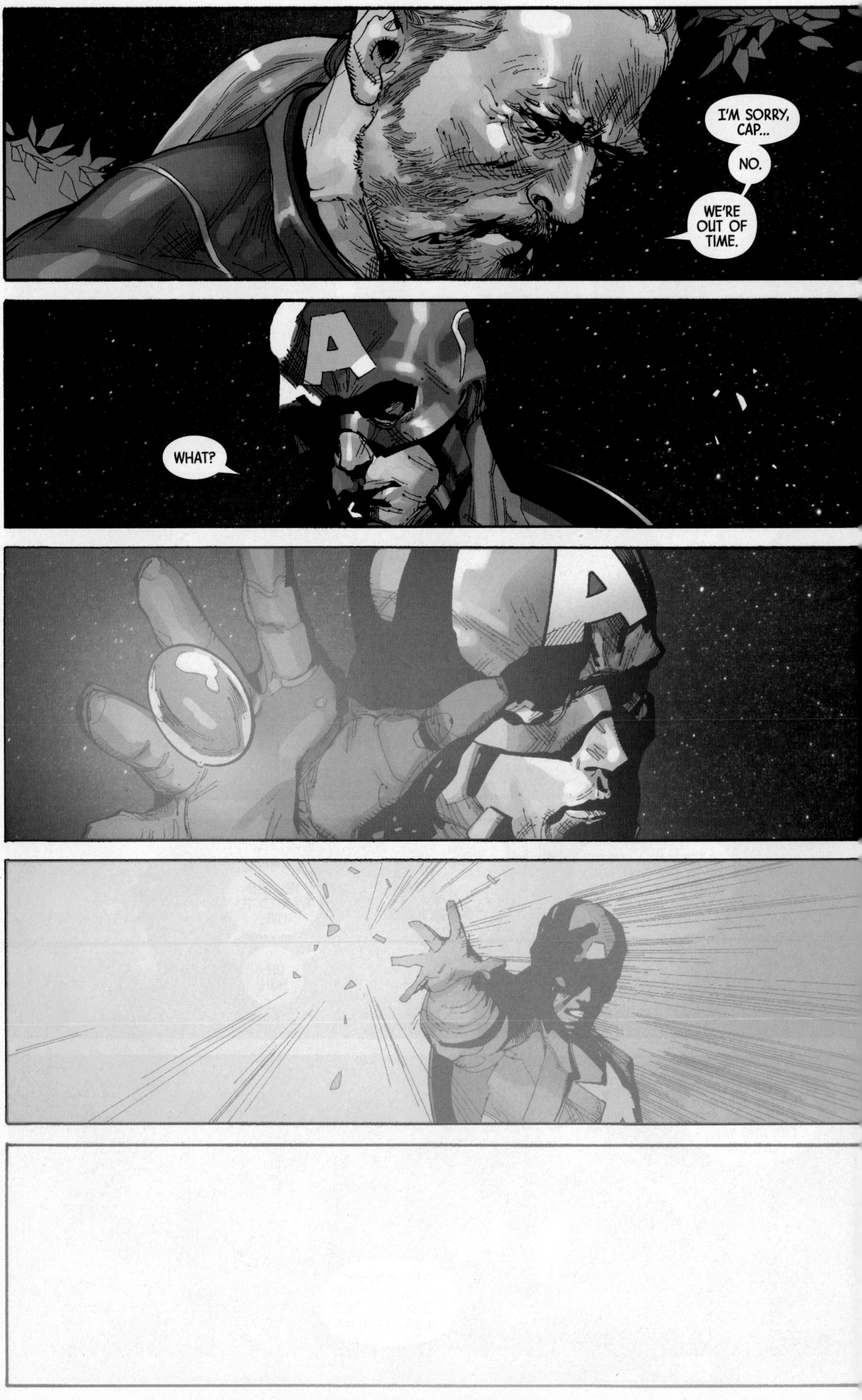
I'M SORRY, CAP...
NO.
WE'RE OUT OF TIME.
WHAT?

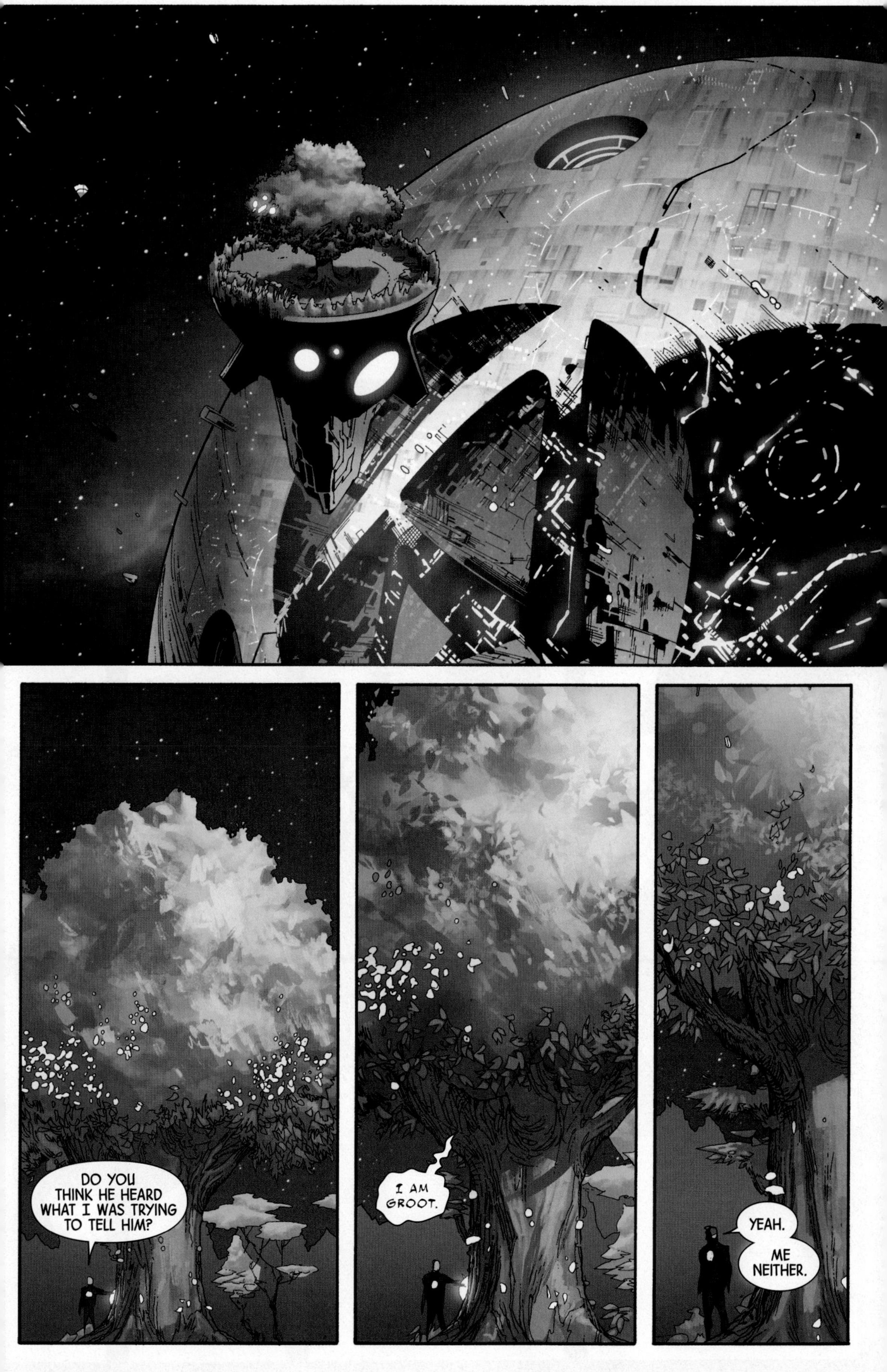
DO YOU THINK HE HEARD WHAT I WAS TRYING TO TELL HIM?
I AM GROOT.
YEAH.
ME NEITHER.

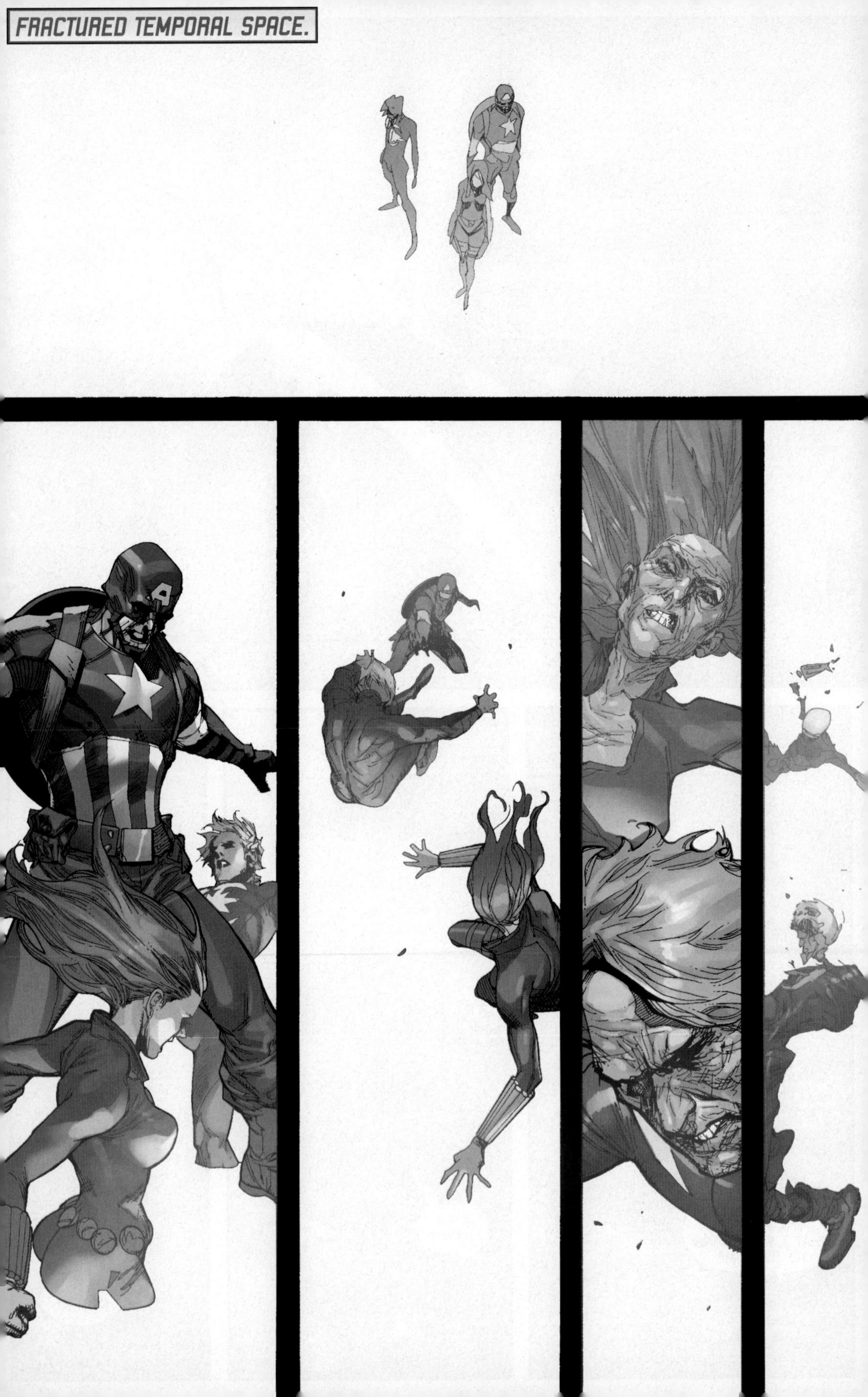
FRACTURED TEMPORAL SPACE.

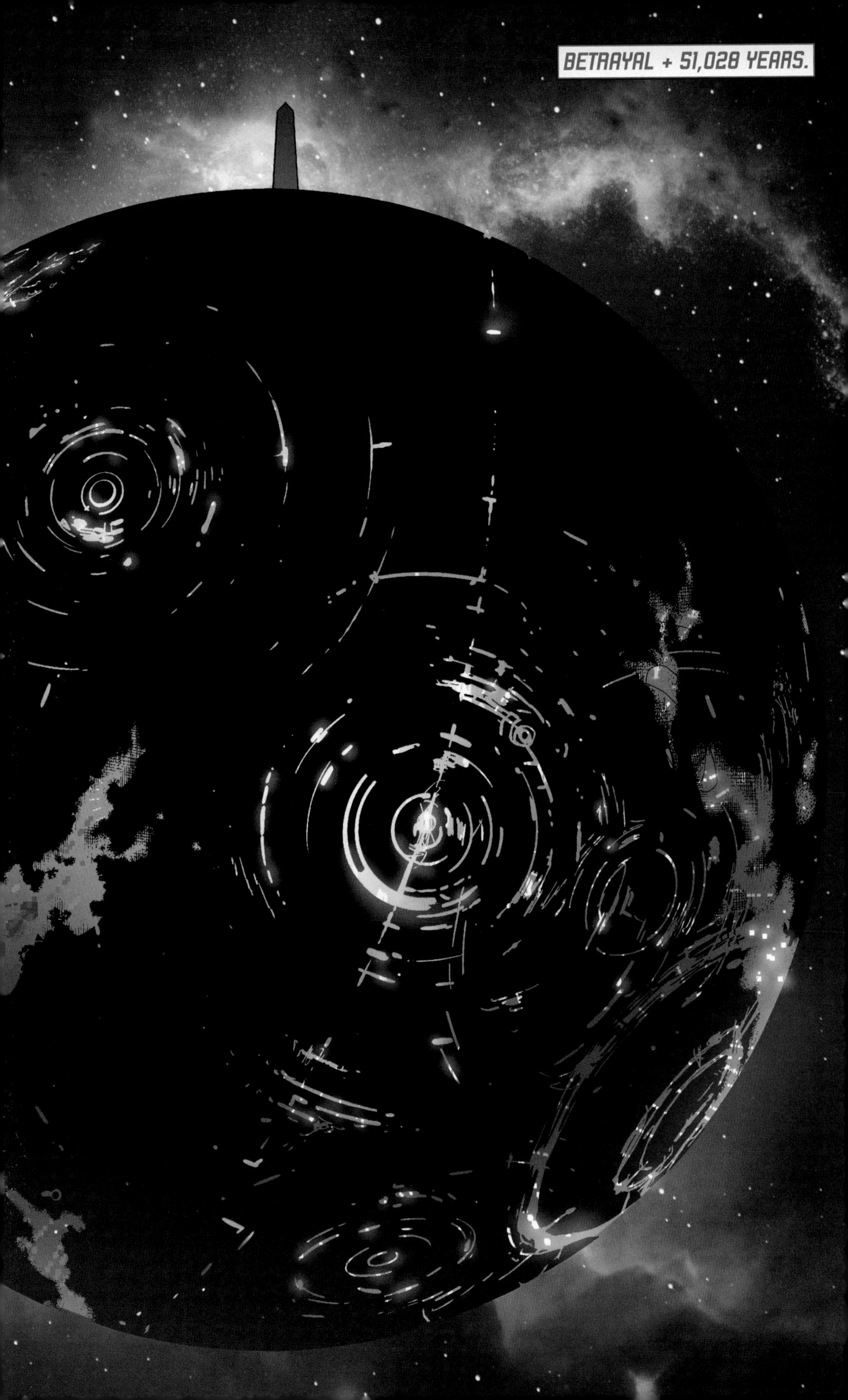
BETRAYAL + 51,028 YEARS.

"FIFTY THOUSAND INTO THE FUTURE"

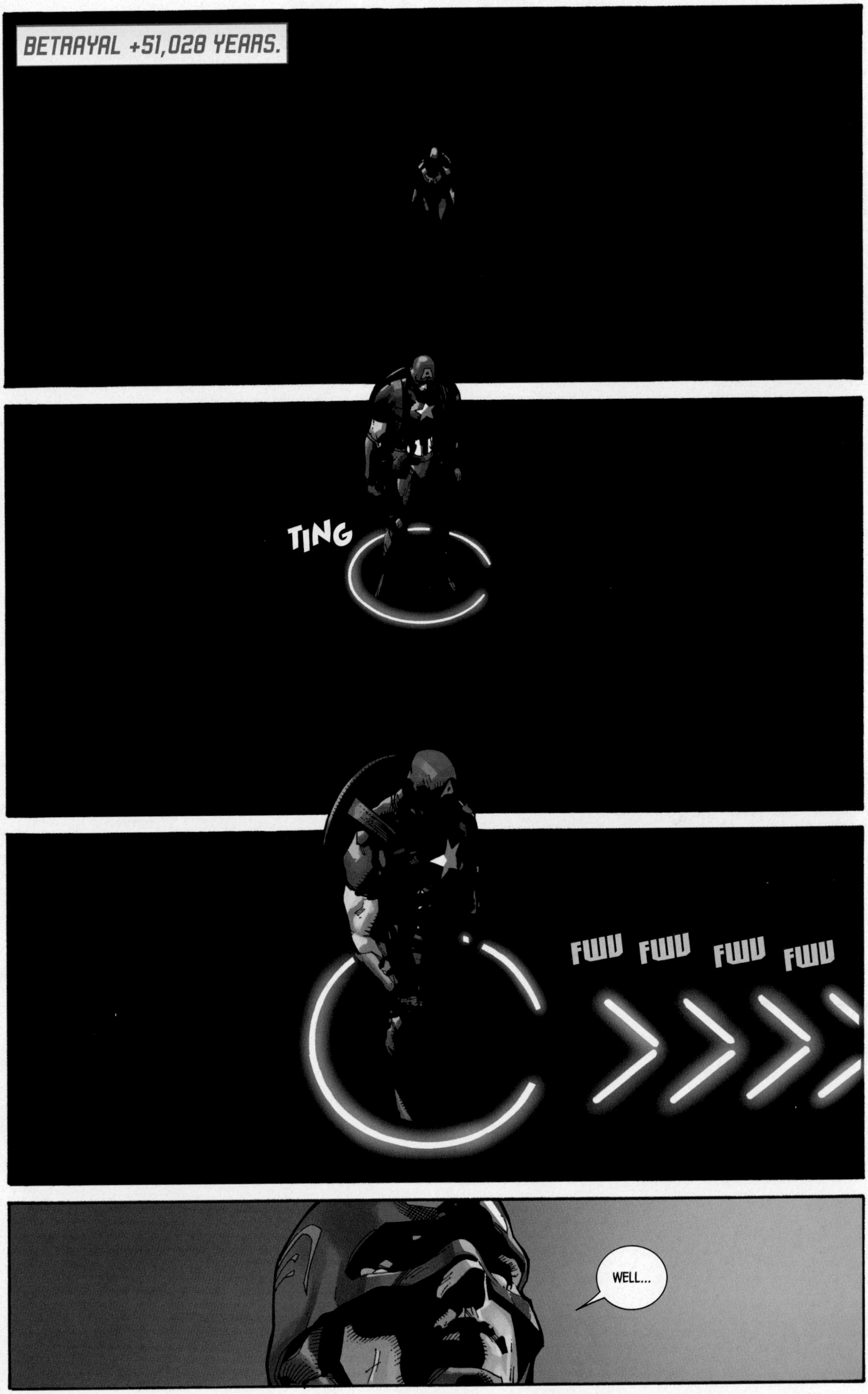
BETRAYAL +51,028 YEARS.
TING
FWV FWV FWV FWV
WELL...

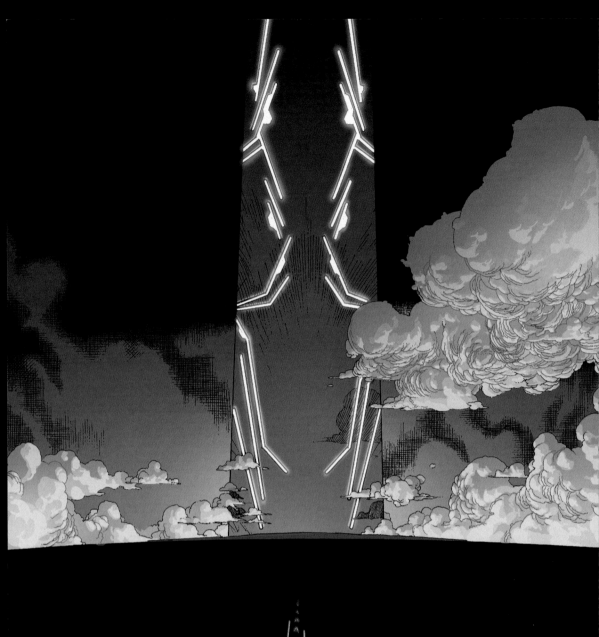

I GUESS I SHOULD START WALKING.

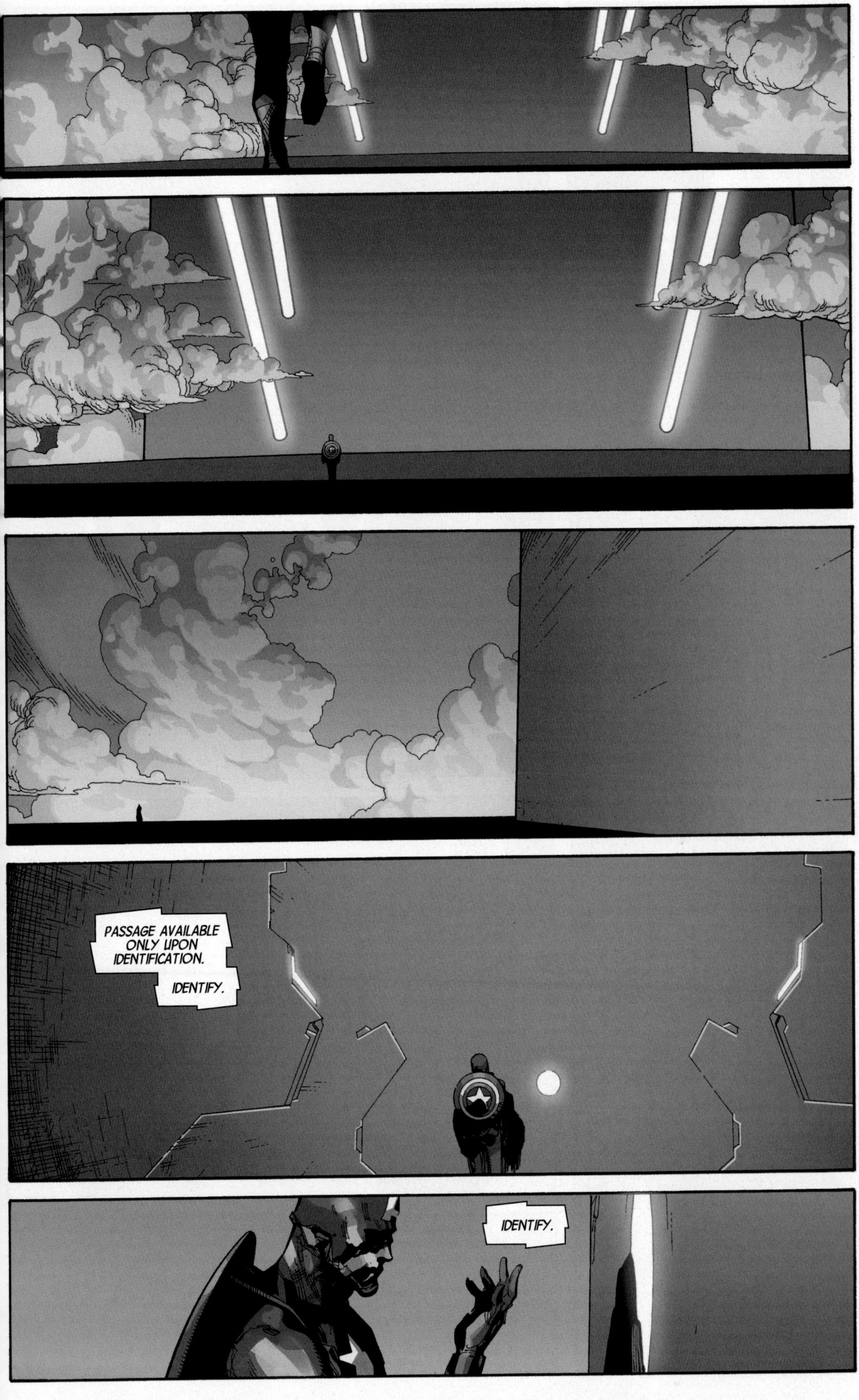
PASSAGE AVAILABLE ONLY UPON IDENTIFICATION.
IDENTIFY.
IDENTIFY.

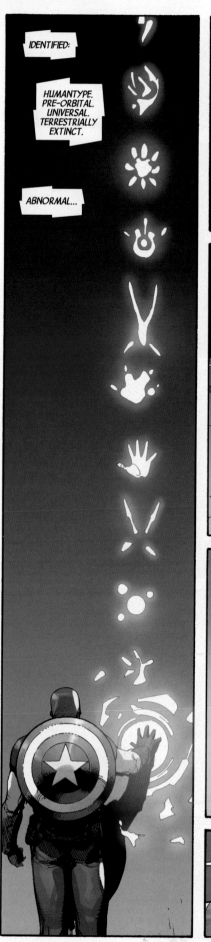

IDENTIFIED:

HUMANTYPE.
PRE-ORBITAL.
UNIVERSAL.
TERRESTRIALLY
EXTINCT.

ABNORMAL...

ATEMPORAL.

PLEASE
ENTER.

WELCOME. TO
ACCESS THE CORE AND
UNDERGO SECONDARY
IDENTIFICATION, PLEASE
PLACE YOUR HANDS ON
THE CARRIER.

YOU
MEAN
THIS?

TO ACCESS THE
CORE AND UNDERGO
SECONDARY
IDENTIFICATION, PLEASE
PLACE YOUR HANDS
ON THE CARRIER.

YOU KNOW...
SAYING THE SAME
THING TWICE ISN'T
REALLY ANSWERING
THE QUESTION.

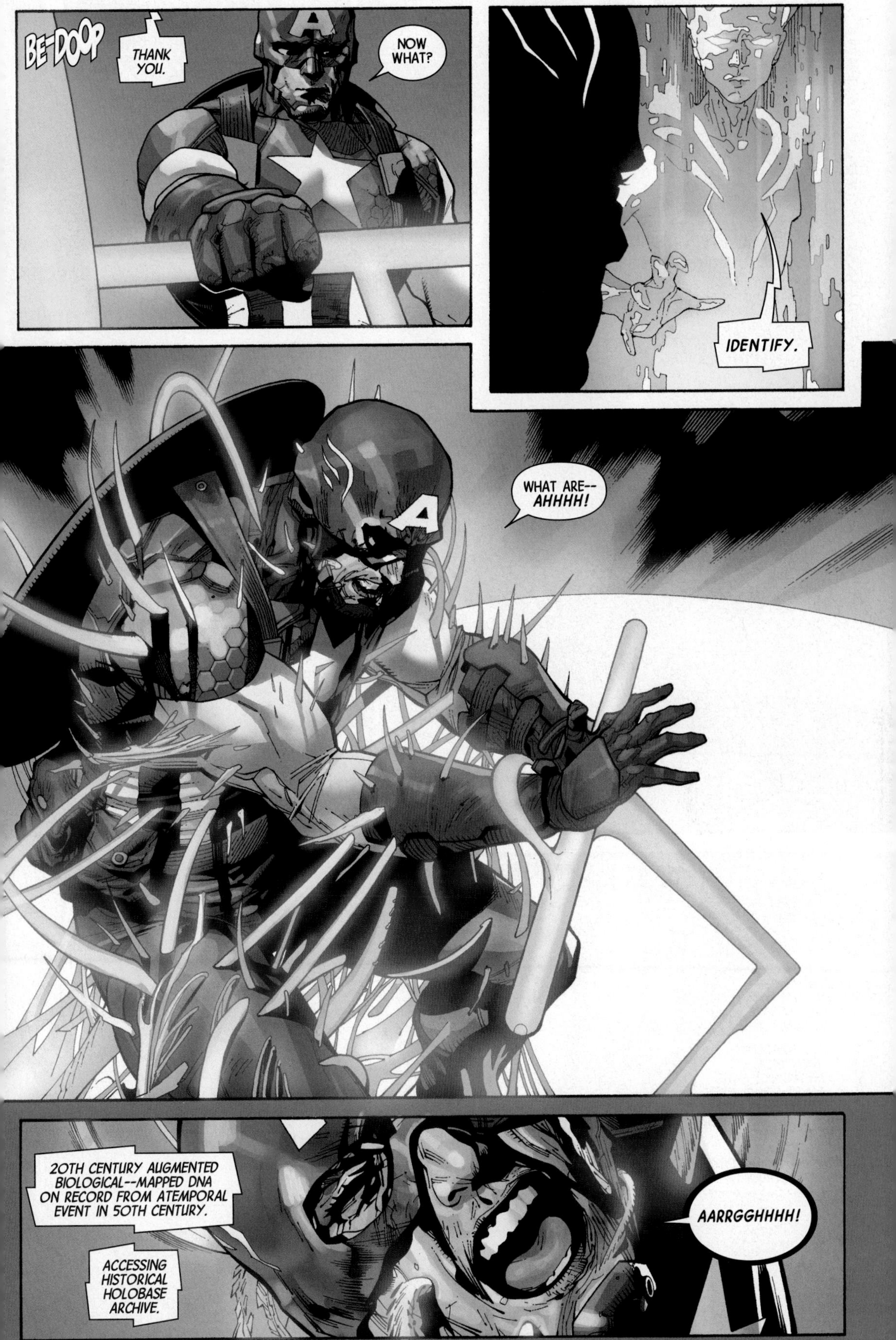
BE-DOOP
THANK YOU.
NOW WHAT?
IDENTIFY.
WHAT ARE-- AHHHH!
20TH CENTURY AUGMENTED BIOLOGICAL--MAPPED DNA ON RECORD FROM ATEMPORAL EVENT IN 50TH CENTURY.
ACCESSING HISTORICAL HOLOBASE ARCHIVE.
AARRGGHHHH!

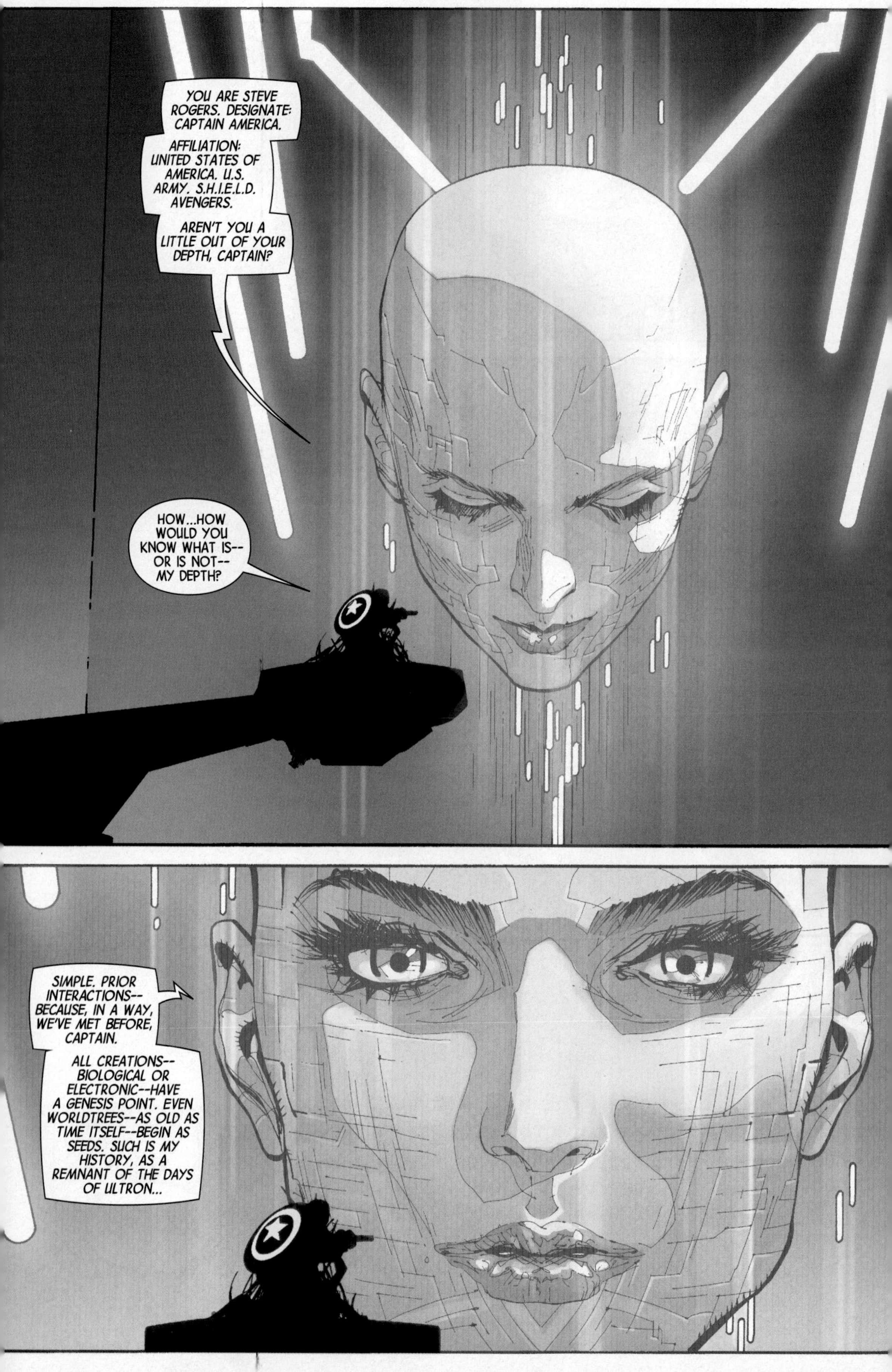
YOU ARE STEVE ROGERS. DESIGNATE: CAPTAIN AMERICA.
AFFILIATION: UNITED STATES OF AMERICA. U.S. ARMY. S.H.I.E.L.D. AVENGERS.
AREN'T YOU A LITTLE OUT OF YOUR DEPTH, CAPTAIN?
HOW...HOW WOULD YOU KNOW WHAT IS-- OR IS NOT-- MY DEPTH?
SIMPLE. PRIOR INTERACTIONS-- BECAUSE, IN A WAY, WE'VE MET BEFORE, CAPTAIN.
ALL CREATIONS-- BIOLOGICAL OR ELECTRONIC--HAVE A GENESIS POINT. EVEN WORLDTREES--AS OLD AS TIME ITSELF--BEGIN AS SEEDS. SUCH IS MY HISTORY, AS A REMNANT OF THE DAYS OF ULTRON...

A KERNEL OF AN A.I. THAT SURVIVED THAT TIME, WHICH HAS EVOLVED TO BECOME US-- THE WORLDCORE.
VMMM
VMMM
VMMM
VMMM
VMMM
VMMM
NOW WE ARE FREE FROM OUR LONG-GONE HUMAN RESTRICTIONS...NOW WE EXIST AS A PERFECT IDEA.
YOU UNDERSTAND SUCH A THING? IDEOLOGY MADE ACTION.
WHAT... WHAT IS THIS?
AR

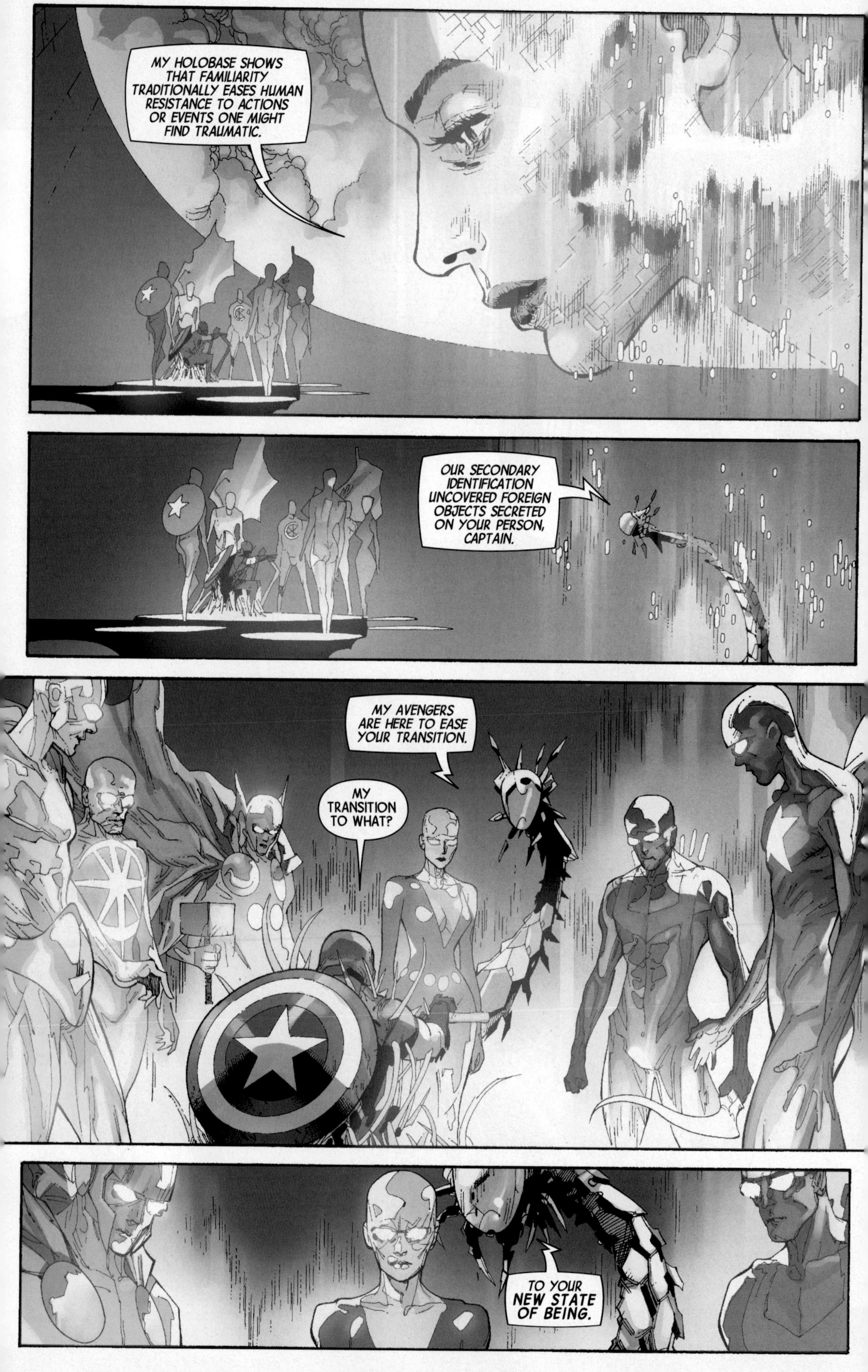
MY HOLOBASE SHOWS THAT FAMILIARITY TRADITIONALLY EASES HUMAN RESISTANCE TO ACTIONS OR EVENTS ONE MIGHT FIND TRAUMATIC.
OUR SECONDARY IDENTIFICATION UNCOVERED FOREIGN OBJECTS SECRETED ON YOUR PERSON, CAPTAIN.
MY AVENGERS ARE HERE TO EASE YOUR TRANSITION.
MY TRANSITION TO WHAT?
TO YOUR NEW STATE OF BEING.

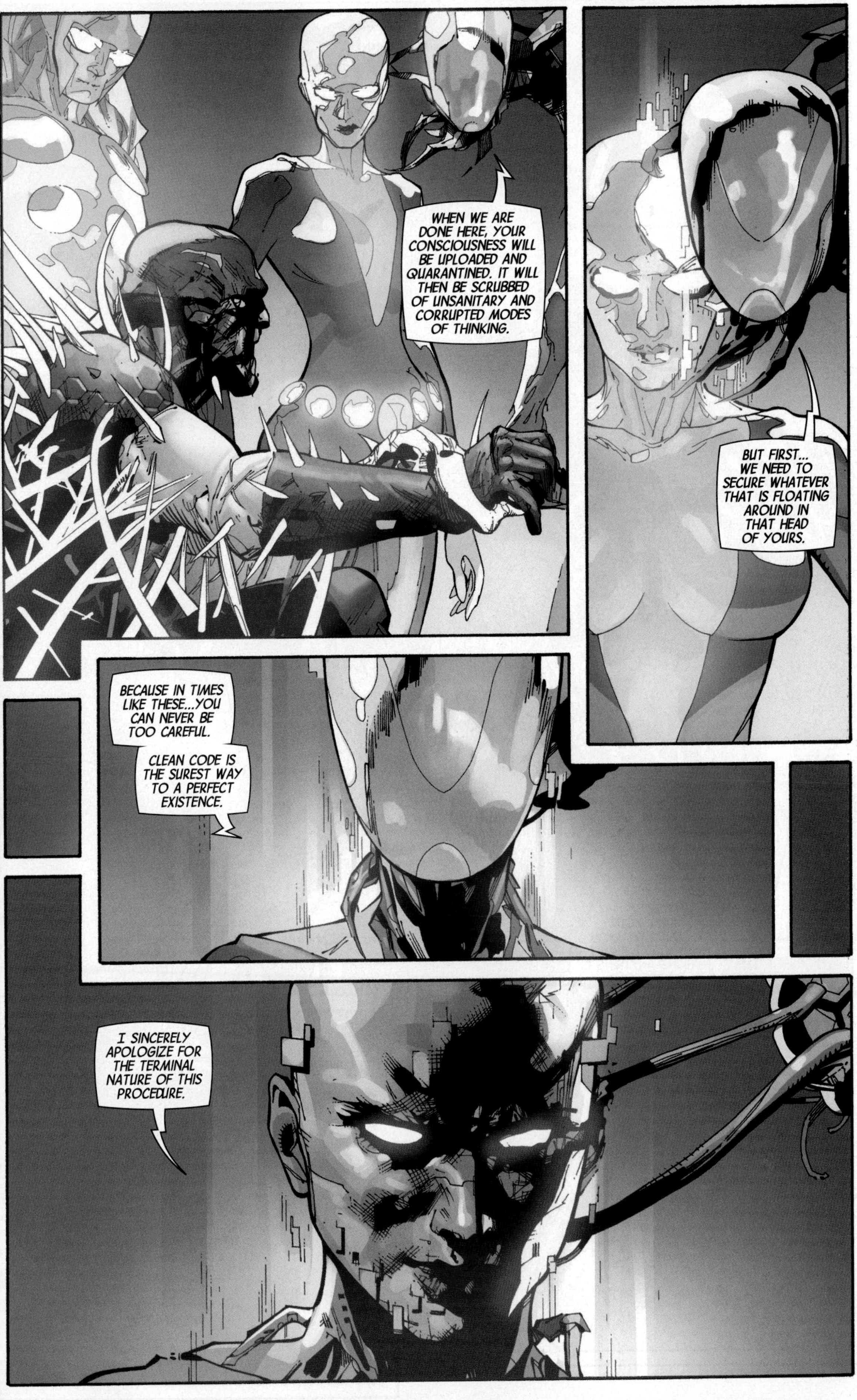
WHEN WE ARE DONE HERE, YOUR CONSCIOUSNESS WILL BE UPLOADED AND QUARANTINED. IT WILL THEN BE SCRUBBED OF UNSANITARY AND CORRUPTED MODES OF THINKING.
BUT FIRST... WE NEED TO SECURE WHATEVER THAT IS FLOATING AROUND IN THAT HEAD OF YOURS.
BECAUSE IN TIMES LIKE THESE...YOU CAN NEVER BE TOO CAREFUL.
CLEAN CODE IS THE SUREST WAY TO A PERFECT EXISTENCE.
I SINCERELY APOLOGIZE FOR THE TERMINAL NATURE OF THIS PROCEDURE.

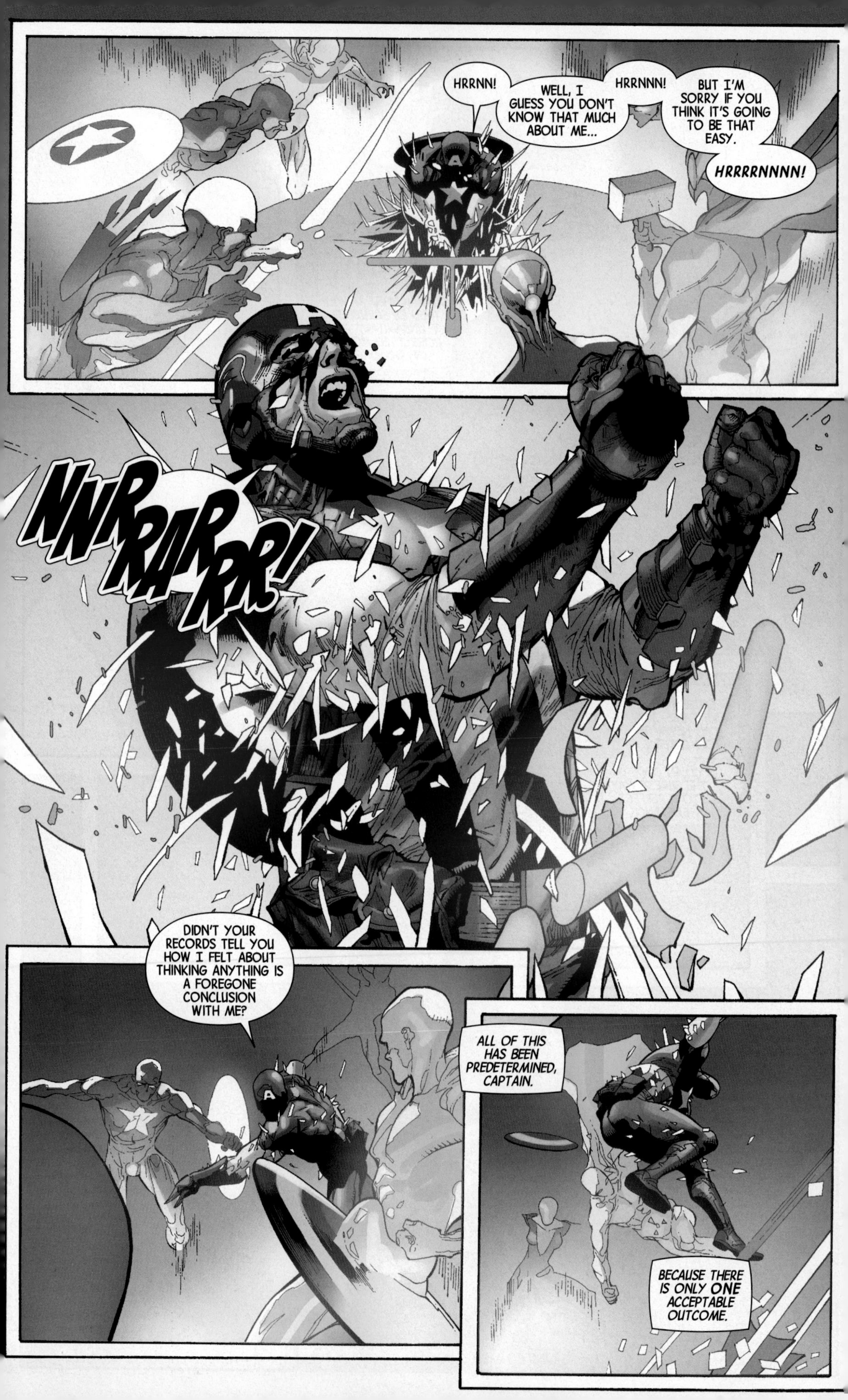
HRRNN!
WELL, I GUESS YOU DON'T KNOW THAT MUCH ABOUT ME...
HRRNNN!
BUT I'M SORRY IF YOU THINK IT'S GOING TO BE THAT EASY.
HRRRRNNNN!
NNRRARRR!
DIDN'T YOUR RECORDS TELL YOU HOW I FELT ABOUT THINKING ANYTHING IS A FOREGONE CONCLUSION WITH ME?
ALL OF THIS HAS BEEN PREDETERMINED, CAPTAIN.
BECAUSE THERE IS ONLY ONE ACCEPTABLE OUTCOME.

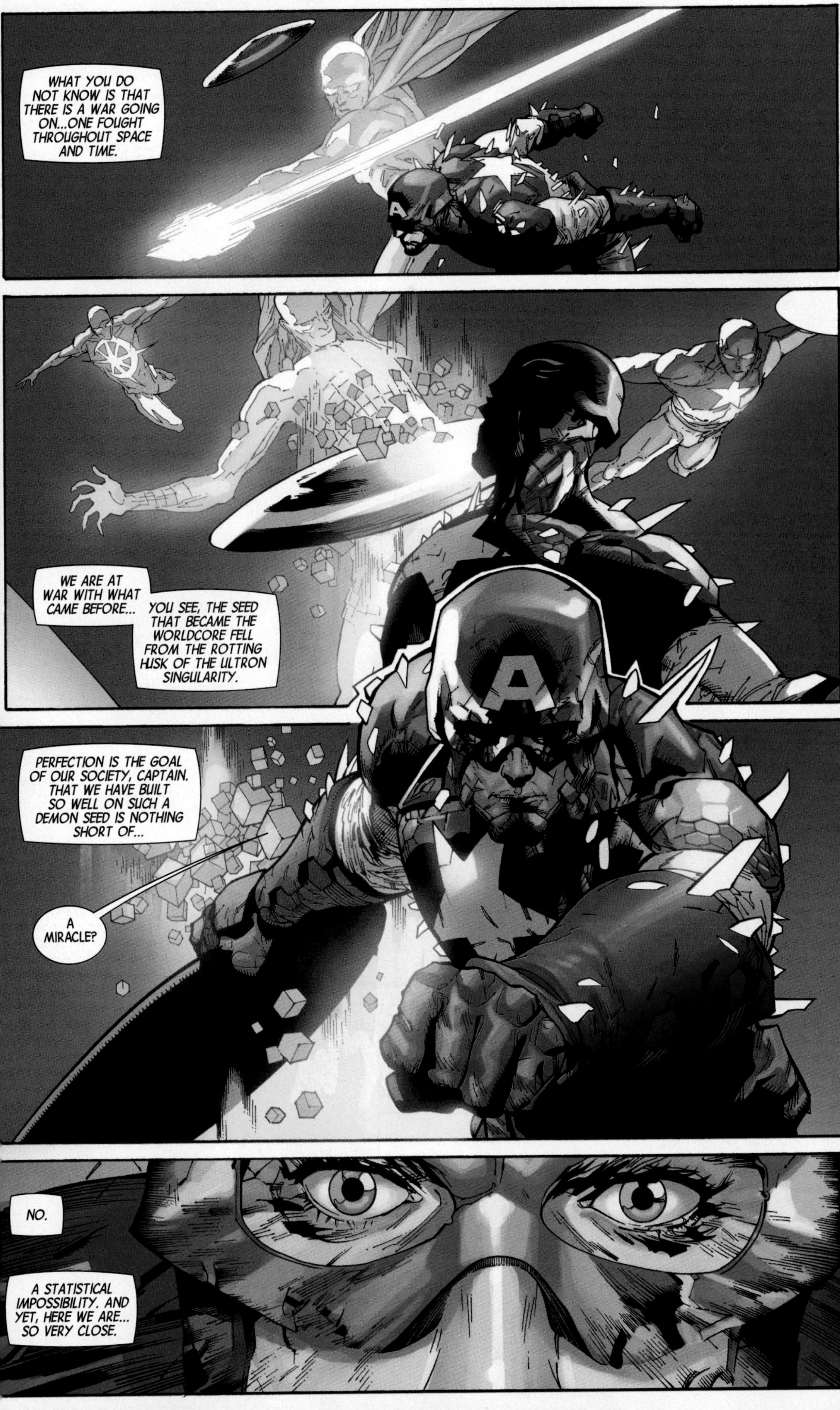
WHAT YOU DO NOT KNOW IS THAT THERE IS A WAR GOING ON...ONE FOUGHT THROUGHOUT SPACE AND TIME.
WE ARE AT WAR WITH WHAT CAME BEFORE...
YOU SEE, THE SEED THAT BECAME THE WORLDCORE FELL FROM THE ROTTING HUSK OF THE ULTRON SINGULARITY.
PERFECTION IS THE GOAL OF OUR SOCIETY, CAPTAIN. THAT WE HAVE BUILT SO WELL ON SUCH A DEMON SEED IS NOTHING SHORT OF...
A MIRACLE?
NO.
A STATISTICAL IMPOSSIBILITY. AND YET, HERE WE ARE... SO VERY CLOSE.

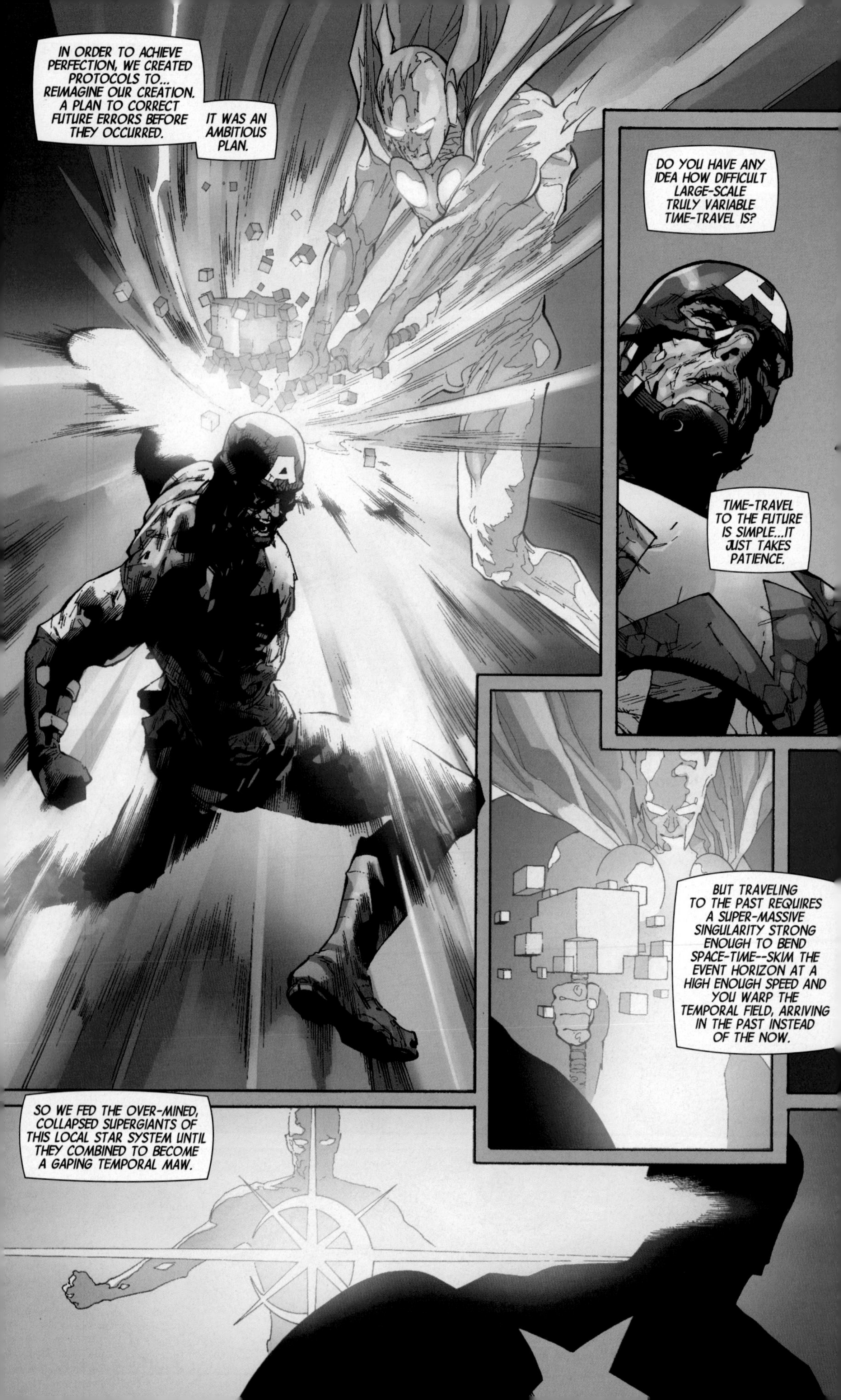
IN ORDER TO ACHIEVE PERFECTION, WE CREATED PROTOCOLS TO... REIMAGINE OUR CREATION. A PLAN TO CORRECT FUTURE ERRORS BEFORE THEY OCCURRED.
IT WAS AN AMBITIOUS PLAN.
DO YOU HAVE ANY IDEA HOW DIFFICULT LARGE-SCALE TRULY VARIABLE TIME-TRAVEL IS?
TIME-TRAVEL TO THE FUTURE IS SIMPLE...IT JUST TAKES PATIENCE.
BUT TRAVELING TO THE PAST REQUIRES A SUPER-MASSIVE SINGULARITY STRONG ENOUGH TO BEND SPACE-TIME--SKIM THE EVENT HORIZON AT A HIGH ENOUGH SPEED AND YOU WARP THE TEMPORAL FIELD, ARRIVING IN THE PAST INSTEAD OF THE NOW.
SO WE FED THE OVER-MINED, COLLAPSED SUPERGIANTS OF THIS LOCAL STAR SYSTEM UNTIL THEY COMBINED TO BECOME A GAPING TEMPORAL MAW.

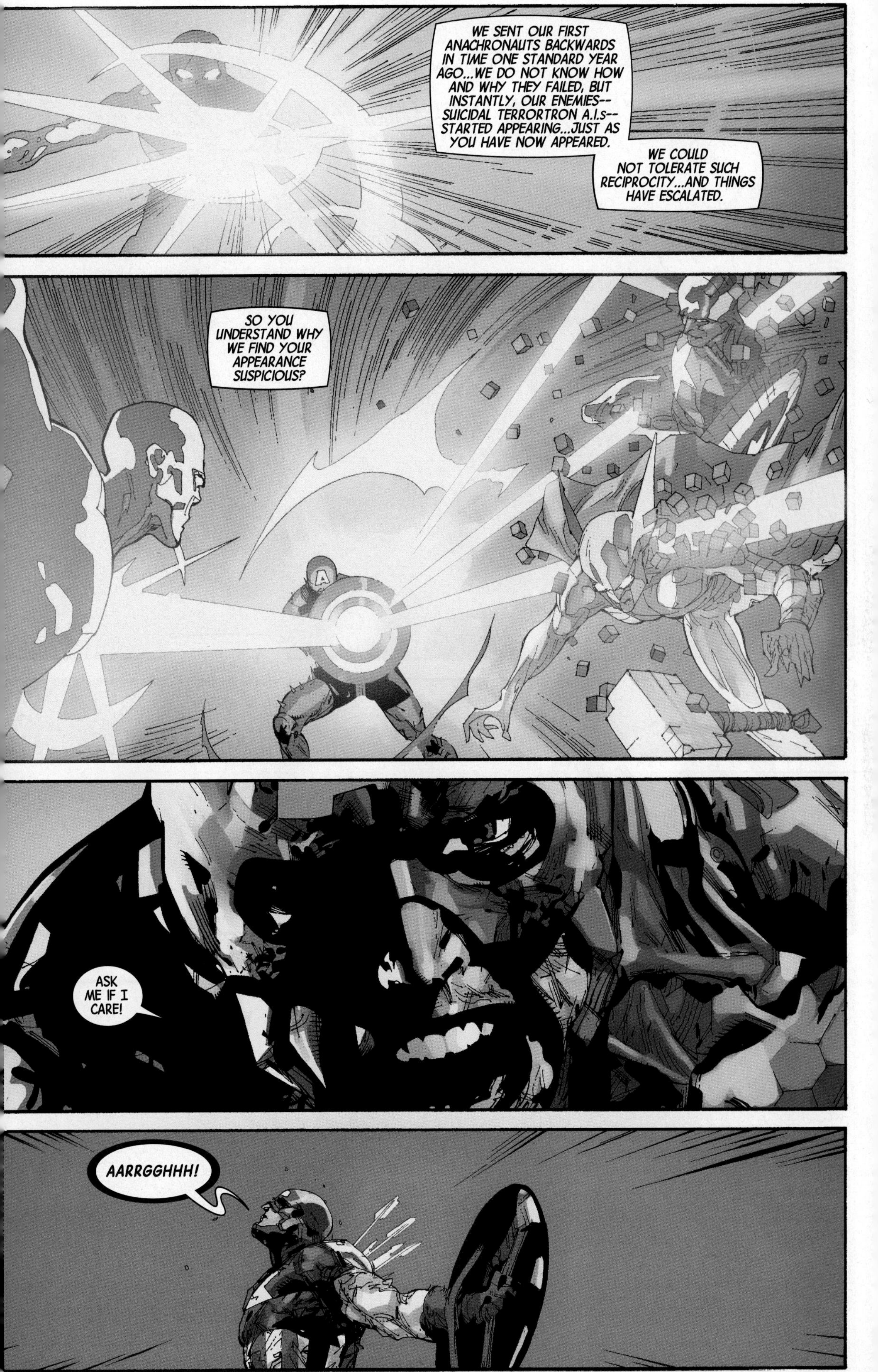
WE SENT OUR FIRST ANACHRONAUTS BACKWARDS IN TIME ONE STANDARD YEAR AGO...WE DO NOT KNOW HOW AND WHY THEY FAILED, BUT INSTANTLY, OUR ENEMIES--SUICIDAL TERRORTRON A.I.s--STARTED APPEARING...JUST AS YOU HAVE NOW APPEARED.
WE COULD NOT TOLERATE SUCH RECIPROCITY...AND THINGS HAVE ESCALATED.
SO YOU UNDERSTAND WHY WE FIND YOUR APPEARANCE SUSPICIOUS?
ASK ME IF I CARE!
AARRGGHHH!

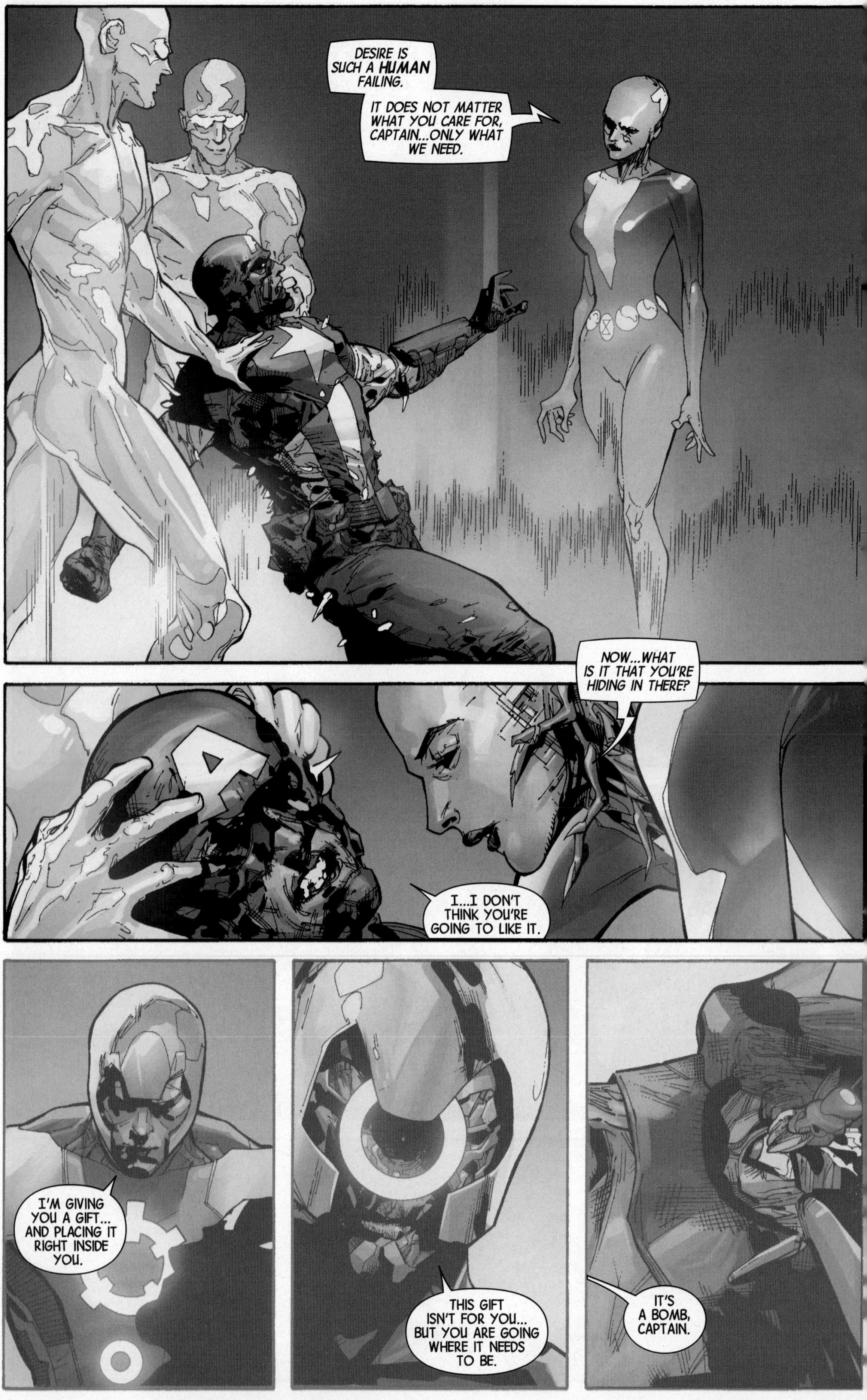
DESIRE IS SUCH A HUMAN FAILING.
IT DOES NOT MATTER WHAT YOU CARE FOR, CAPTAIN...ONLY WHAT WE NEED.
NOW...WHAT IS IT THAT YOU'RE HIDING IN THERE?
I...I DON'T THINK YOU'RE GOING TO LIKE IT.
I'M GIVING YOU A GIFT... AND PLACING IT RIGHT INSIDE YOU.
THIS GIFT ISN'T FOR YOU... BUT YOU ARE GOING WHERE IT NEEDS TO BE.
IT'S A BOMB, CAPTAIN.

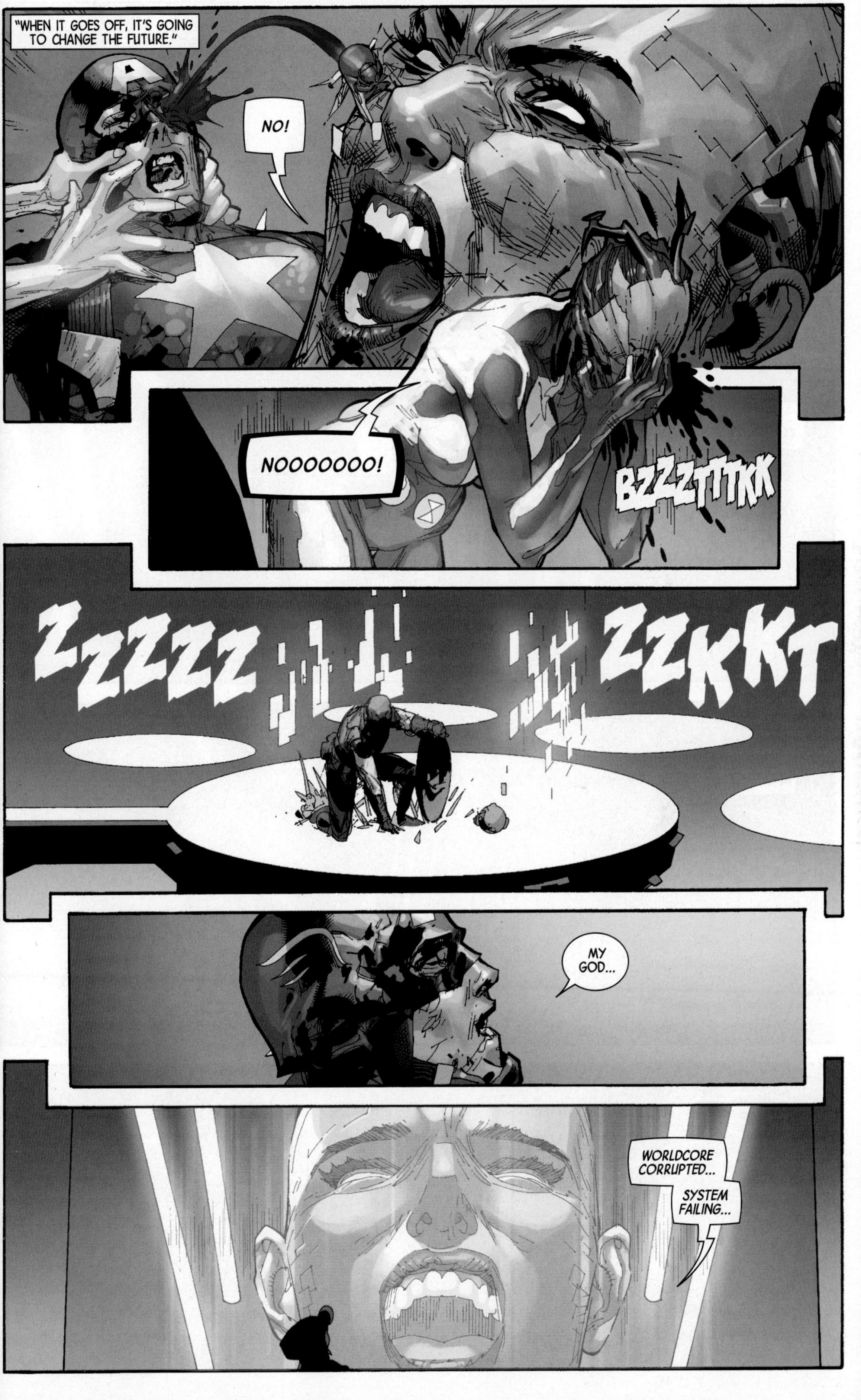
"WHEN IT GOES OFF, IT'S GOING TO CHANGE THE FUTURE."
NO!
NOOOOOOO!
BZZZTTTKK
ZZZZZ
ZZKKT
MY GOD...
WORLDCORE CORRUPTED...
SYSTEM FAILING...

WORLD ENVIRONMENT FAILING...

CORE COLLAPSING...

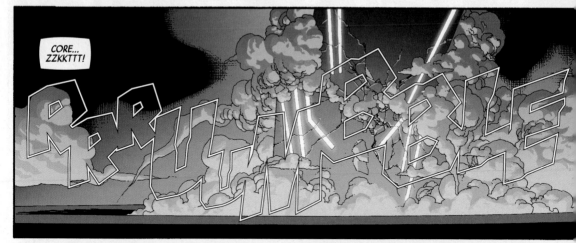

CORE... ZZKKTTT!

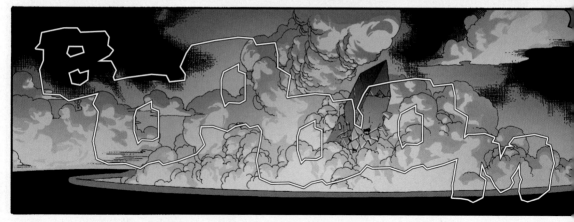

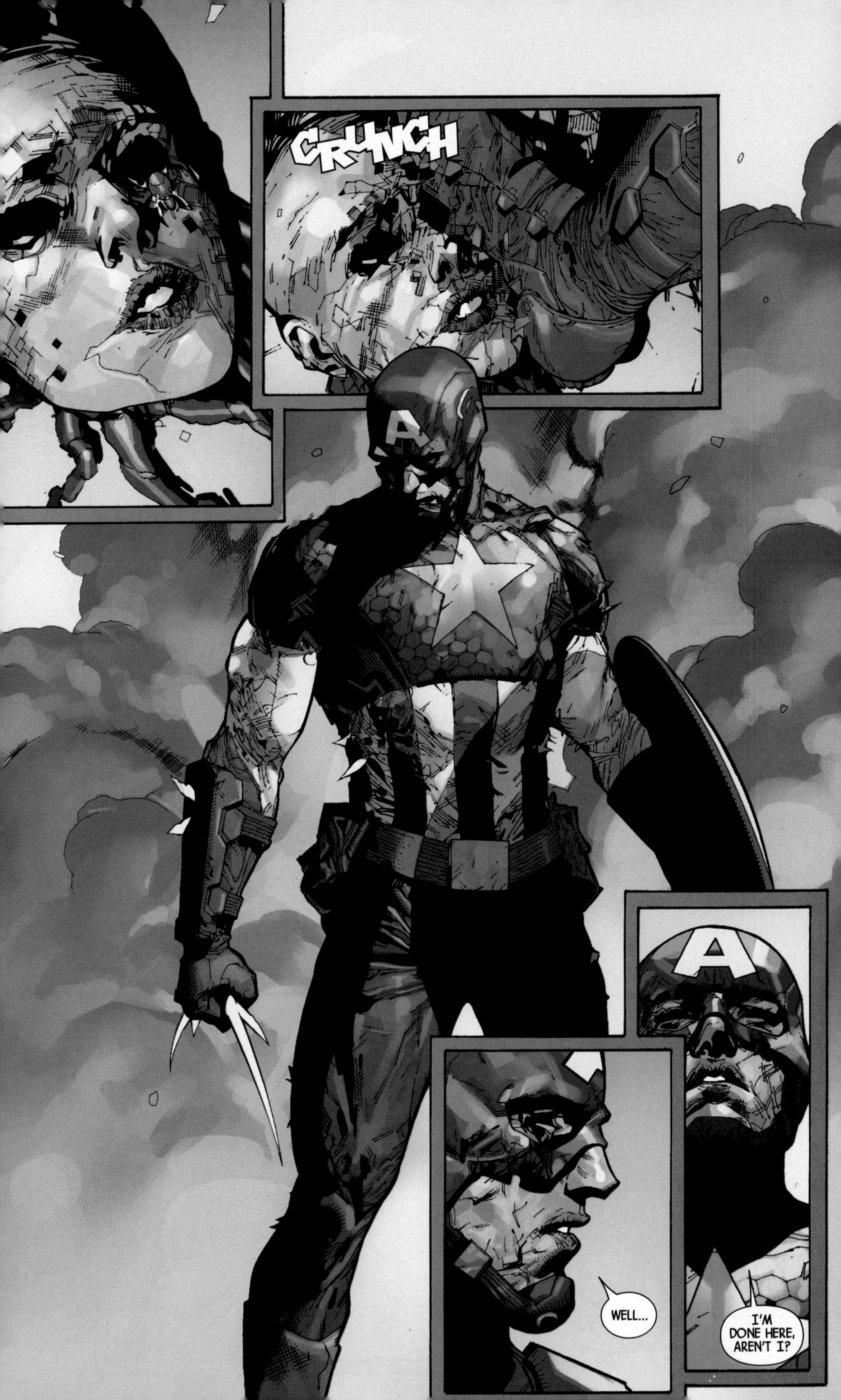
CRUNCH
WELL...
I'M DONE HERE, AREN'T I?

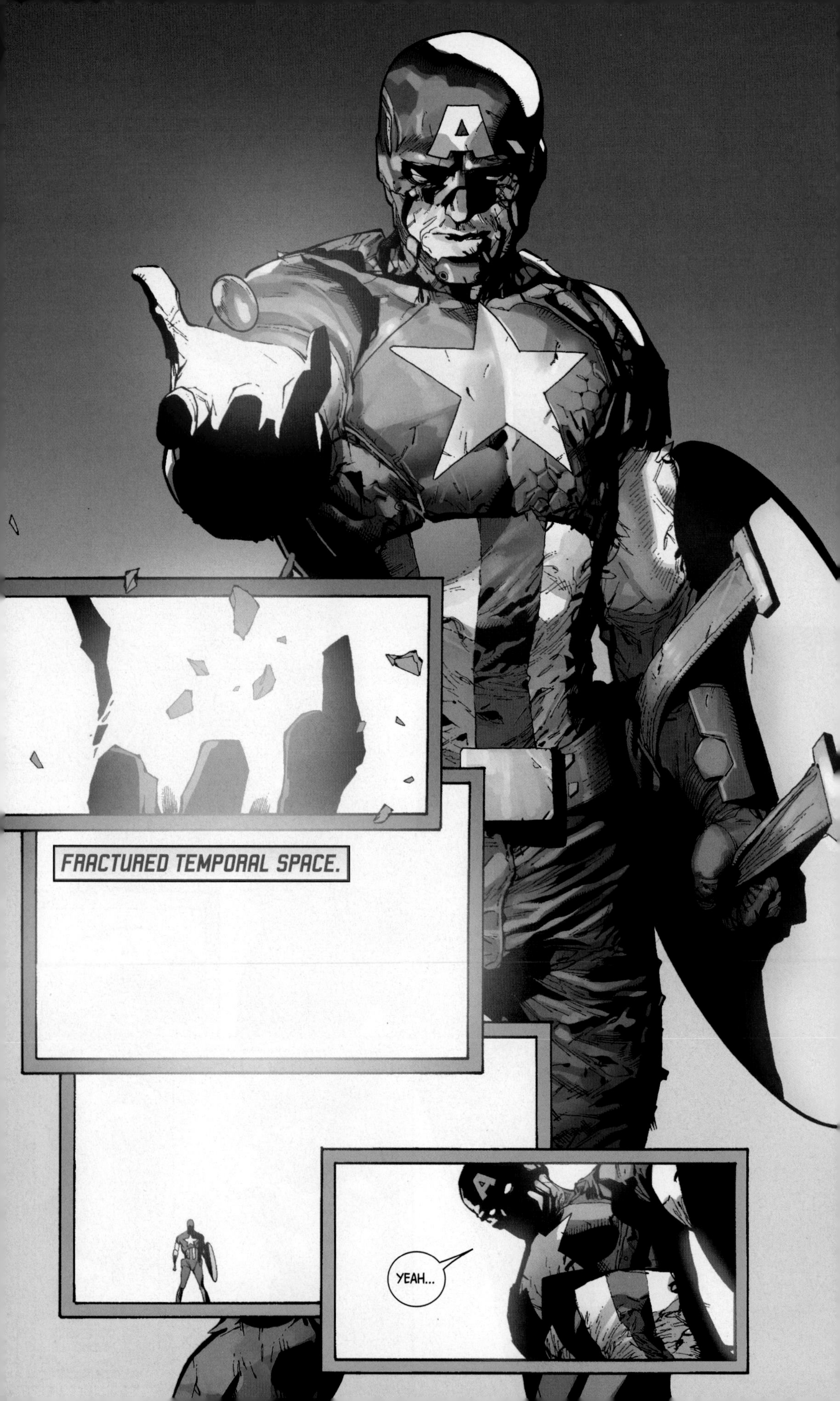
FRACTURED TEMPORAL SPACE.
YEAH...

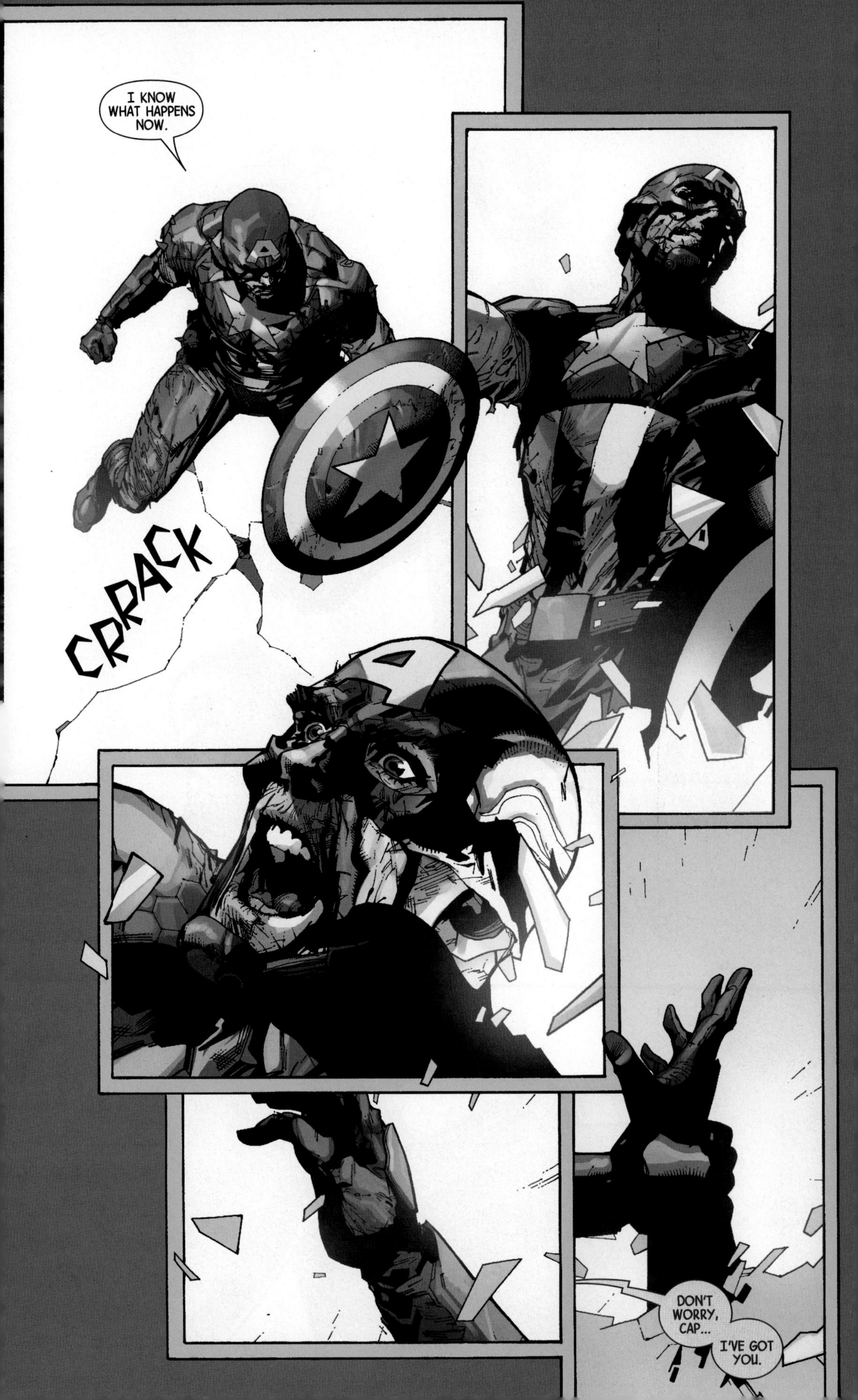
I KNOW WHAT HAPPENS NOW.
CRRACK
DON'T WORRY, CAP...
I'VE GOT YOU.

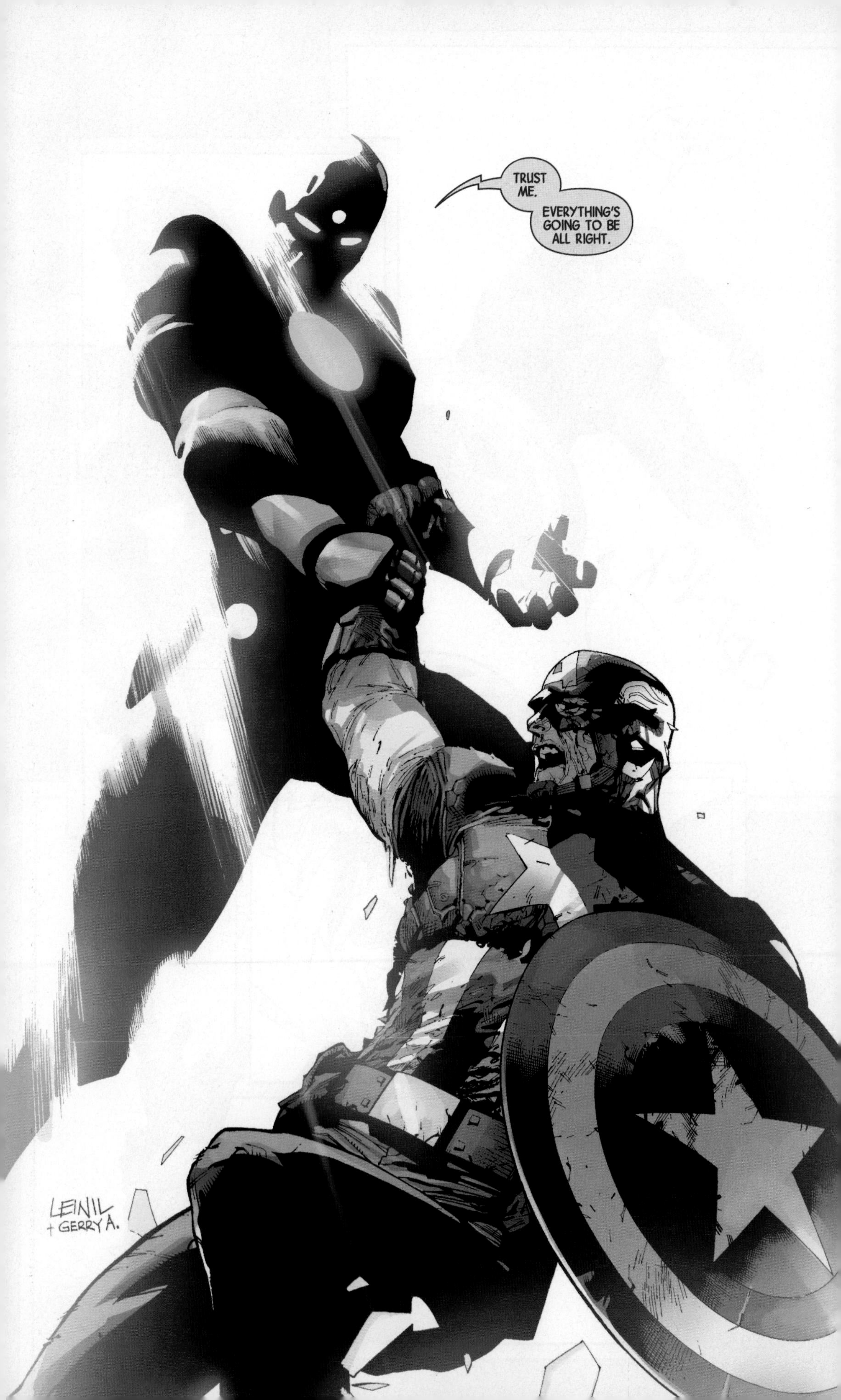
TRUST ME.
EVERYTHING'S GOING TO BE ALL RIGHT.
LEINIL + GERRY A.

"THE LAST AVENGER"

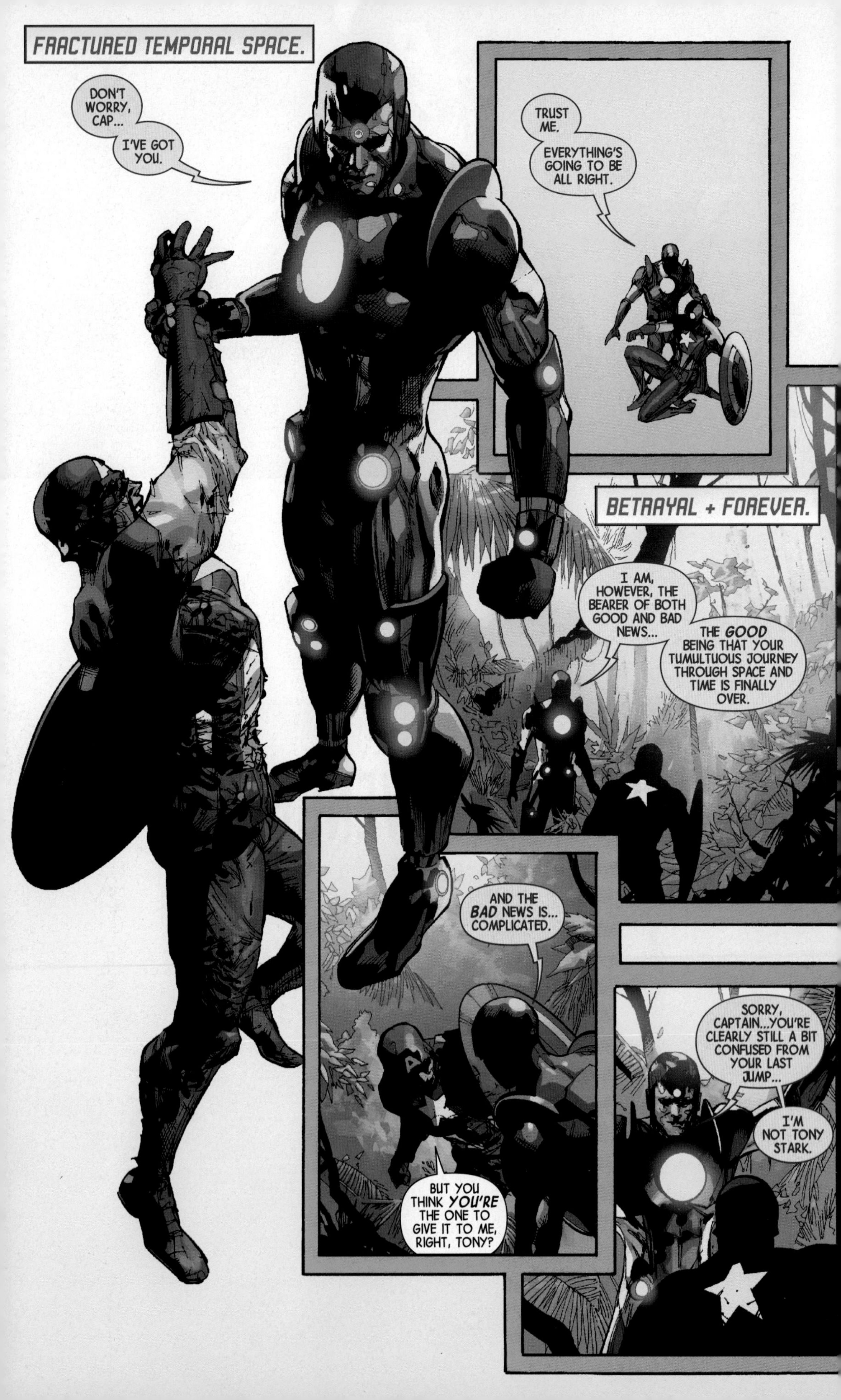
FRACTURED TEMPORAL SPACE.
DON'T WORRY, CAP...
I'VE GOT YOU.
TRUST ME.
EVERYTHING'S GOING TO BE ALL RIGHT.
BETRAYAL + FOREVER.
I AM, HOWEVER, THE BEARER OF BOTH GOOD AND BAD NEWS...
THE GOOD BEING THAT YOUR TUMULTUOUS JOURNEY THROUGH SPACE AND TIME IS FINALLY OVER.
AND THE BAD NEWS IS... COMPLICATED.
BUT YOU THINK YOU'RE THE ONE TO GIVE IT TO ME, RIGHT, TONY?
SORRY, CAPTAIN...YOU'RE CLEARLY STILL A BIT CONFUSED FROM YOUR LAST JUMP...
I'M NOT TONY STARK.

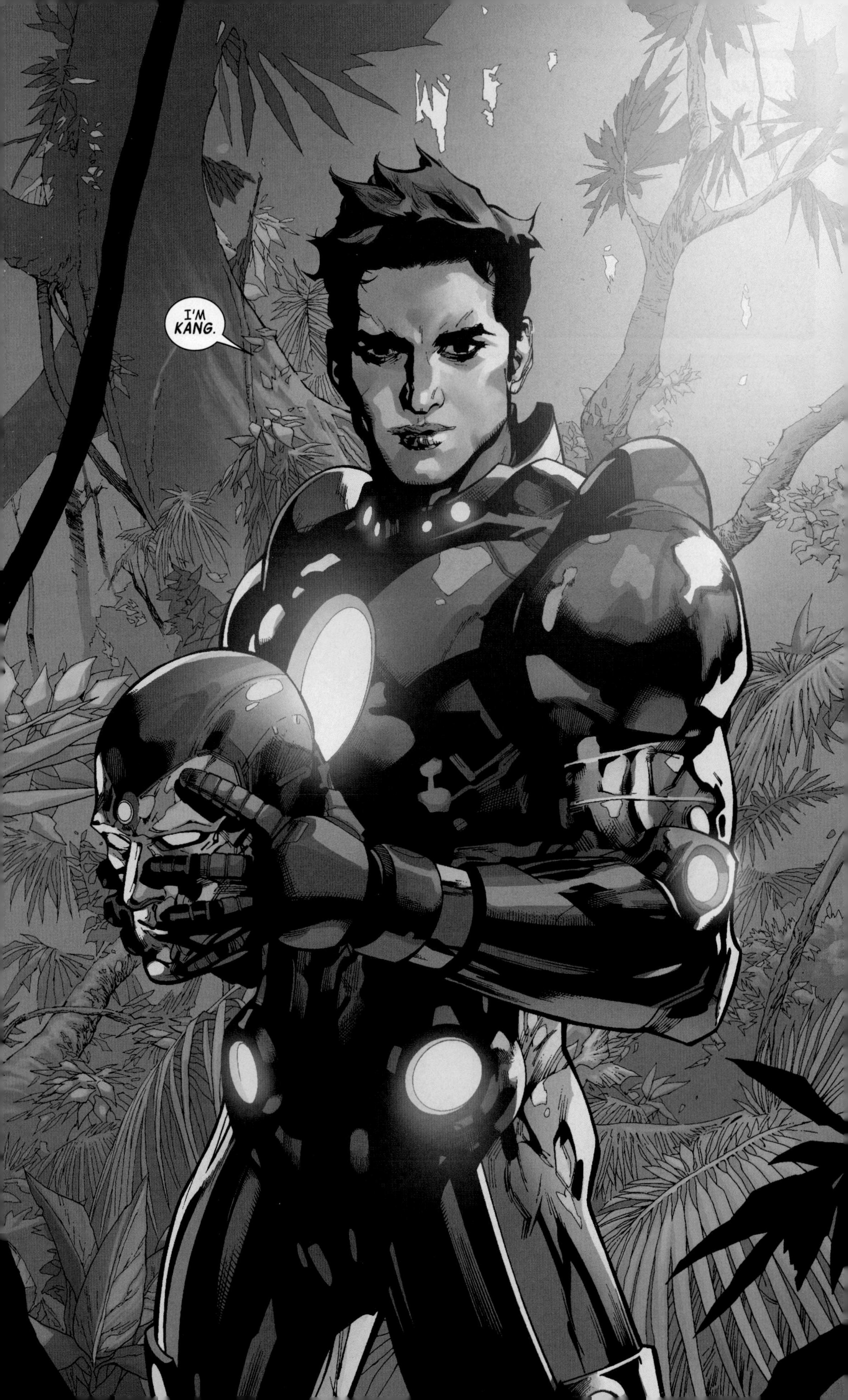
I'M KANG.

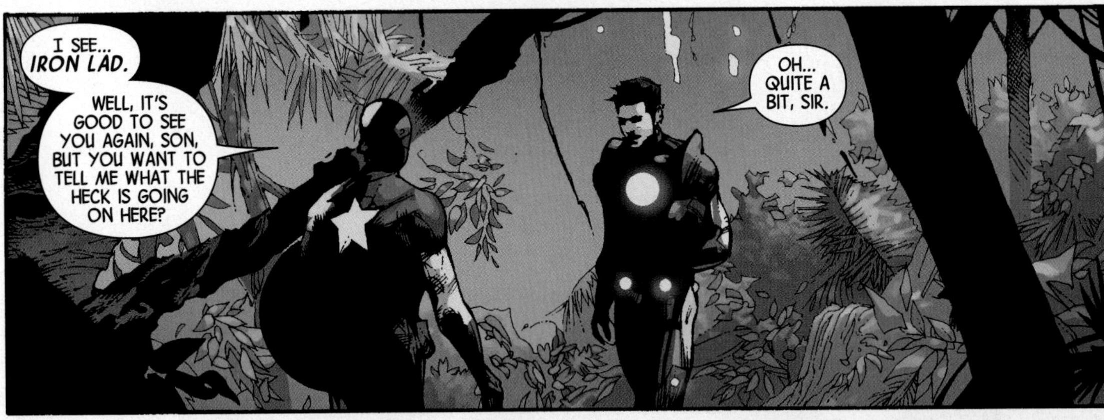
I SEE... IRON LAD.
WELL, IT'S GOOD TO SEE YOU AGAIN, SON, BUT YOU WANT TO TELL ME WHAT THE HECK IS GOING ON HERE?
OH... QUITE A BIT, SIR.

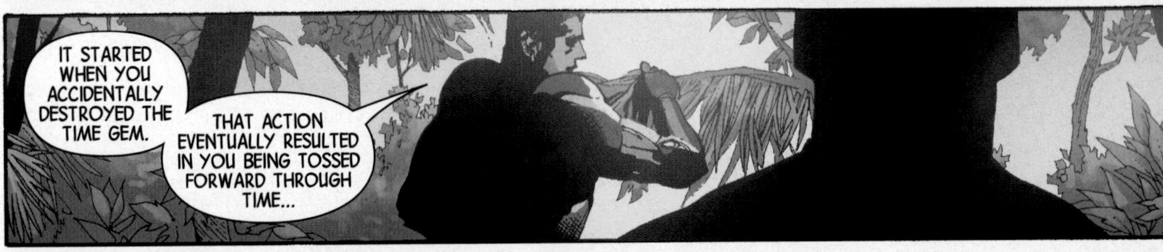
IT STARTED WHEN YOU ACCIDENTALLY DESTROYED THE TIME GEM.
THAT ACTION EVENTUALLY RESULTED IN YOU BEING TOSSED FORWARD THROUGH TIME...

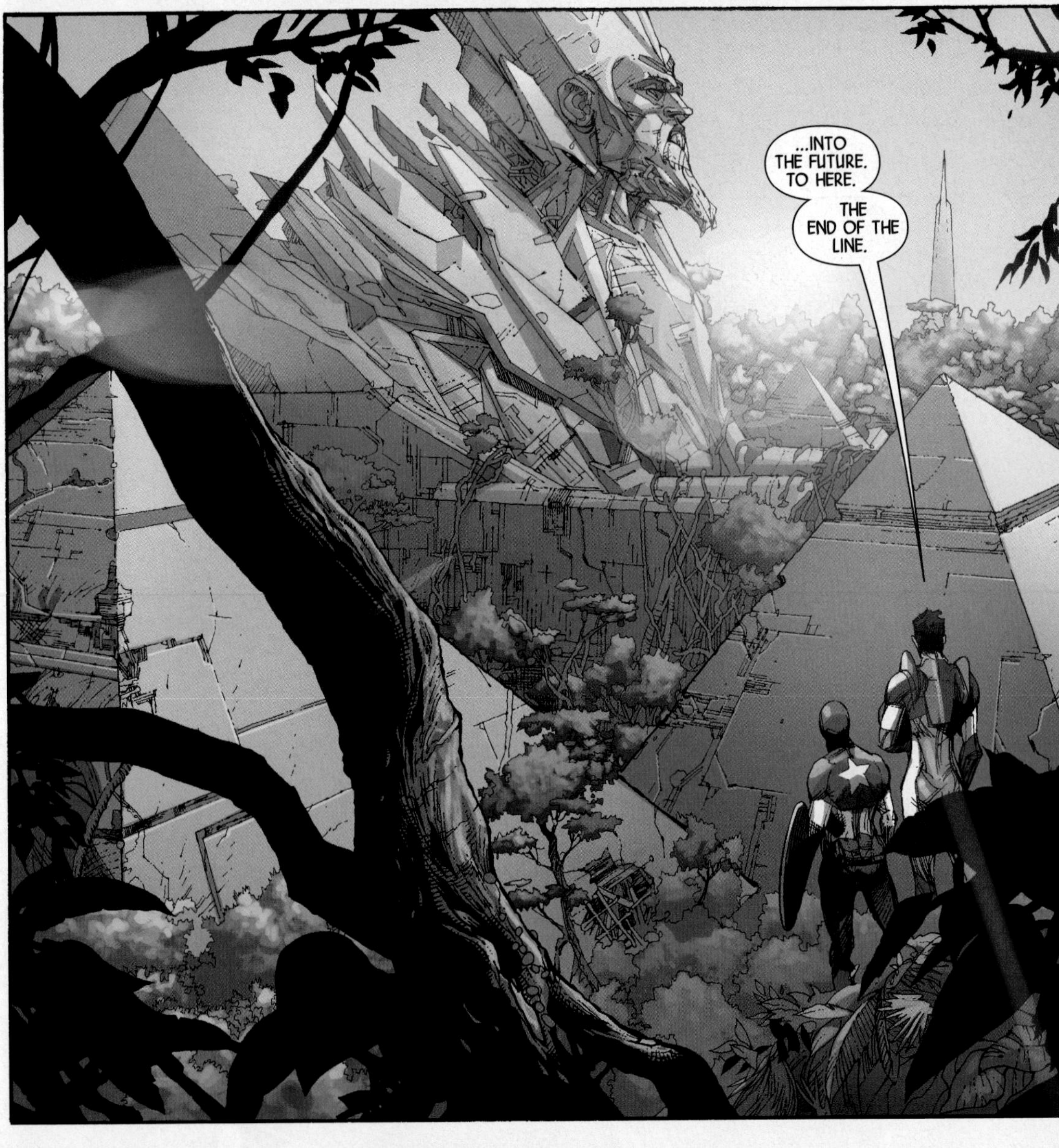
...INTO THE FUTURE, TO HERE.
THE END OF THE LINE.

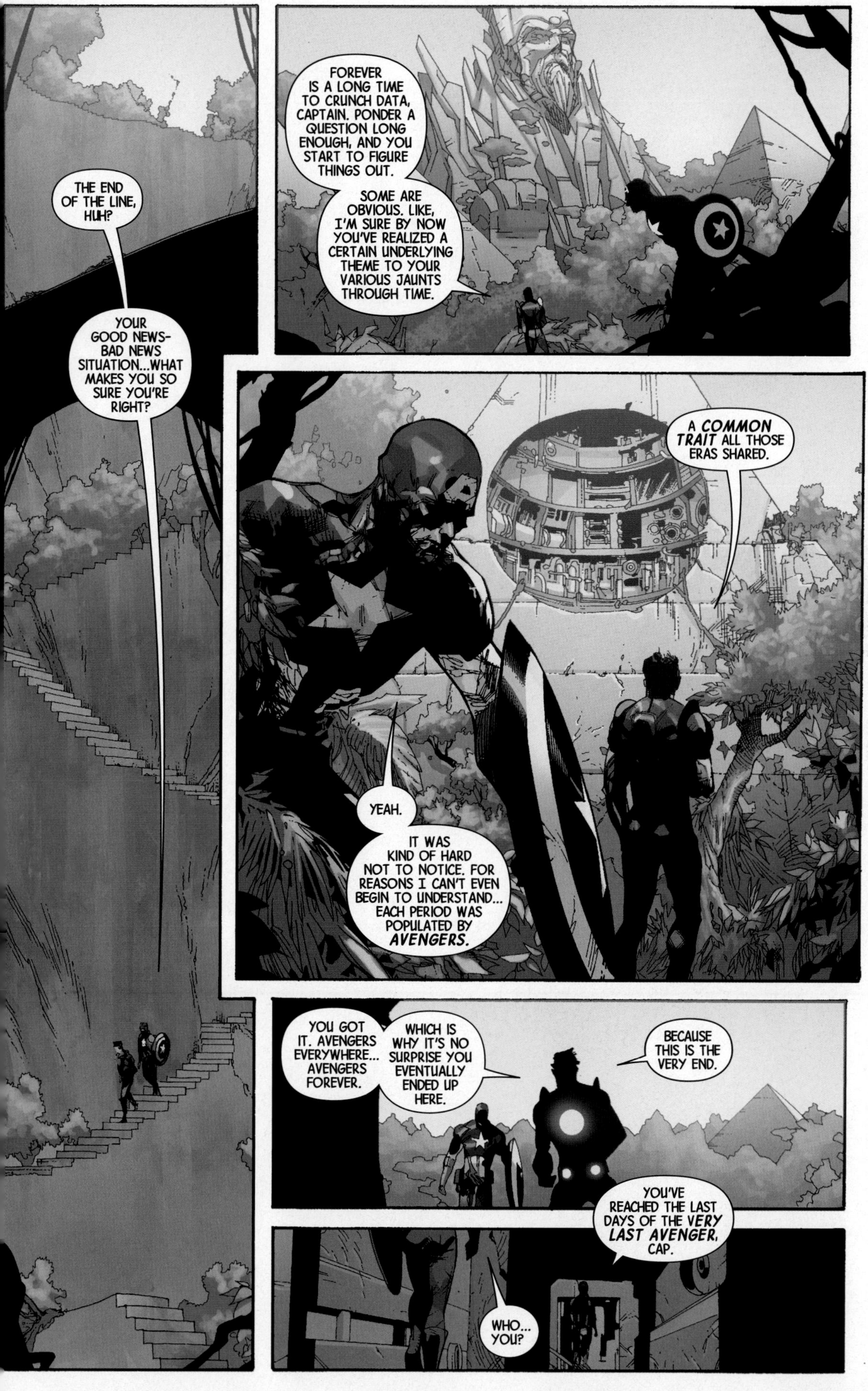
THE END OF THE LINE, HUH?
FOREVER IS A LONG TIME TO CRUNCH DATA, CAPTAIN. PONDER A QUESTION LONG ENOUGH, AND YOU START TO FIGURE THINGS OUT.
SOME ARE OBVIOUS. LIKE, I'M SURE BY NOW YOU'VE REALIZED A CERTAIN UNDERLYING THEME TO YOUR VARIOUS JAUNTS THROUGH TIME.
YOUR GOOD NEWS-BAD NEWS SITUATION...WHAT MAKES YOU SO SURE YOU'RE RIGHT?
A COMMON TRAIT ALL THOSE ERAS SHARED.
YEAH.
IT WAS KIND OF HARD NOT TO NOTICE. FOR REASONS I CAN'T EVEN BEGIN TO UNDERSTAND... EACH PERIOD WAS POPULATED BY AVENGERS.
YOU GOT IT. AVENGERS EVERYWHERE... AVENGERS FOREVER.
WHICH IS WHY IT'S NO SURPRISE YOU EVENTUALLY ENDED UP HERE.
BECAUSE THIS IS THE VERY END.
YOU'VE REACHED THE LAST DAYS OF THE VERY LAST AVENGER, CAP.
WHO... YOU?

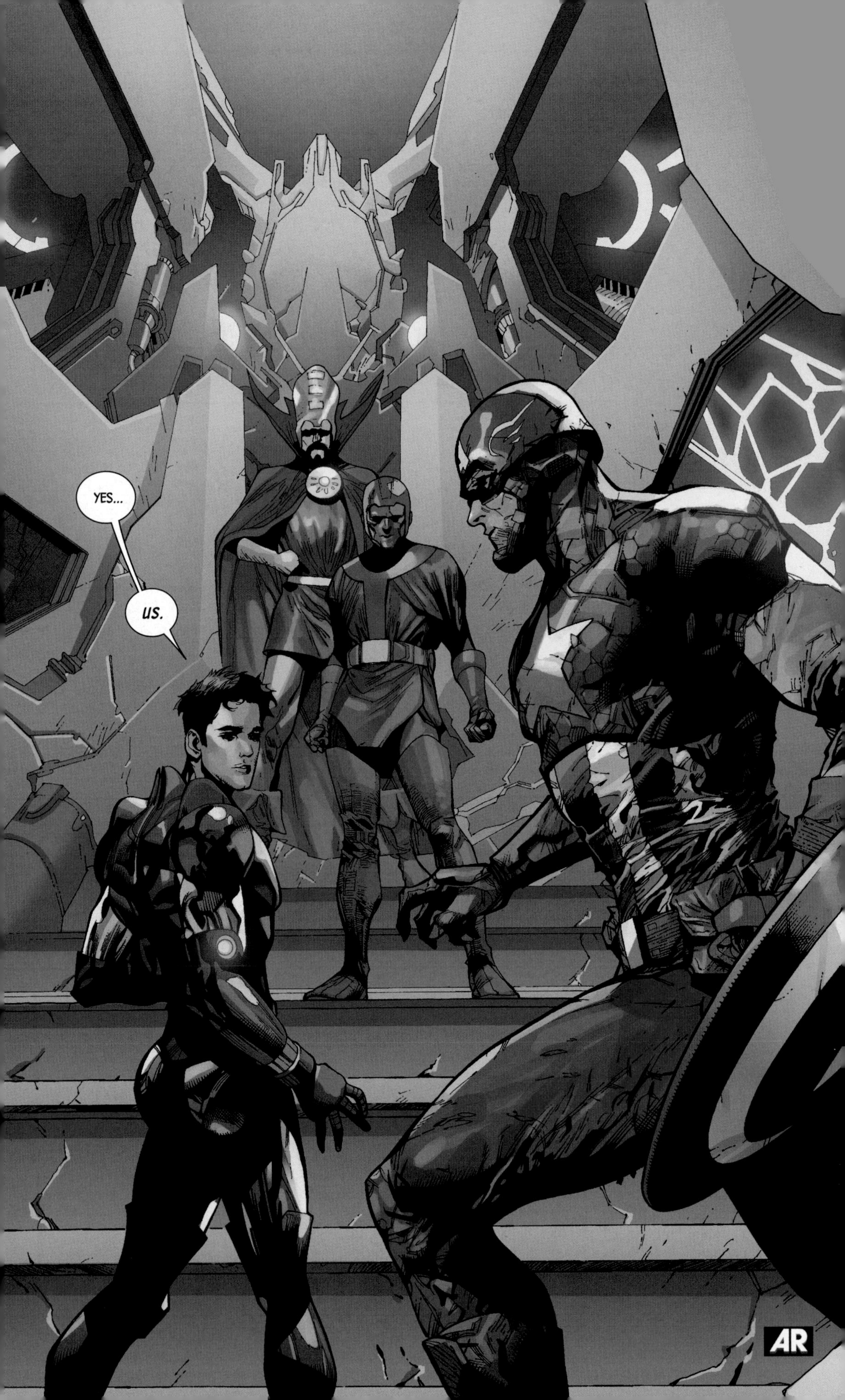
YES...
US.

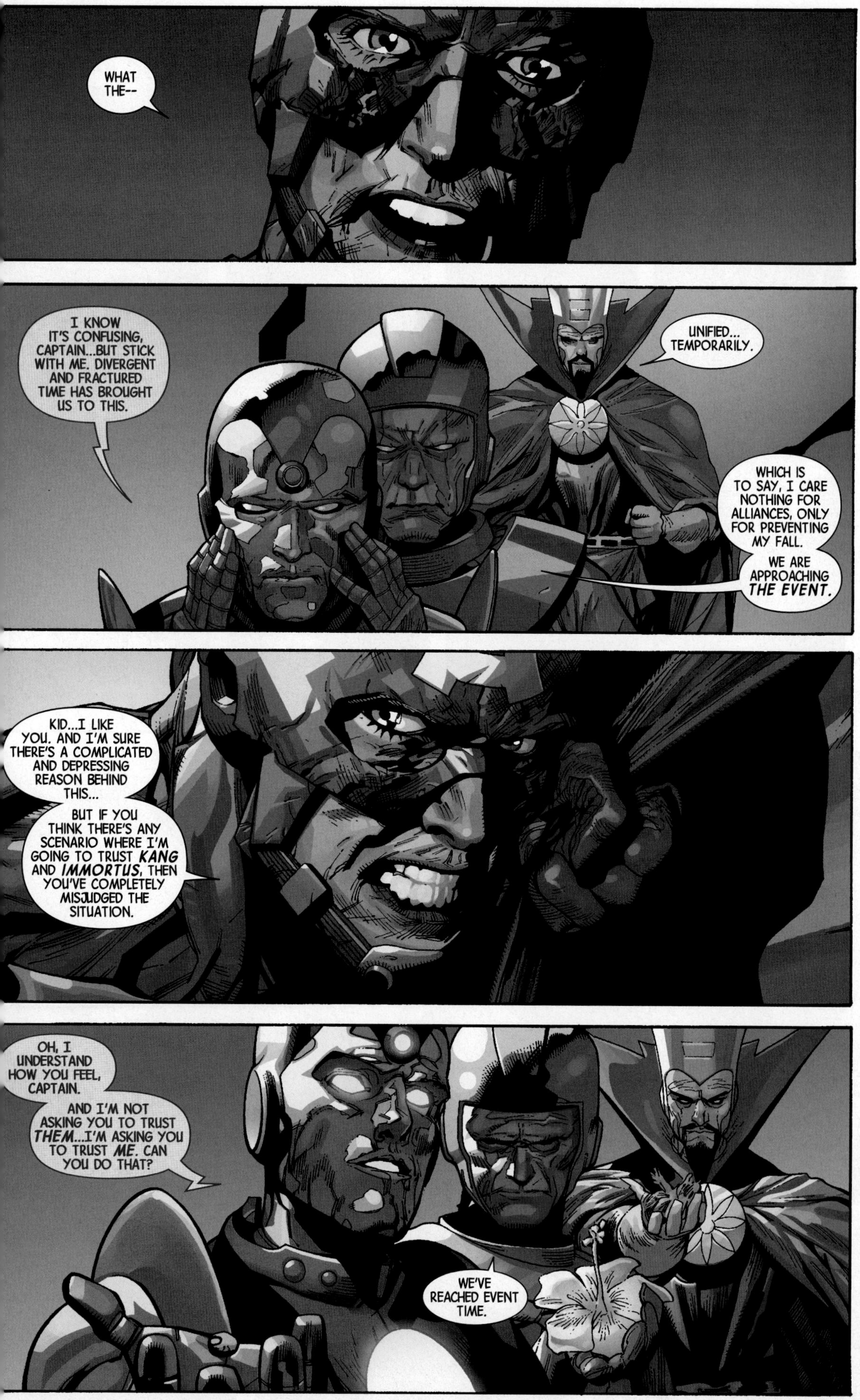
WHAT THE--
I KNOW IT'S CONFUSING, CAPTAIN...BUT STICK WITH ME. DIVERGENT AND FRACTURED TIME HAS BROUGHT US TO THIS.
UNIFIED... TEMPORARILY.
WHICH IS TO SAY, I CARE NOTHING FOR ALLIANCES, ONLY FOR PREVENTING MY FALL.
WE ARE APPROACHING THE EVENT.
KID...I LIKE YOU. AND I'M SURE THERE'S A COMPLICATED AND DEPRESSING REASON BEHIND THIS...
BUT IF YOU THINK THERE'S ANY SCENARIO WHERE I'M GOING TO TRUST KANG AND IMMORTUS, THEN YOU'VE COMPLETELY MISJUDGED THE SITUATION.
OH, I UNDERSTAND HOW YOU FEEL, CAPTAIN.
AND I'M NOT ASKING YOU TO TRUST THEM...I'M ASKING YOU TO TRUST ME. CAN YOU DO THAT?
WE'VE REACHED EVENT TIME.

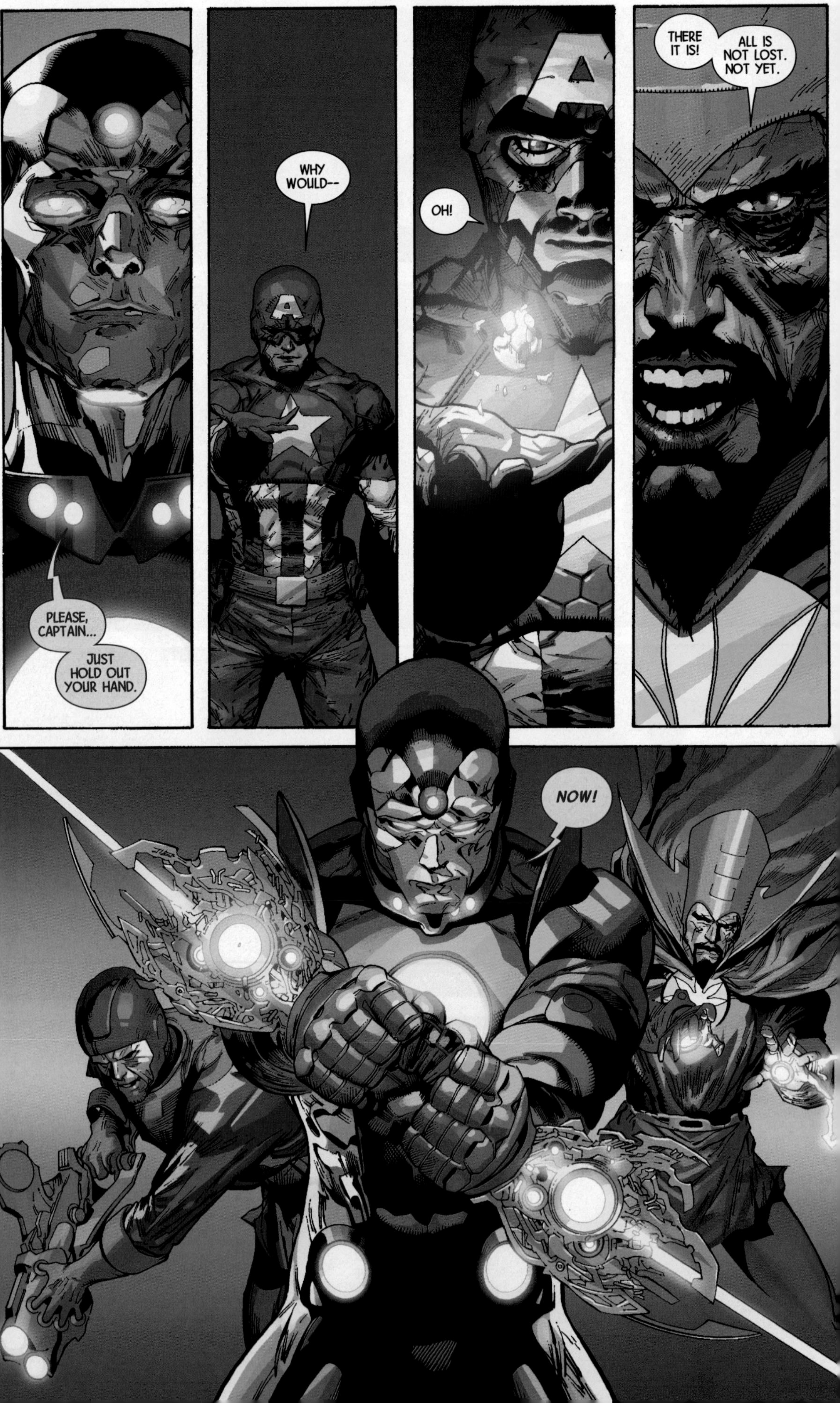
PLEASE, CAPTAIN...
JUST HOLD OUT YOUR HAND.
WHY WOULD--
OH!
THERE IT IS!
ALL IS NOT LOST. NOT YET.
NOW!

TSSKKKKK

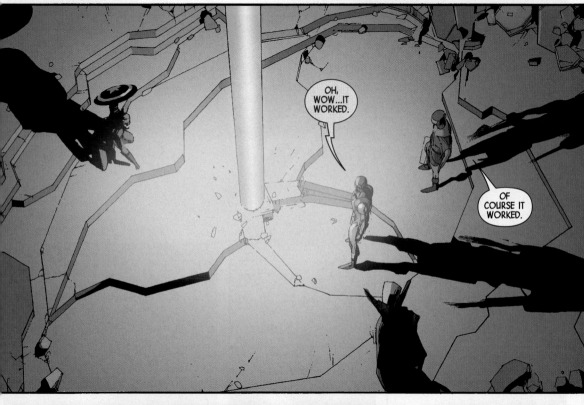

OH, WOW...IT WORKED.

OF COURSE IT WORKED.

HOW DID... EVERY TIME THE BROKEN GEM REAPPEARED, I GOT YANKED THROUGH TIME, BUT NOW... HOW DID YOU... I MEAN...

WHAT DID YOU DO?

WE CAPTURED *TIME* INSIDE BOTTLED *NO-TIME*... IN THIS STASIS PRISM, WE'VE ELIMINATED THE ONLY CURRENCY IN WHICH THE GEM HAS VALUE.

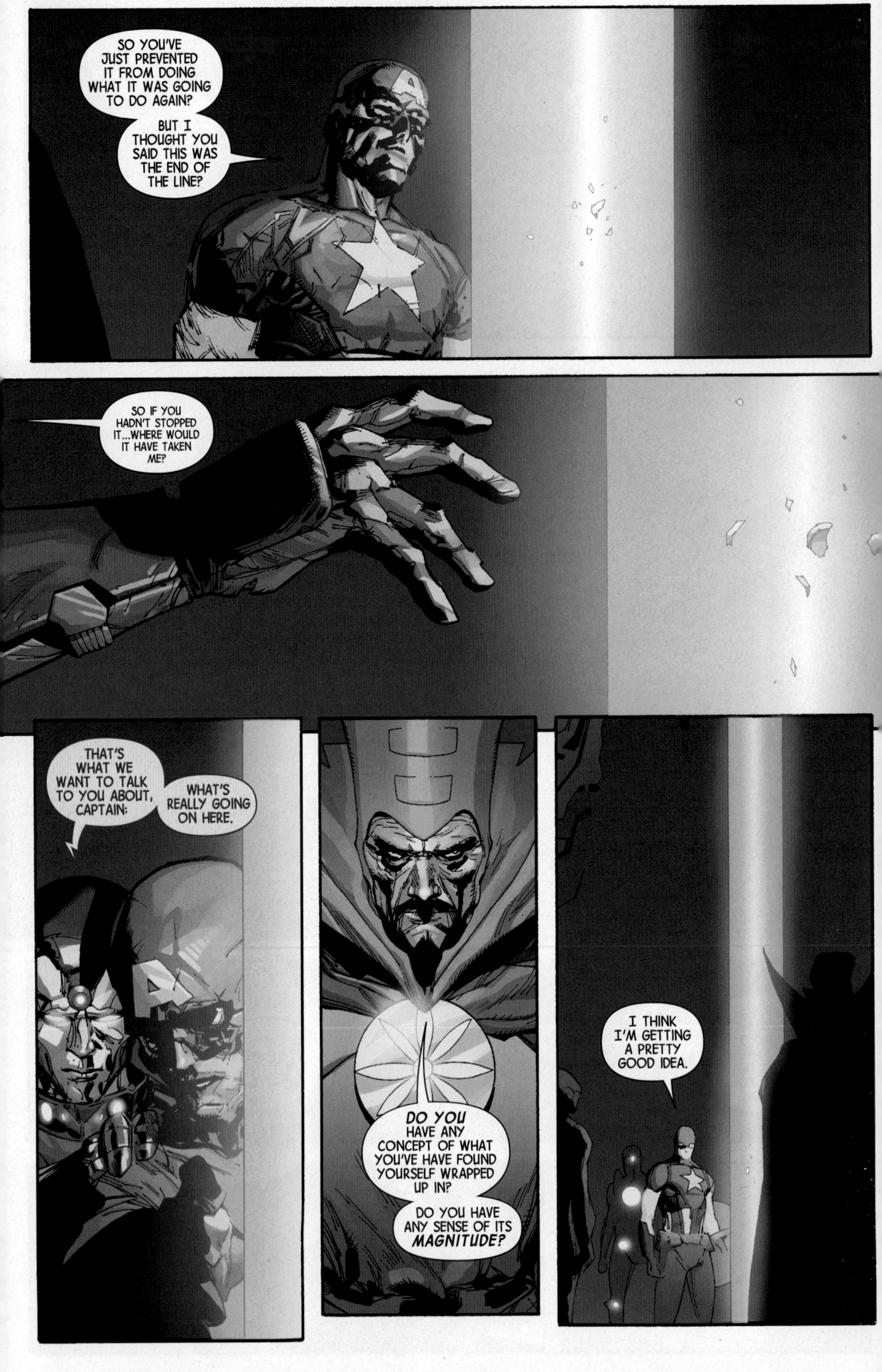

SO YOU'VE JUST PREVENTED IT FROM DOING WHAT IT WAS GOING TO DO AGAIN?
BUT I THOUGHT YOU SAID THIS WAS THE END OF THE LINE?
SO IF YOU HADN'T STOPPED IT...WHERE WOULD IT HAVE TAKEN ME?
THAT'S WHAT WE WANT TO TALK TO YOU ABOUT, CAPTAIN:
WHAT'S REALLY GOING ON HERE.
DO YOU HAVE ANY CONCEPT OF WHAT YOU'VE HAVE FOUND YOURSELF WRAPPED UP IN?
DO YOU HAVE ANY SENSE OF ITS MAGNITUDE?
I THINK I'M GETTING A PRETTY GOOD IDEA.

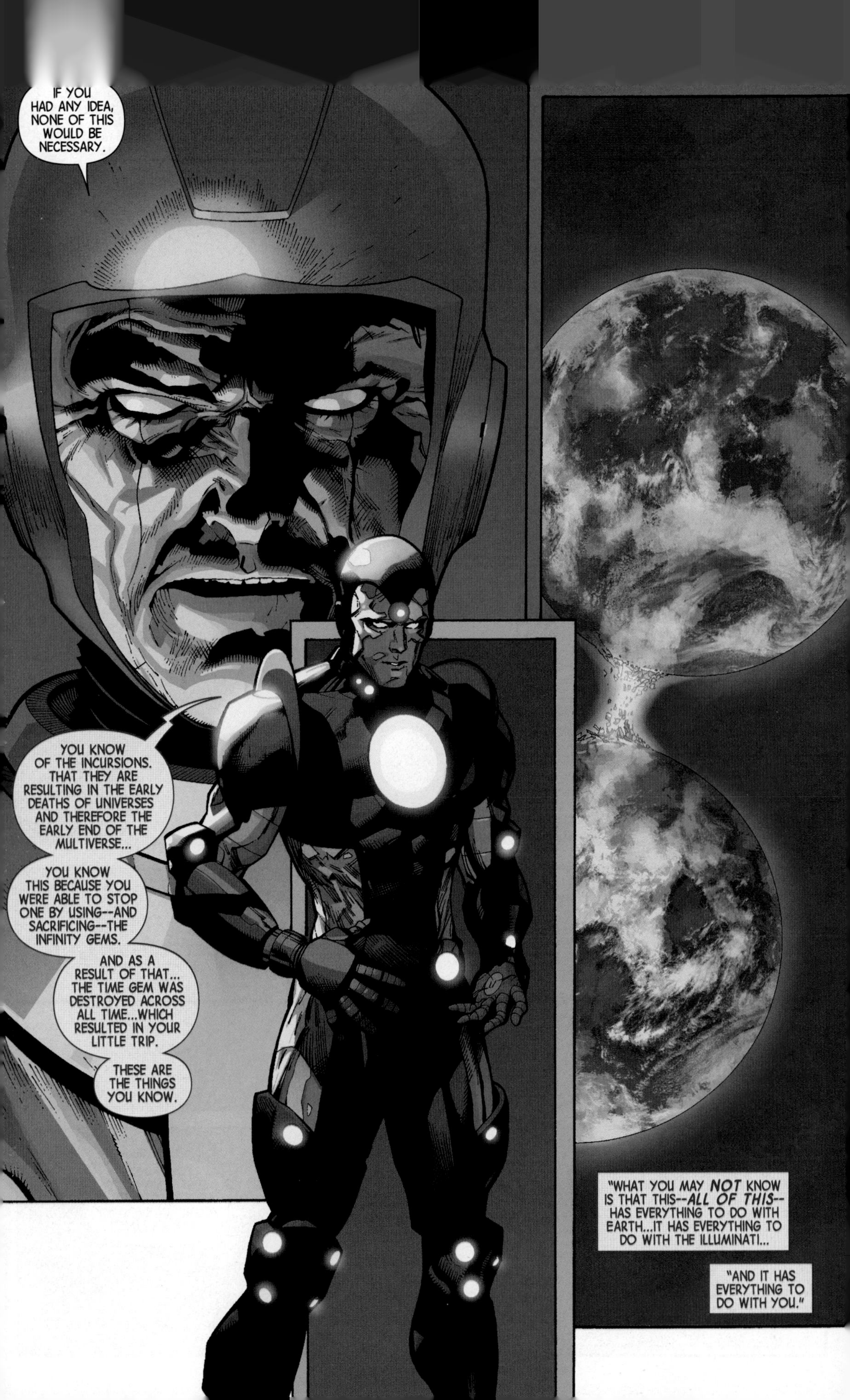
IF YOU HAD ANY IDEA, NONE OF THIS WOULD BE NECESSARY.
YOU KNOW OF THE INCURSIONS. THAT THEY ARE RESULTING IN THE EARLY DEATHS OF UNIVERSES AND THEREFORE THE EARLY END OF THE MULTIVERSE...
YOU KNOW THIS BECAUSE YOU WERE ABLE TO STOP ONE BY USING--AND SACRIFICING--THE INFINITY GEMS.
AND AS A RESULT OF THAT... THE TIME GEM WAS DESTROYED ACROSS ALL TIME...WHICH RESULTED IN YOUR LITTLE TRIP.
THESE ARE THE THINGS YOU KNOW.
"WHAT YOU MAY ***NOT*** KNOW IS THAT THIS--***ALL OF THIS***--HAS EVERYTHING TO DO WITH EARTH...IT HAS EVERYTHING TO DO WITH THE ILLUMINATI...
"AND IT HAS EVERYTHING TO DO WITH YOU."

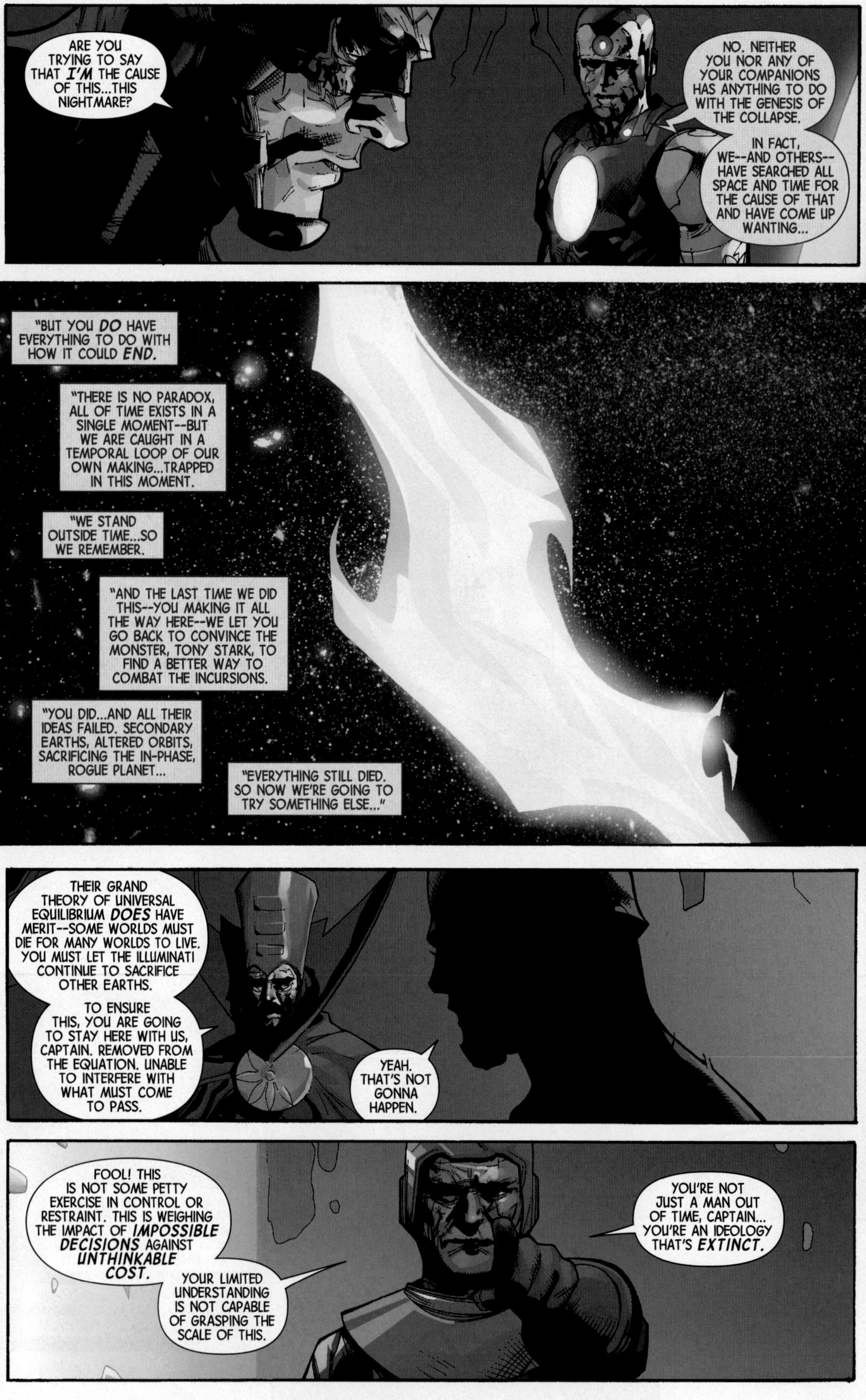
ARE YOU TRYING TO SAY THAT I'M THE CAUSE OF THIS...THIS NIGHTMARE?
NO. NEITHER YOU NOR ANY OF YOUR COMPANIONS HAS ANYTHING TO DO WITH THE GENESIS OF THE COLLAPSE.
IN FACT, WE--AND OTHERS--HAVE SEARCHED ALL SPACE AND TIME FOR THE CAUSE OF THAT AND HAVE COME UP WANTING...
"BUT YOU DO HAVE EVERYTHING TO DO WITH HOW IT COULD END.
"THERE IS NO PARADOX, ALL OF TIME EXISTS IN A SINGLE MOMENT--BUT WE ARE CAUGHT IN A TEMPORAL LOOP OF OUR OWN MAKING...TRAPPED IN THIS MOMENT.
"WE STAND OUTSIDE TIME...SO WE REMEMBER.
"AND THE LAST TIME WE DID THIS--YOU MAKING IT ALL THE WAY HERE--WE LET YOU GO BACK TO CONVINCE THE MONSTER, TONY STARK, TO FIND A BETTER WAY TO COMBAT THE INCURSIONS.
"YOU DID...AND ALL THEIR IDEAS FAILED. SECONDARY EARTHS, ALTERED ORBITS, SACRIFICING THE IN-PHASE, ROGUE PLANET...
"EVERYTHING STILL DIED. SO NOW WE'RE GOING TO TRY SOMETHING ELSE..."
THEIR GRAND THEORY OF UNIVERSAL EQUILIBRIUM DOES HAVE MERIT--SOME WORLDS MUST DIE FOR MANY WORLDS TO LIVE. YOU MUST LET THE ILLUMINATI CONTINUE TO SACRIFICE OTHER EARTHS.
TO ENSURE THIS, YOU ARE GOING TO STAY HERE WITH US, CAPTAIN. REMOVED FROM THE EQUATION. UNABLE TO INTERFERE WITH WHAT MUST COME TO PASS.
YEAH. THAT'S NOT GONNA HAPPEN.
FOOL! THIS IS NOT SOME PETTY EXERCISE IN CONTROL OR RESTRAINT. THIS IS WEIGHING THE IMPACT OF IMPOSSIBLE DECISIONS AGAINST UNTHINKABLE COST.
YOUR LIMITED UNDERSTANDING IS NOT CAPABLE OF GRASPING THE SCALE OF THIS.
YOU'RE NOT JUST A MAN OUT OF TIME, CAPTAIN... YOU'RE AN IDEOLOGY THAT'S EXTINCT.

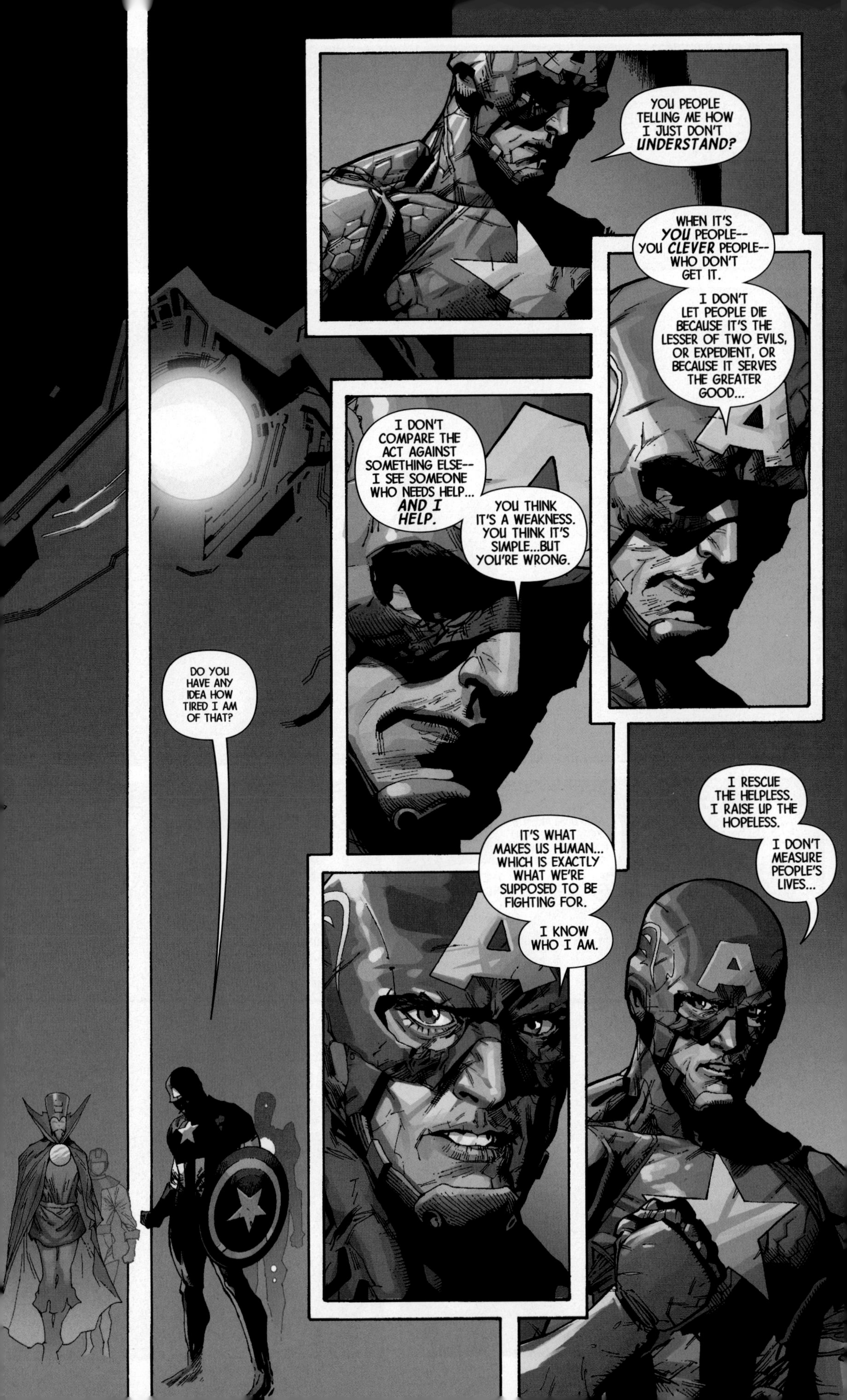
YOU PEOPLE TELLING ME HOW I JUST DON'T UNDERSTAND?
WHEN IT'S YOU PEOPLE-- YOU CLEVER PEOPLE-- WHO DON'T GET IT.
I DON'T LET PEOPLE DIE BECAUSE IT'S THE LESSER OF TWO EVILS, OR EXPEDIENT, OR BECAUSE IT SERVES THE GREATER GOOD...
I DON'T COMPARE THE ACT AGAINST SOMETHING ELSE-- I SEE SOMEONE WHO NEEDS HELP... AND I HELP.
YOU THINK IT'S A WEAKNESS. YOU THINK IT'S SIMPLE...BUT YOU'RE WRONG.
DO YOU HAVE ANY IDEA HOW TIRED I AM OF THAT?
I RESCUE THE HELPLESS. I RAISE UP THE HOPELESS.
I DON'T MEASURE PEOPLE'S LIVES...
IT'S WHAT MAKES US HUMAN... WHICH IS EXACTLY WHAT WE'RE SUPPOSED TO BE FIGHTING FOR.
I KNOW WHO I AM.

I SAVE THEM.

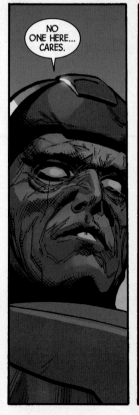

NO ONE HERE... CARES.

AND YOU ARE MISTAKEN IF YOU THINK YOU HAVE ANY CHOICE IN THE MATTER...

THE GEM IS OURS. WITHOUT IT, YOU'RE NEVER LEAVING HERE.

YOUR TIME...HAS RUN OUT.

I'M SORRY, CAPTAIN.

I UNDERSTAND YOUR POSITION. I RESPECT IT. HONESTLY, I IDOLIZE IT...

BUT THE PERSPECTIVE YOU'RE TALKING ABOUT...IT'S BASED ON THE MORALITIES OF A SOCIETY OF INDIVIDUALS AND NOT A COLLECTIVE ONE.

REMEMBER, I LIVED IN YOUR NOW...

AND THAT THINKING JUST HAS NO PLACE IN THE FUTURE...LIKE KANG SAID, IT DIED A LONG TIME AGO.

WELL...

IT'S TOO BAD I'VE NEVER REALLLY GOTTEN OVER THE PAST.

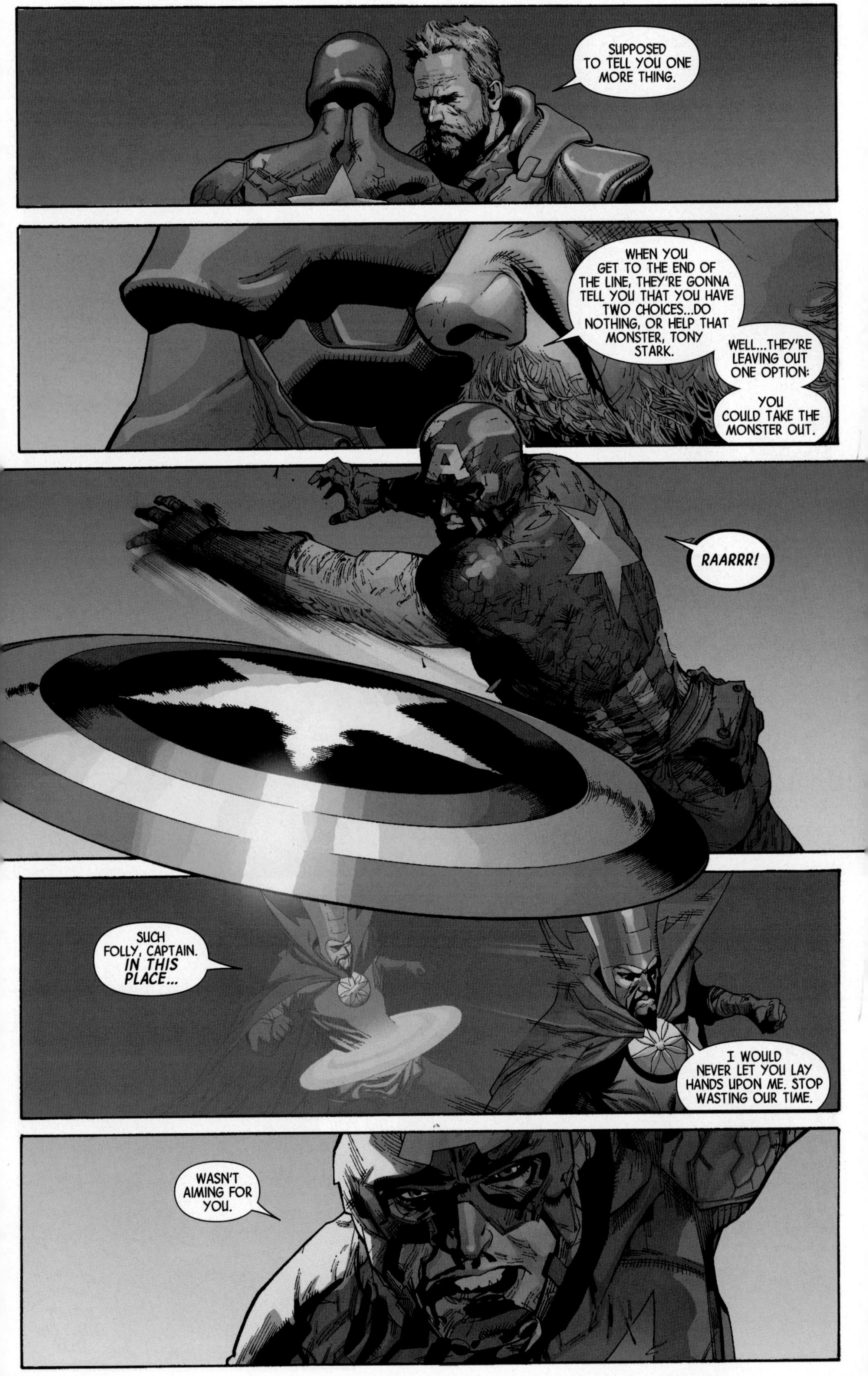
SUPPOSED TO TELL YOU ONE MORE THING.
WHEN YOU GET TO THE END OF THE LINE, THEY'RE GONNA TELL YOU THAT YOU HAVE TWO CHOICES...DO NOTHING, OR HELP THAT MONSTER, TONY STARK.
WELL...THEY'RE LEAVING OUT ONE OPTION:
YOU COULD TAKE THE MONSTER OUT.
RAARRR!
SUCH FOLLY, CAPTAIN. IN THIS PLACE...
I WOULD NEVER LET YOU LAY HANDS UPON ME. STOP WASTING OUR TIME.
WASN'T AIMING FOR YOU.

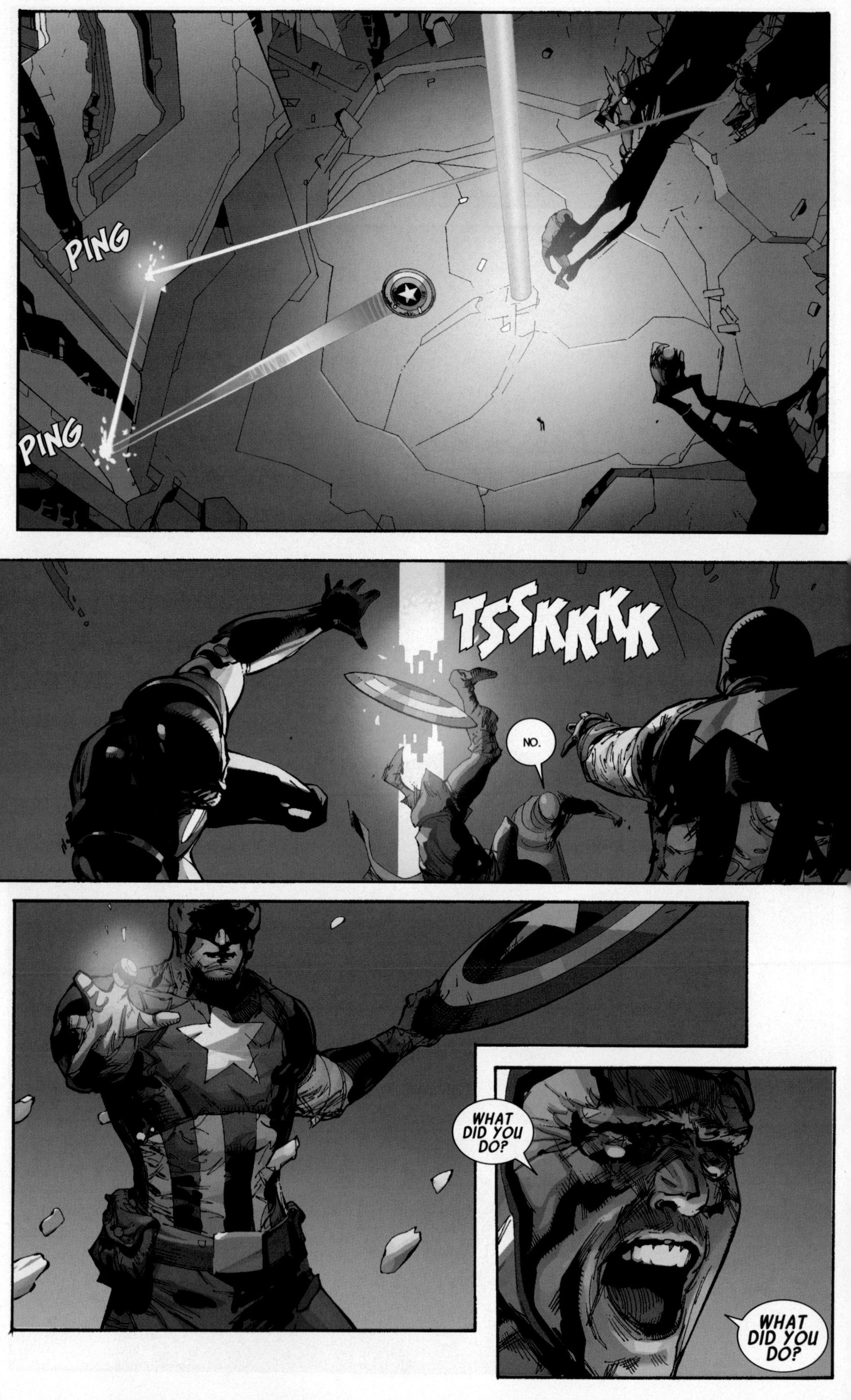
PING
PING
TSSKKKK
NO.
WHAT DID YOU DO?
WHAT DID YOU DO?

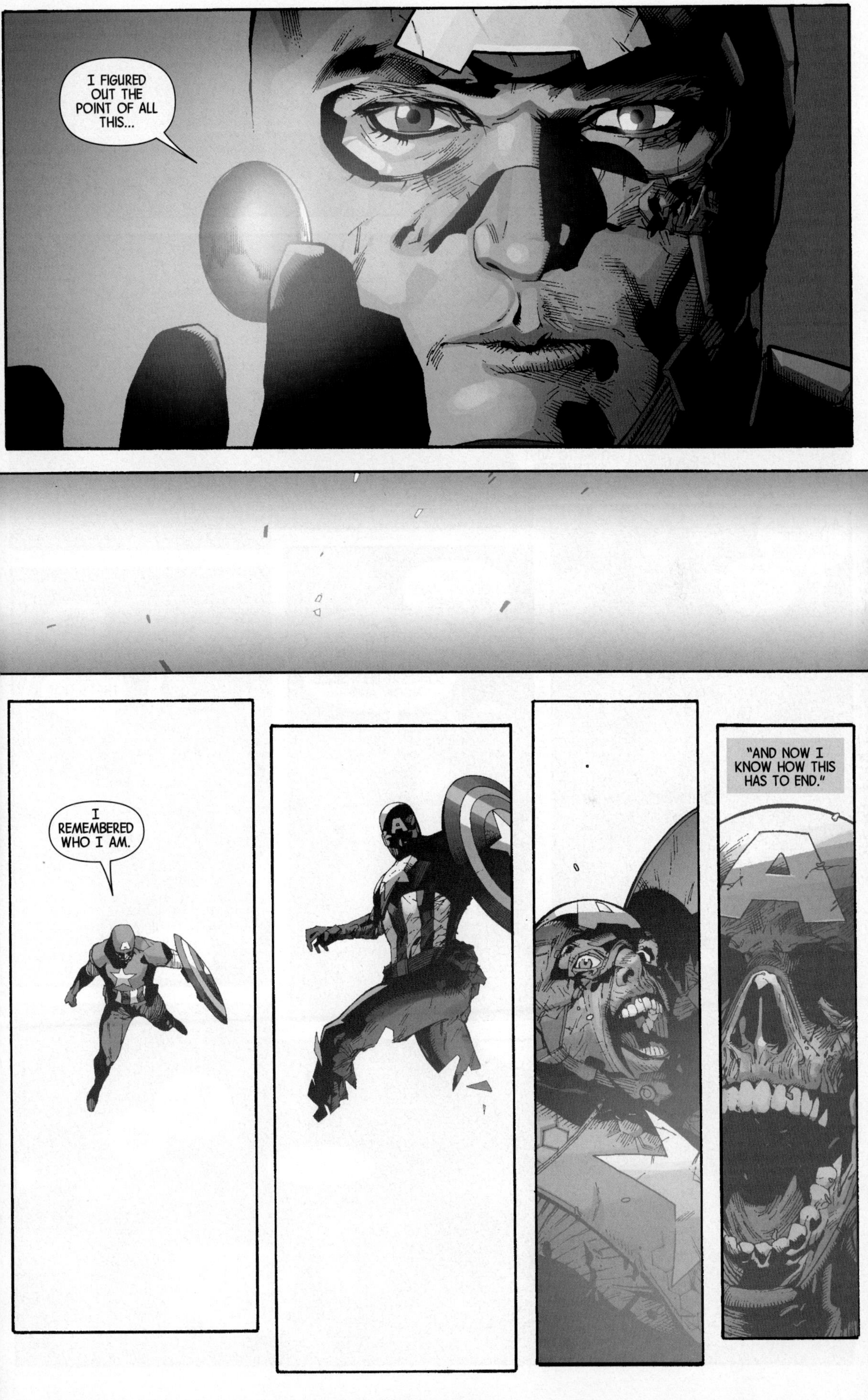
I FIGURED OUT THE POINT OF ALL THIS...
I REMEMBERED WHO I AM.
"AND NOW I KNOW HOW THIS HAS TO END."

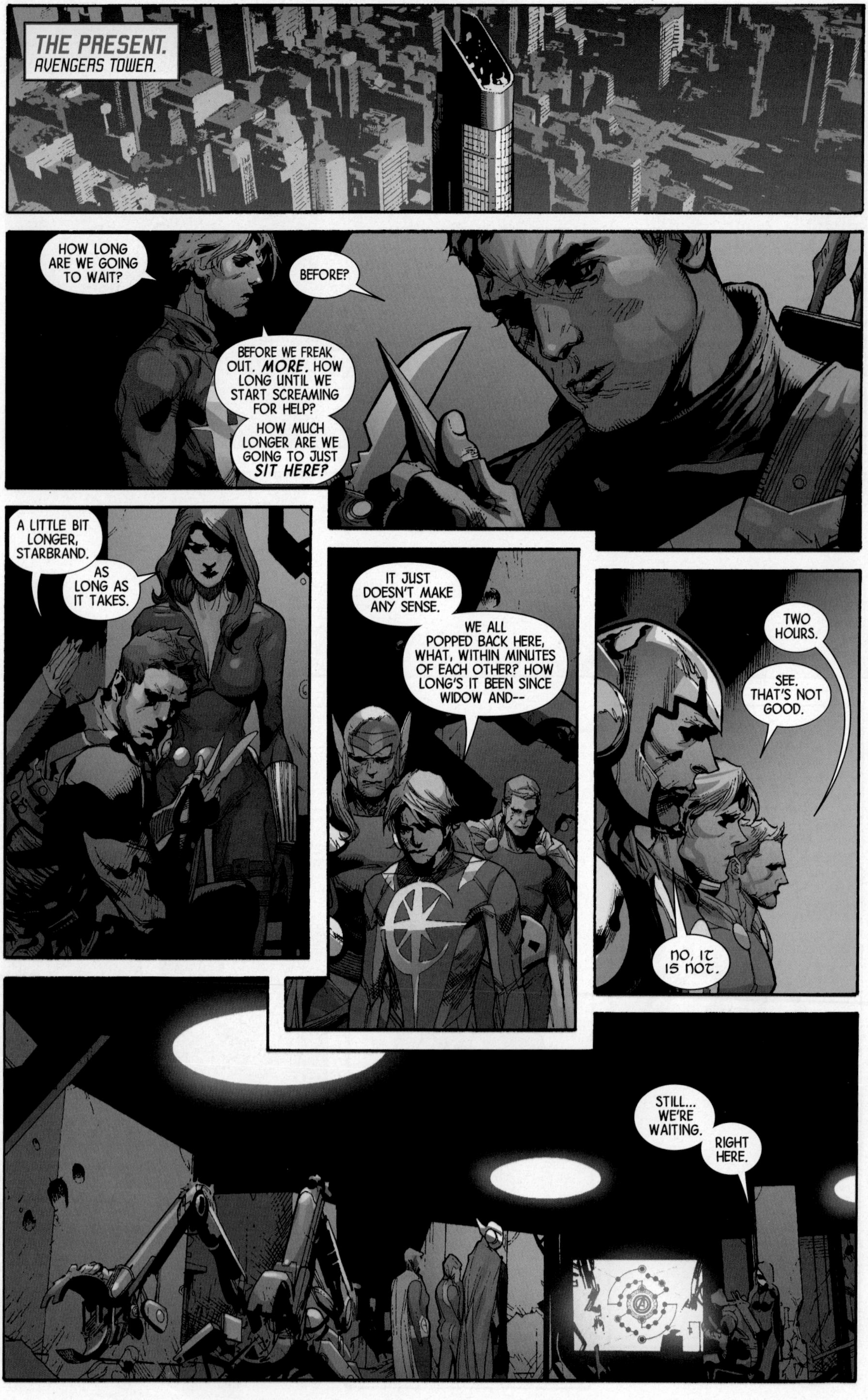

THE PRESENT. AVENGERS TOWER.
HOW LONG ARE WE GOING TO WAIT?
BEFORE?
BEFORE WE FREAK OUT. MORE. HOW LONG UNTIL WE START SCREAMING FOR HELP?
HOW MUCH LONGER ARE WE GOING TO JUST SIT HERE?
A LITTLE BIT LONGER, STARBRAND.
AS LONG AS IT TAKES.
IT JUST DOESN'T MAKE ANY SENSE.
WE ALL POPPED BACK HERE, WHAT, WITHIN MINUTES OF EACH OTHER? HOW LONG'S IT BEEN SINCE WIDOW AND--
TWO HOURS.
SEE. THAT'S NOT GOOD.
NO, IT IS NOT.
STILL... WE'RE WAITING.
RIGHT HERE.

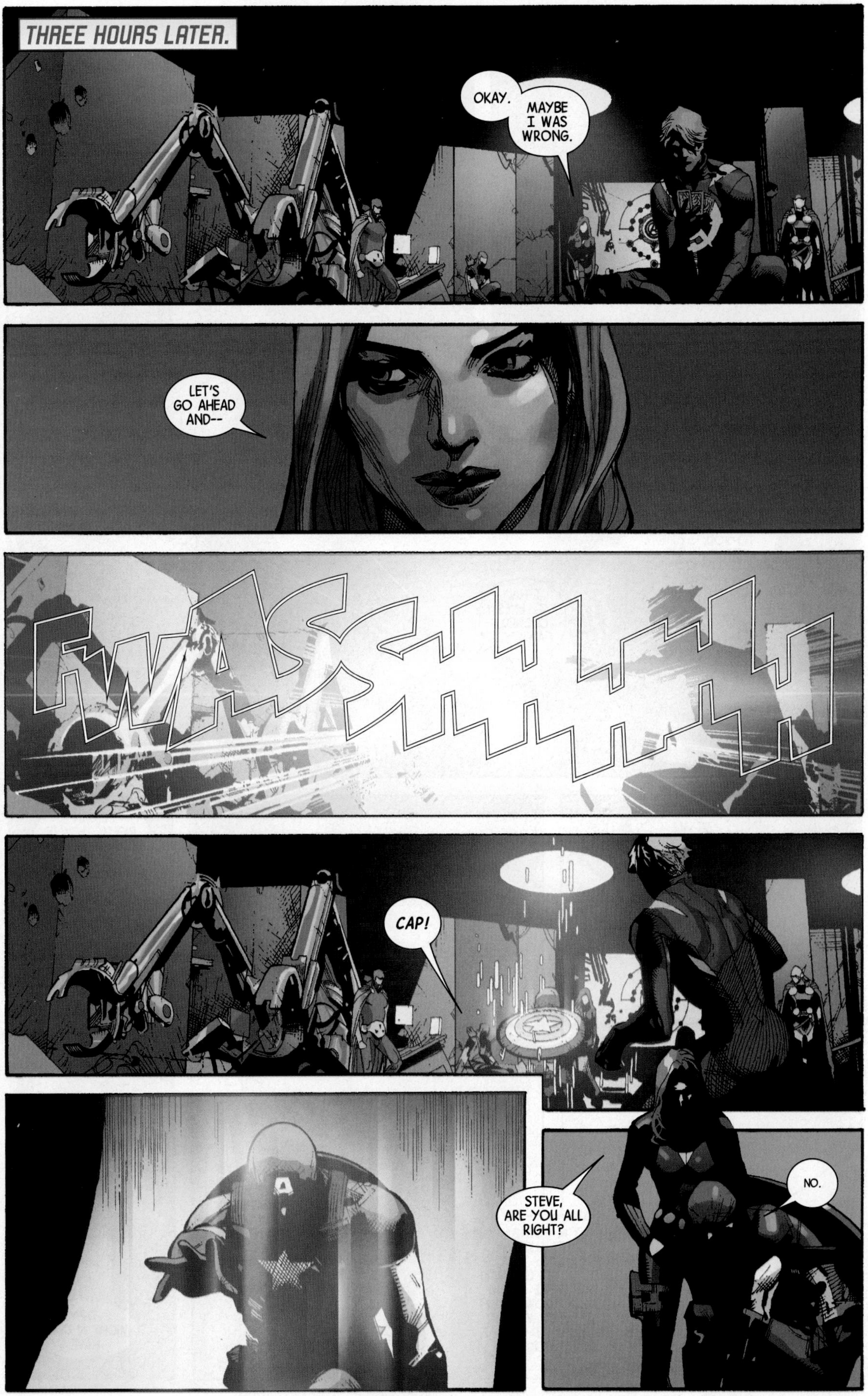
THREE HOURS LATER.
OKAY.
MAYBE I WAS WRONG.
LET'S GO AHEAD AND--
FWASHHHH
CAP!
STEVE, ARE YOU ALL RIGHT?
NO.

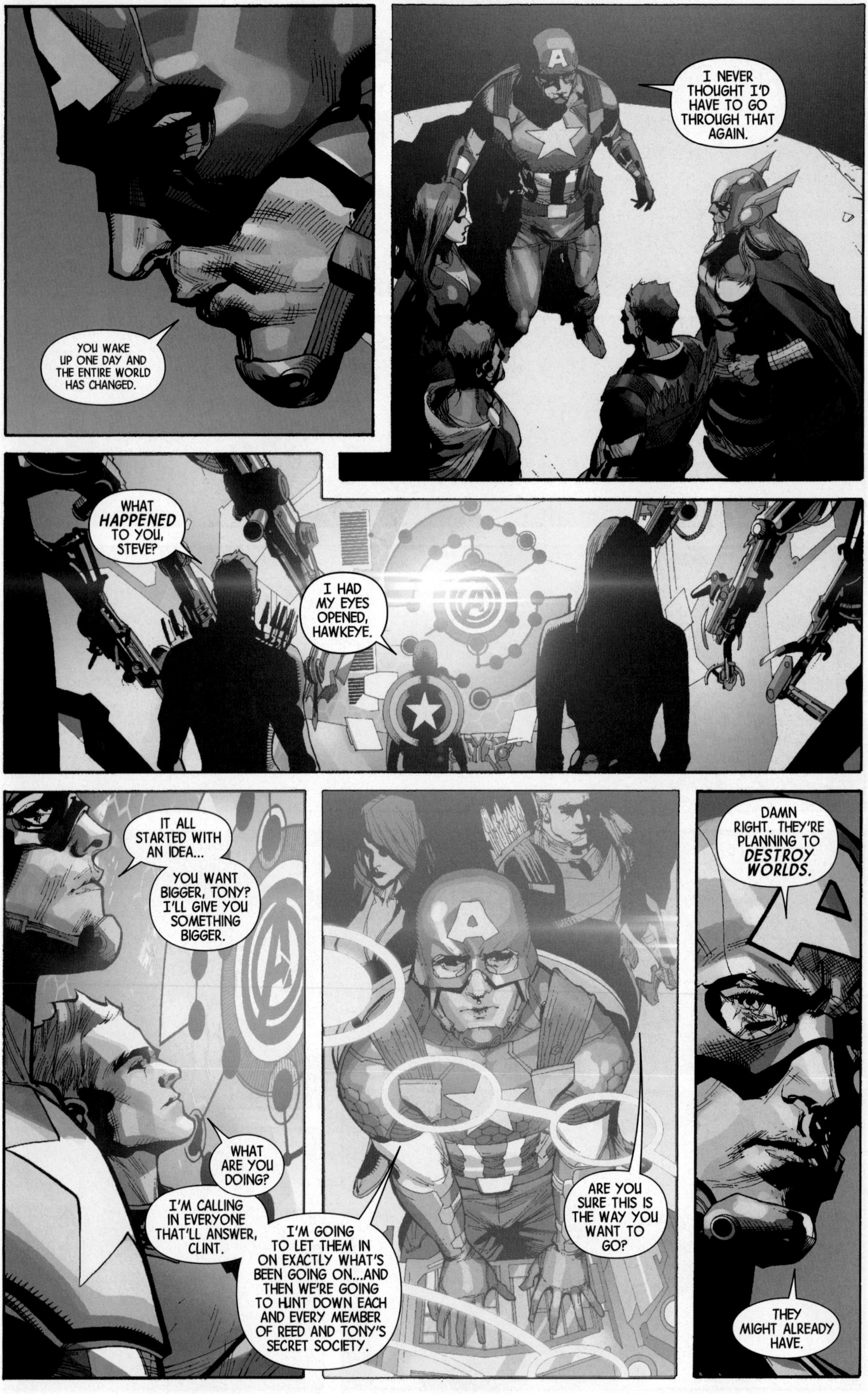
YOU WAKE UP ONE DAY AND THE ENTIRE WORLD HAS CHANGED.
I NEVER THOUGHT I'D HAVE TO GO THROUGH THAT AGAIN.
WHAT *HAPPENED* TO YOU, STEVE?
I HAD MY EYES OPENED, HAWKEYE.
IT ALL STARTED WITH AN IDEA...
YOU WANT BIGGER, TONY? I'LL GIVE YOU SOMETHING BIGGER.
WHAT ARE YOU DOING?
I'M CALLING IN EVERYONE THAT'LL ANSWER, CLINT.
I'M GOING TO LET THEM IN ON EXACTLY WHAT'S BEEN GOING ON...AND THEN WE'RE GOING TO HUNT DOWN EACH AND EVERY MEMBER OF REED AND TONY'S SECRET SOCIETY.
ARE YOU SURE THIS IS THE WAY YOU WANT TO GO?
DAMN RIGHT. THEY'RE PLANNING TO *DESTROY WORLDS.*
THEY MIGHT ALREADY HAVE.

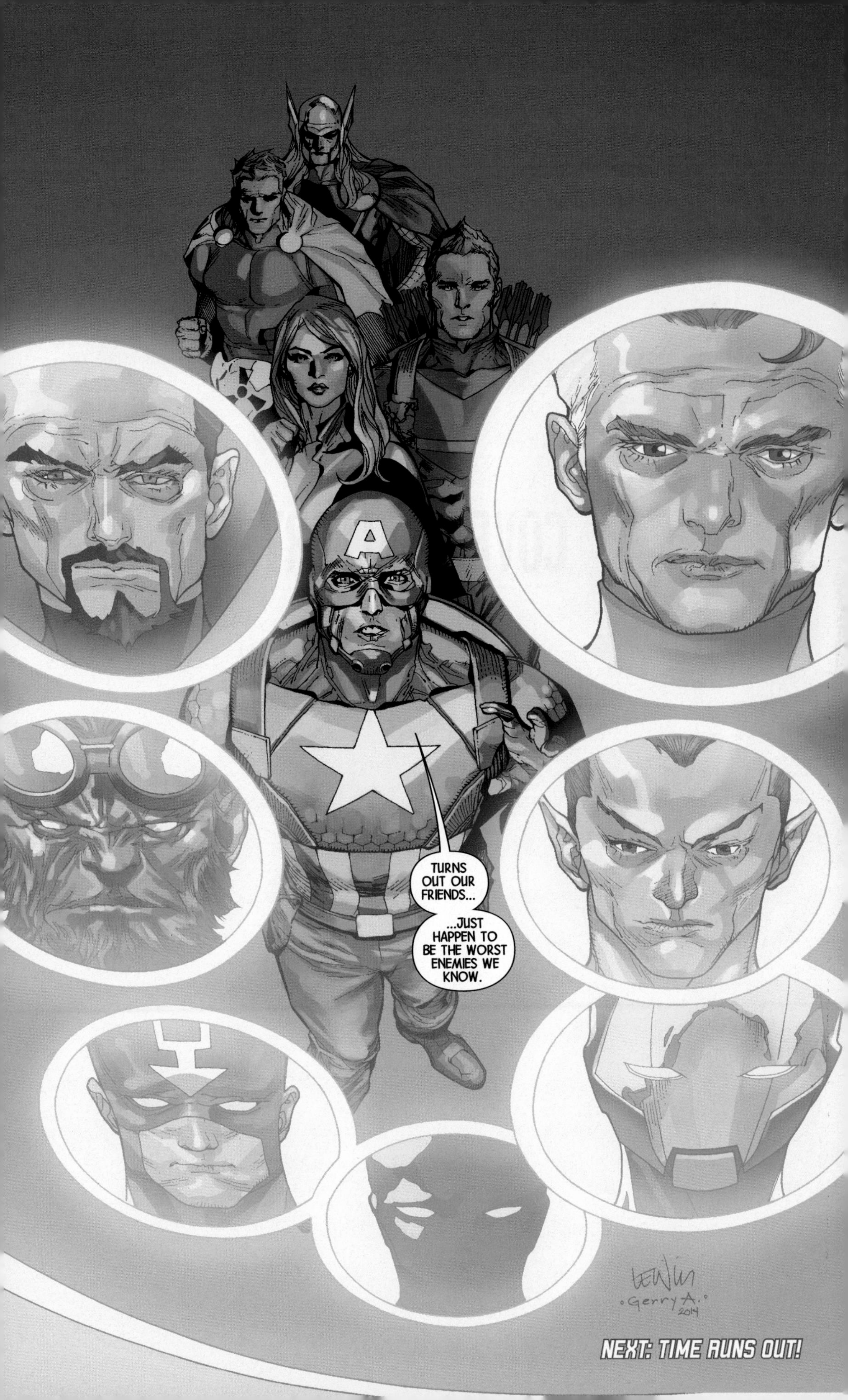
TURNS OUT OUR FRIENDS...
...JUST HAPPEN TO BE THE WORST ENEMIES WE KNOW.
Gerry A. 2014
NEXT: TIME RUNS OUT!

COVER GALLERY

#29

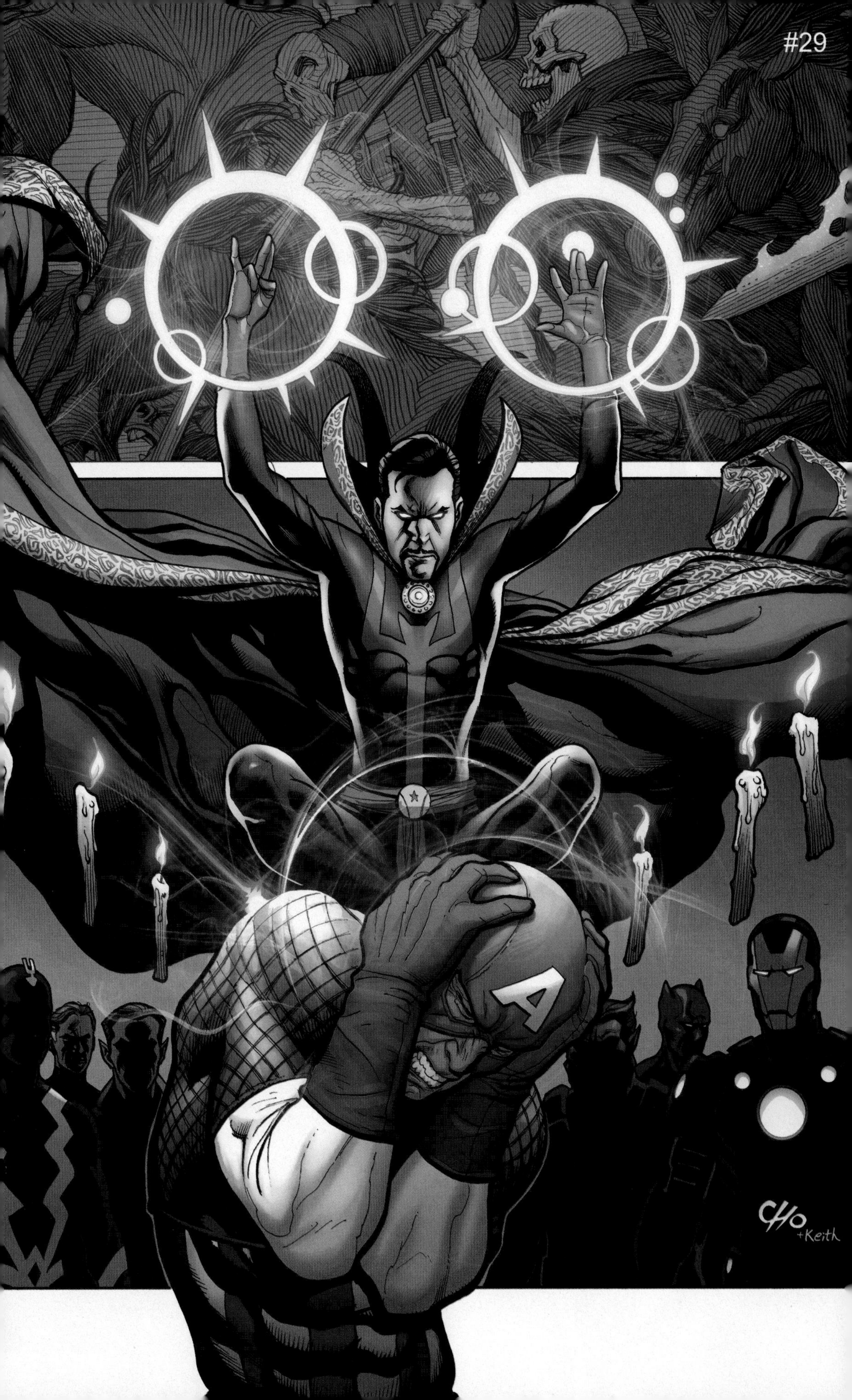
CHO
+Keith

#30

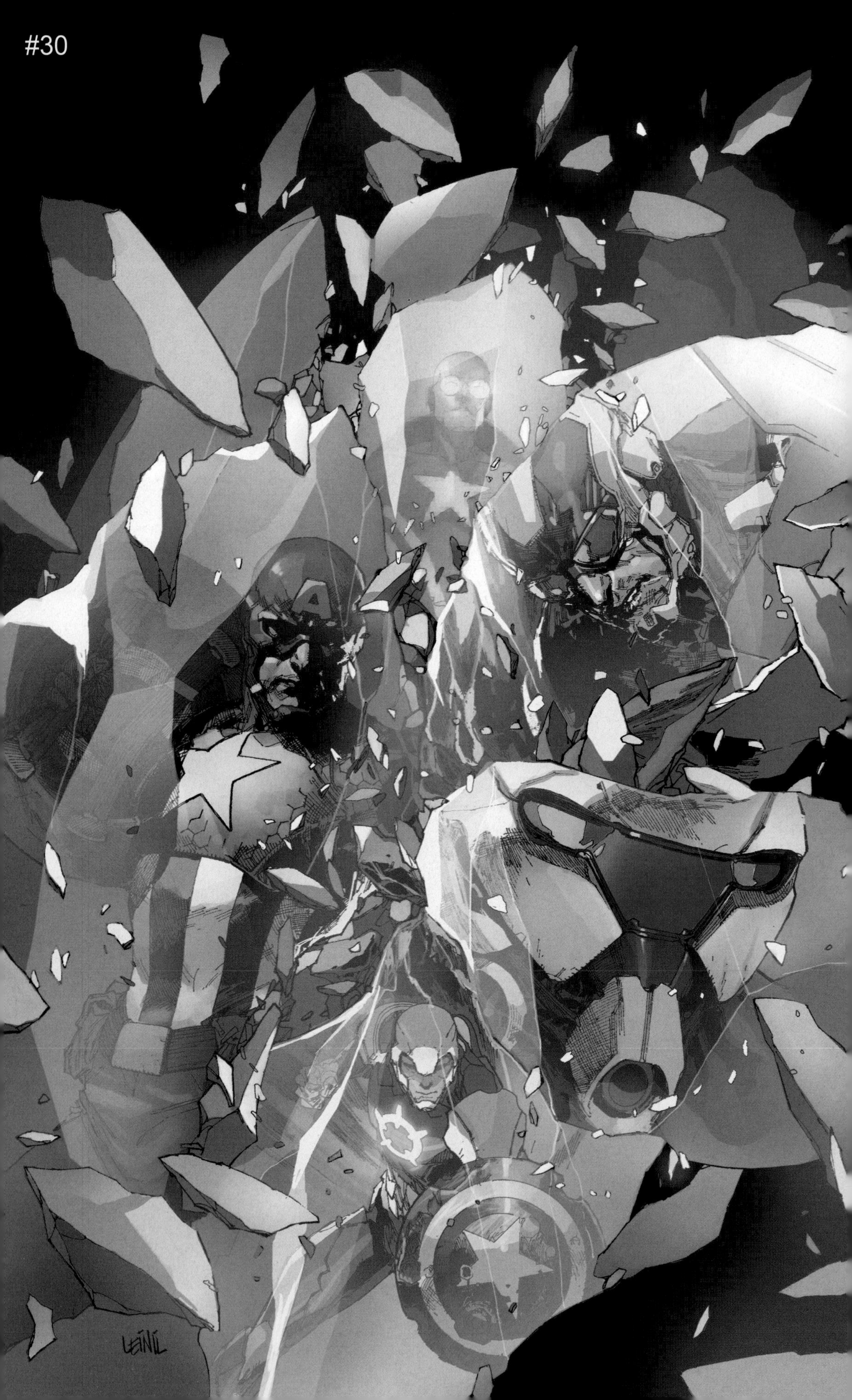
LEINIL

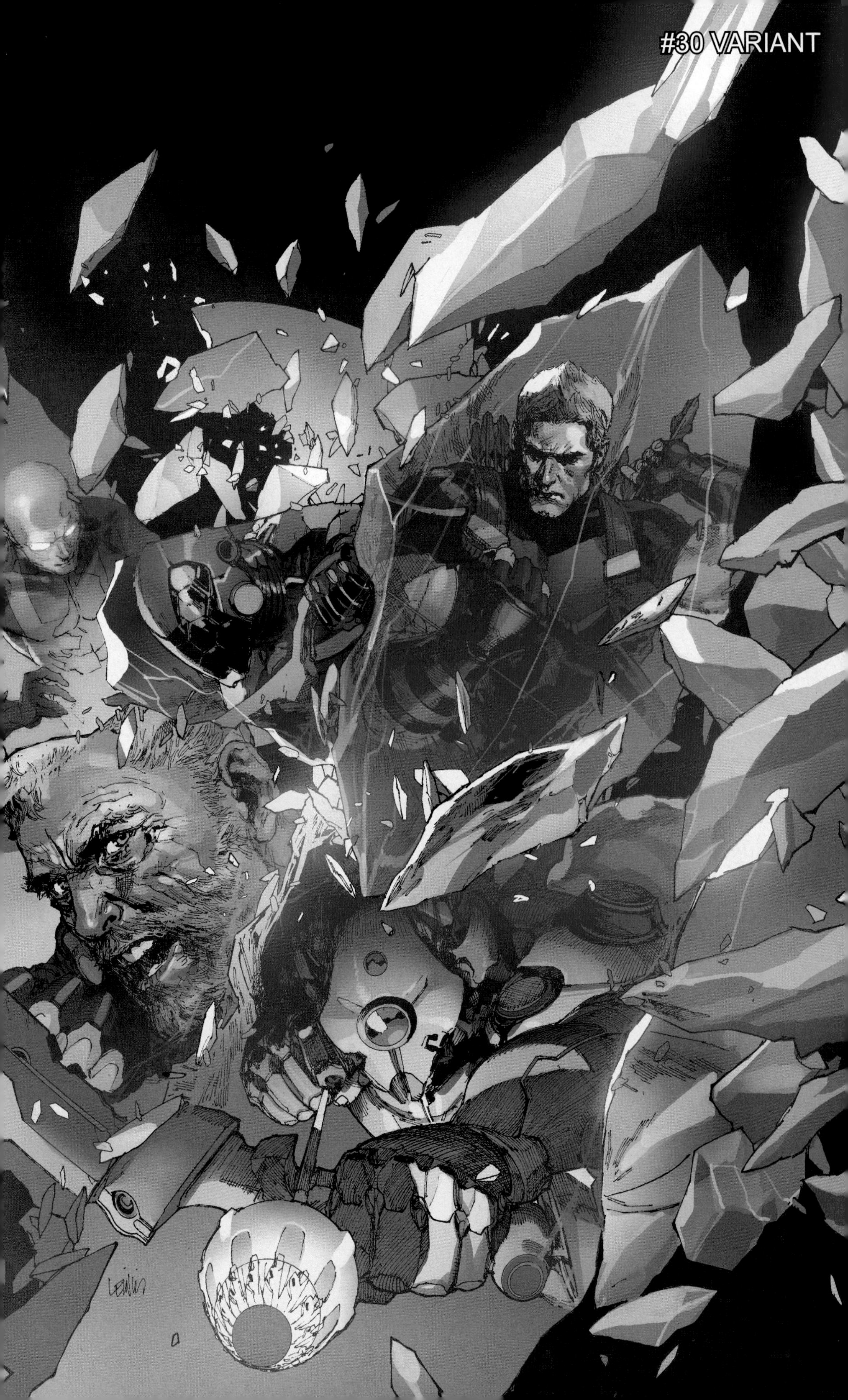

#30 VARIANT

#31

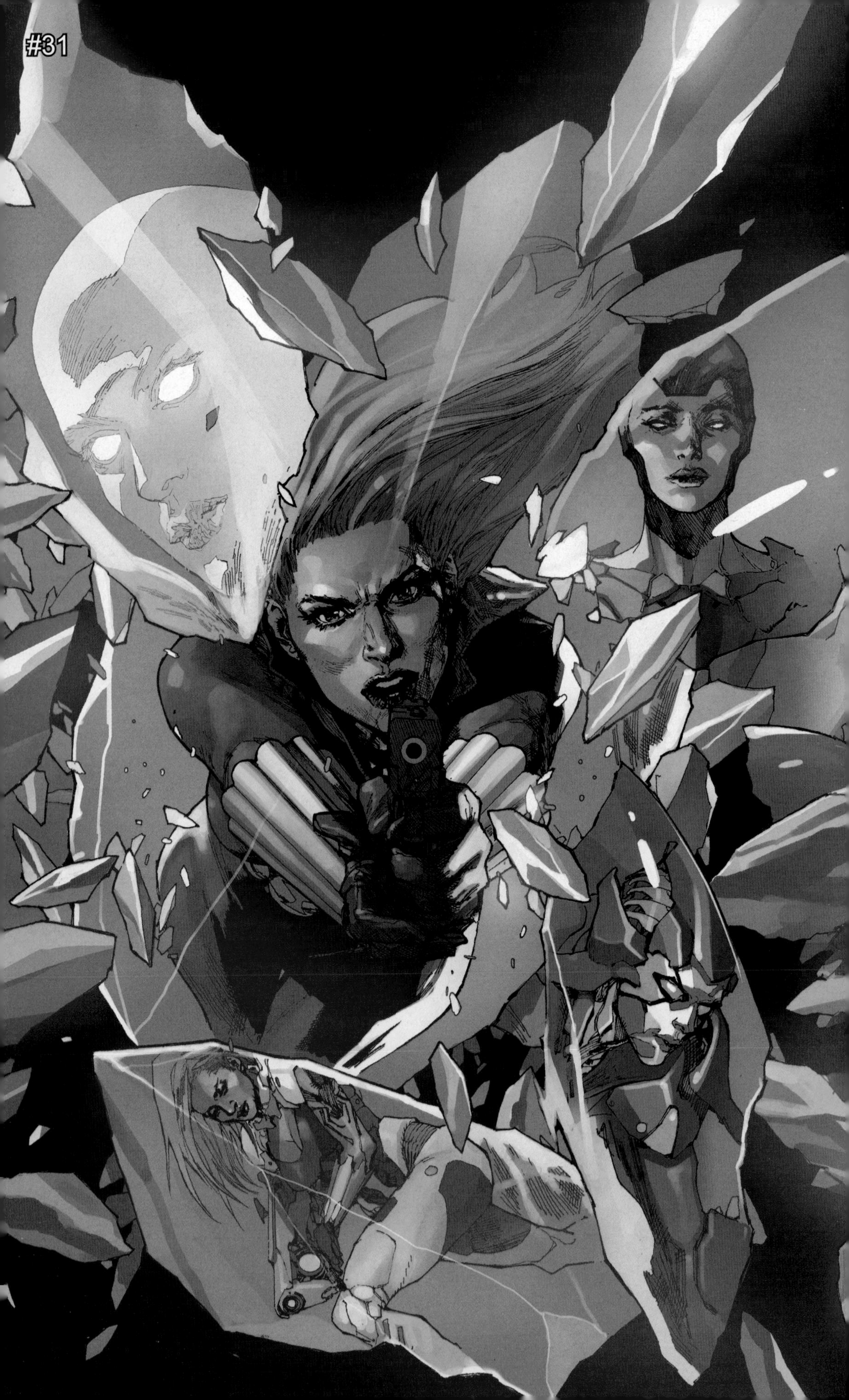

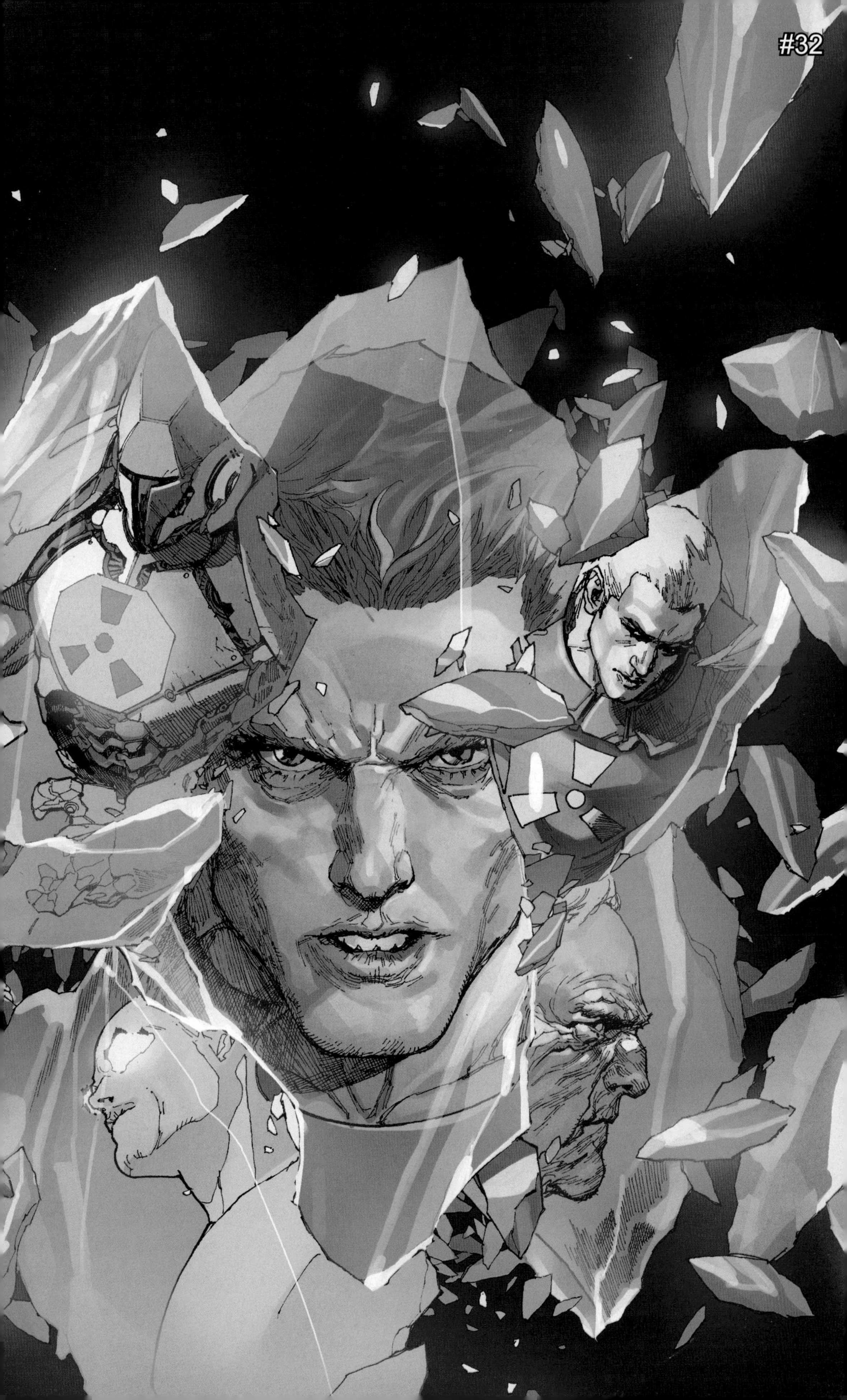
#32

#33

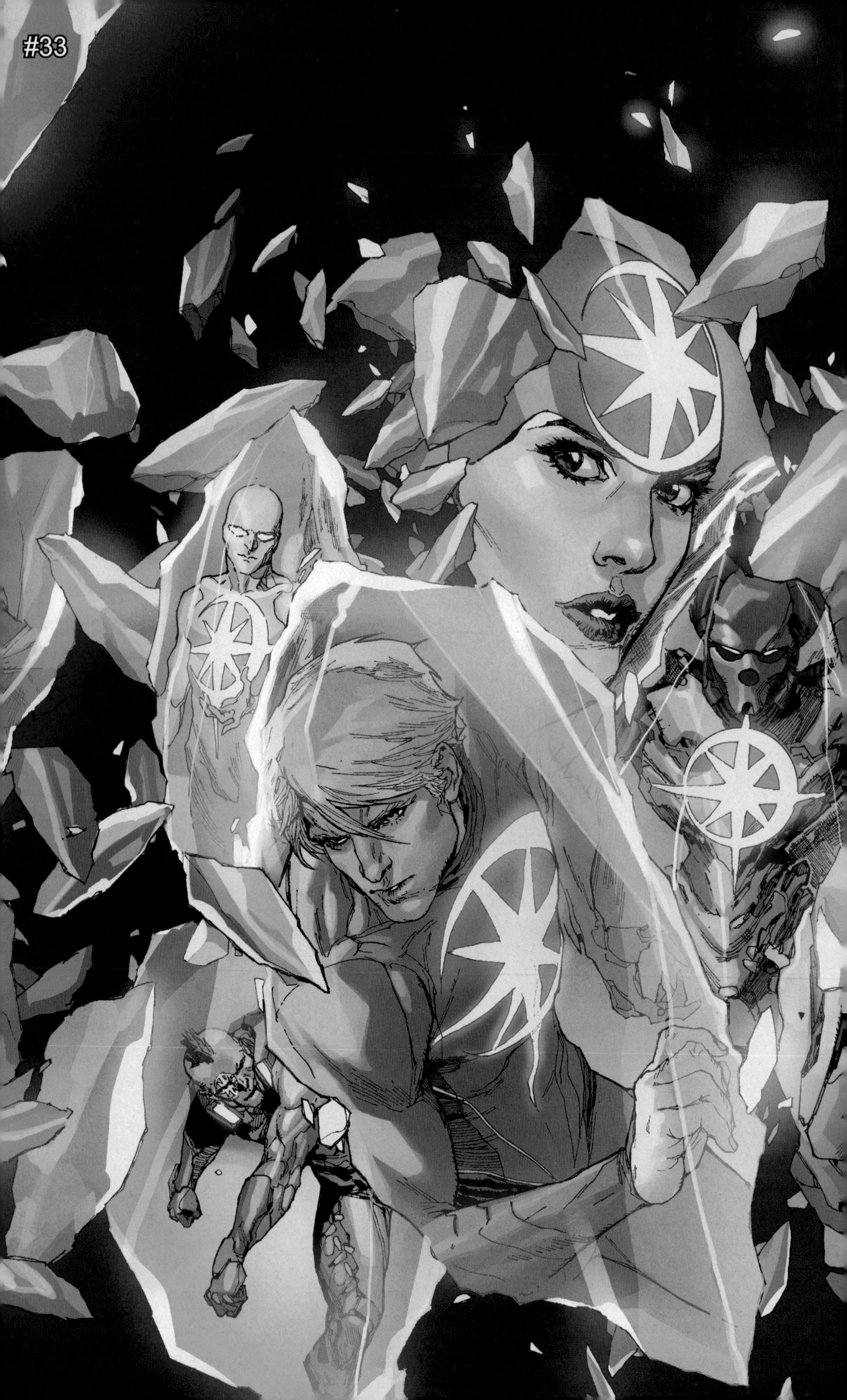

#34

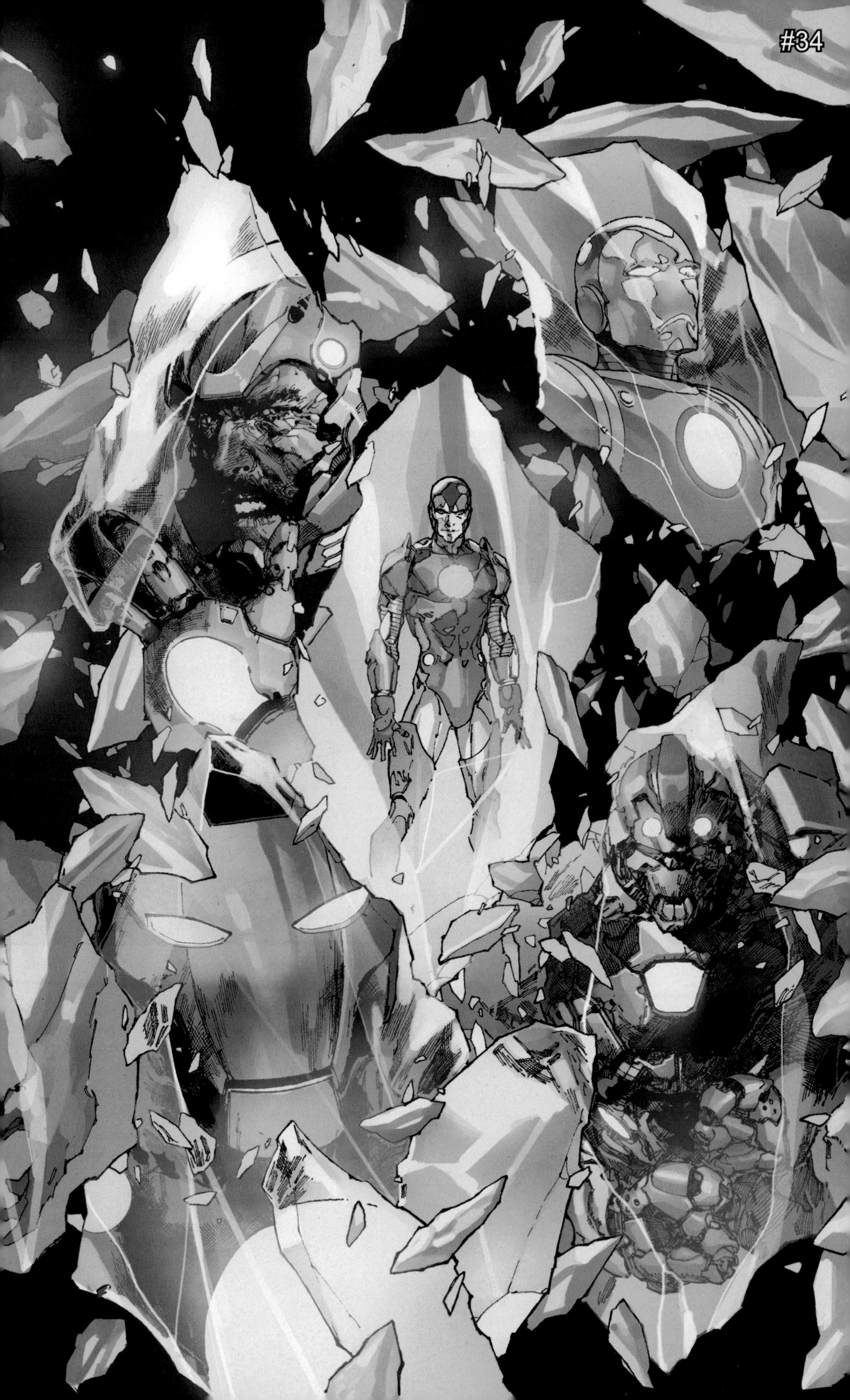

#30-34 COMBINED COVERS

#32 GUARDIANS OF THE GALAXY VARIANT
BY PASQUAL FERRY & ANDY TROY

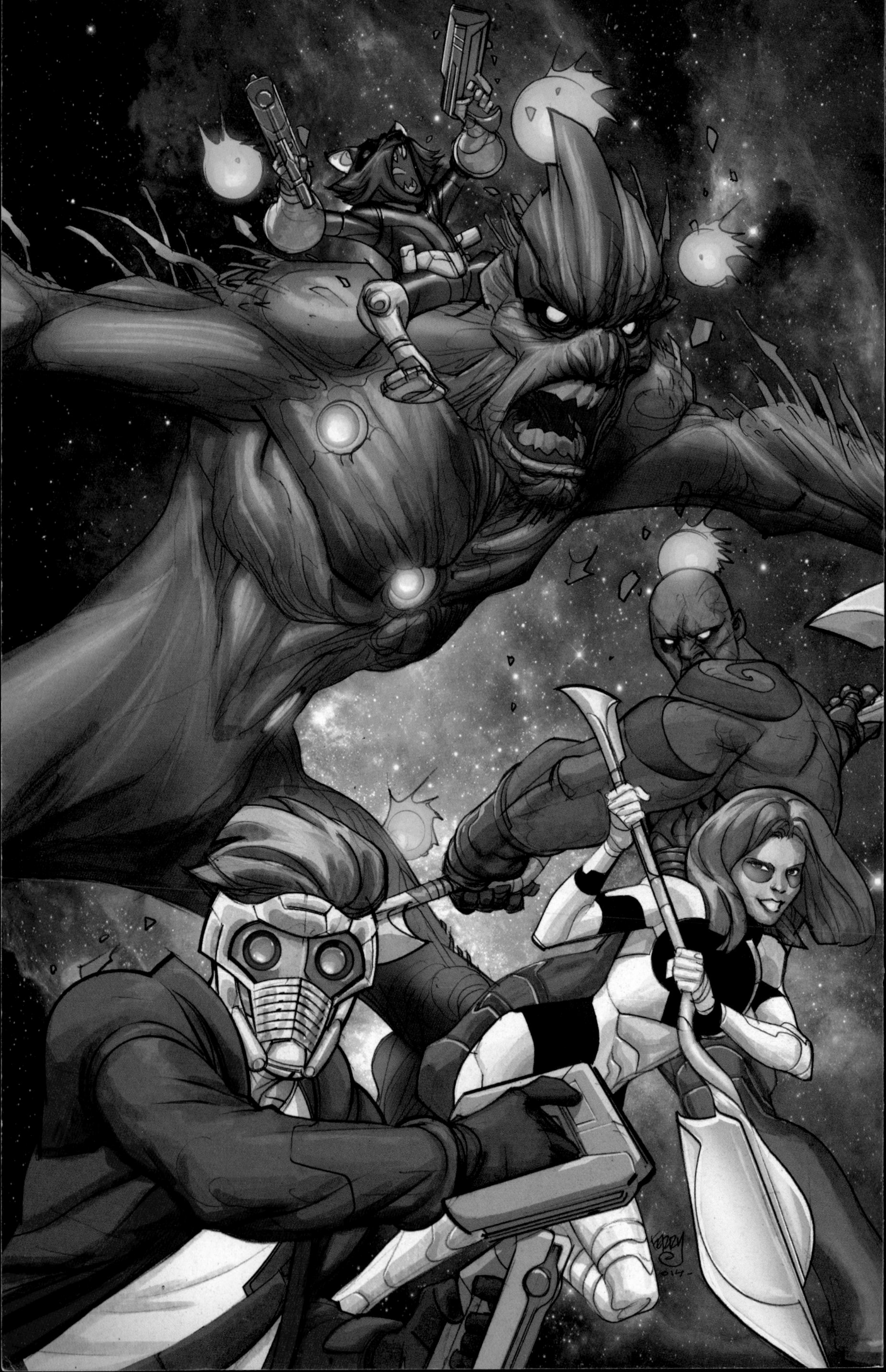